PHARMACEUTICAL CAREERS

PHARMACEUTICAL CAREERS

Neelam Singla

JPS Kohli

PharmaMed Press

An Imprint of BSP Books Pvt. Ltd.

4-4-309/316, Giriraj Lane,

Sultan Bazar, Hyderabad - 500 095.

Pharmaceutical Careers

by Neelam Singla and JPS Kohli

Published by:

PharmaMed Press

An Imprint of BSP Books Pvt. Ltd.

4-4-309/316, Giriraj Lane, Sultan Bazar, Hyderabad - 500 095.

Phone: 040-23445688; Fax: 91+40-23445611

E-mail: info@pharmamedpress.net

www.bspbooks.net/www.pharmamedpress.net

ISBN: 978-93-90211-89-0 (Hardback)

Preface

This art and science of making medicines is believed to be evolved in India and it has century's old tradition of practicing Pharmacy. The profession traditionally recognized and perceived as dispensing medicines has undergone a significant paradigm shift and transformed to a revolutionized industry. Pharmaceutical industry has seen the robust growth in last two and half decades. There are vast and rewarding array of opportunities within this ever evolving field and offers a first career choice for the desiring students.

Growing up in pharma field and my role as a teacher of pharmaceutical sciences, I have closely seen that the students who chose pharmacy as a profession always had medical as the first choice. One of the reasons can be that we as pharmacy professionals could not highlight the vital contribution and role of our profession and motivate the prospective students.

The thought inspired me to make an honest and optimistic attempt to demonstrate the presence of Indian pharma industry to students who are in the midst of making a decision for their career choice. This will stimulate their interest in a profession which has huge social impact with respect to public health concerns.

The information given in the chapters will establish a baseline and comprehensive understanding regarding opportunities, description of the work, role and responsibilities in different specialized areas of this profession.

Detailed information regarding the courses offered, selection criterion, and website of the top 50 pharmacy institutes in India is incorporated. This will help the students to get an idea and evaluate the possibilities while choosing their career option.

This book is also written with a thought in mind for those students who are pursuing their career in pharmacy. I always found them curious, intelligent, informed and thoughtful. The content will further help them to assess their potential and align their career options based upon their capabilities, aptitude and personality for the need of 21st century pharmaceutical industry.

This book highlights the integration of education, research and practice at the level of college education system and can be seen as a roadmap from education to employment.

Authors

Acknowledgements

I would like to express my sincere gratitude to Mr. Jupinder Kohli for his insightful inputs, brilliant illustrations and reviews. He truly was the powerhouse behind the completion of this book. My sincere thanks to husband Ajay, for sharing his elaborate professional experience and constructive criticism while developing this work. I would also like to acknowledge the assistance from Ms. Sunyana Jain in data compilation. Finally, I would like to thank my daughter Saumya, for her assistance in proof reading and editing the text.

Your support is truly invaluable.

CONTENTS

1 Introduction to Pharmaceutical Sciences

1.1 ORIGINS

a. Ancient Civilizations – World

When humans evolved as a society and started experimenting with food gathering, identifying and eventually growing their own food, especially grains, they also started experimenting with treatments for their ailments. Perhaps the earliest ailments may have a lot to do with injuries – during hunting and fighting – the quest for treatments kept on increasing as they must have realized that many ailments could be treated with simple herbs etc. It is imagined that such treatments must have evolved localized in their original places and subsequently transferred to other places with development of trade.

According to ancient legend, Chinese emperor Shennong is credited as founder of Chinese herbal medicine when he composed the *Shennong Bencao Jing* or The Divine Farmer's Herb-Root Classic in about 2700 BCE. While this composition is lost in time, a copy of this made in 500 CE survives and it details about 365 herbs. It was compiled during the Han dynasty. Around 168 BCE a manuscript described as "Recipes for 52 Ailments" was sealed into a tomb in Mawangdui that included prescriptions for specific ailments (discovered in 1973).

Similarly, ancient Egyptians had the Papyrus Ebers, one of the earliest known herbals dating to 1550 BCE and based on sources, dating back a further 500 to 2000 years. The earliest Sumerian cuneiform clay tablets dated about 2500 BCE give descriptions of various medicines. Inscribed Assyrian tablets dated 668–626 BCE list about 250 vegetable drugs.

A little later, around 400 BCE, Hippocrates was a renowned physician who learned his craft from his father and grandfather (who were also physicians), used about 400 drugs, most being of plant origin. It is claimed by many that the ancient Greeks obtained a large part of their corpus of knowledge from Egypt and Mesopotamia, which they supplemented further with their own experimentation. Aristotle's pupil Theophrastus (371–287 BCE) in his *Historia Plantarum*, (Enquiry into Plants) which was based primarily on Aristotle's notes, deals specifically with medicinal herbs and their uses in the Ninth Book (chapter). In 4th century BCE another Greek physician called Diocles of Carystus studied medicinal properties of plants and wrote a composition detailing medicinal properties of plants. In fact the period around 330 BCE could be considered as golden era of Greek medicine when written herbals were introduced by the physicians Herophilus, Mantias, Andreas of Karystos, Appolonius Mys, and Nicander.

The Greek physician Pedanius Dioscorides wrote a five volume book detailing about 500 medicinal plants in his native Greek in the 1st century CE. The Latin translation *De Materia Medica* was used a basis for many medieval texts. Similarly, Pliny the Elder's (23–79 CE) Naturalis Historia (c. 77–79 CE) is a collection of the information contained in about 2000 scrolls detailing, among other things, medicinal plants. Aelius Galenus or Claudius Galenus (Galen) (129- 217 CE) wrote the work *De Simplicibus* which is considered a milestone in medical literature. Later Apuleius also wrote extensively and his texts also contained the alternative names for plants in several languages. It dates to about 400 CE and a surviving copy dates to about 600 CE.

Fig 1.1 An apothecary publically preparing the drug theriac, under the supervision of a physician
Source: Wikimedia Commons (Library reference: ICV No 11019, Photo number: V0010760)

Galen in fact was a Greek physician who was born in Pergamon which was earlier part of the Greek empire and had now come under the Roman Byzantine Empire (in present day Turkey). By the end of his lifetime, the Western Roman Empire had crumbled and the eastern Byzantine Empire was close to being under Islam in a few hundred years and therefore his works particularly and of other earlier Greek physicians had a great influence in the later Islamic world. The Arabic translations of these works formed the basis of Islamic medicine which was then further developed along scientific lines of research. Such system of medicine is therefore still known as Unani medicine (Unani means Greek in

Arabic). It was also heavily influenced by Ayurveda from the Indian subcontinent whose knowledge had percolated westwards into Middle East.

Muhammad ibn Zakariya Razi (865–915) promoted the medical uses of chemical compounds. Abu al-Qasim al-Zahrawi (936–1013) developed medicines by sublimation and distillation. His *Liber servitoris* provides recipes and explains how to prepare the 'simples' from which complex drugs were compounded. Sabur Ibn Sahl (d 869), initiated the pharmacopoeia, describing a large number of treatments for ailments. Al-Biruni (973–1050) wrote one of the most valuable Islamic works on pharmacology, entitled *Kitab al-Saydanah fi al-Tibb* (Book of Pharmacy in the Healing Art), in which he detailed the properties of drugs and outlined the role of pharmacy and the functions and duties of the pharmacist. It lists synonyms for drug names in Syriac, Persian, Greek, Baluchi, Afghan, Kurdi, and some Indian languages. Avicenna, too, described no less than 700 preparations, their properties, modes of action, and their indications. He devoted in fact a whole volume to simple drugs in The Canon of Medicine. Al-Biruni was a contemporary of Ibn Sina (Avicenna) and they corresponded with each other frequently. Of great impact were also the works by al-Maridini of Baghdad and Cairo, and Ibn al-Wafid (1008–1074). Al-Muwaffaq in the 10th century wrote The Foundations of the True Properties of Remedies, amongst others describing arsenious oxide, and being acquainted with silicic acid.

b. Ancient Civilization - India

Perhaps the earliest system of medicine in the world was Ayurveda, which was already highly codified and scientifically developed at the time of its inception, thought to be around 1500 BCE. Ayurveda is a Sanskrit word meaning knowledge of life. The uniqueness of Ayurveda is that it is inexorably linked with Hindu religious texts which imparts it, both an advantage and a disadvantage. The advantage is that it is approved as genuine source of information with the faith of the Hindu masses firmly behind it. The disadvantage is that it is a part of Hindu religious tradition that is part of oral history (*Shruti*) rather than written or composed (*Smriti*) and hence to ascribe a date to such system is difficult.

The oldest Ayurvedic text can be said to be from Charak called Charaka Samhita and it was followed by the Sushruta Samhita around 1500 BCE. It is claimed that the book by Charak was first taught by Atreya, and then subsequently codified by Agnivesh, revised by Charak, and the manuscripts that survive into the modern era are based on one edited by Dridhabala. In *Sushruta Samhita*, the source of all such medical knowledge is claimed to be from Dhanvantari, Hindu god of Ayurveda, who incarnated himself as a king of Varanasi and taught medicine to a group of physicians, including Sushruta. Sushruta was a physician who taught in a school in Kashi (Varanasi) in parallel to another medical school in Taxila (on Jhelum river). Except for some topics, both discuss similar subjects such as General Principles, Pathology, Diagnosis, Anatomy, Sensorial Prognosis, Therapeutics, Pharmaceutics and ToxicologyThe Sushruta and Charaka texts differ in one major aspect, with Sushruta Samhita providing the foundation of surgery, while Charaka Samhita being primarily a foundation of medicine.

Ayurveda classifies seven basic tissues (*dhatu*), which are plasma (*rasa*), blood (*rakta*), muscles (*māmsa*), fat (*meda*), bone (*asthi*), marrow (*majja*), and semen (*shukra*). Like the medicine of classical antiquity, Ayurveda has historically divided bodily substances into five classical elements (Sanskrit *panchabhuta*), viz. earth, water, fire, air and ether. There are also twenty *gunas* (qualities or characteristics) which are considered to be inherent in all substances. These are organized in ten pairs: heavy/light, cold/hot, unctuous/dry, dull/sharp, stable/mobile, soft/hard, non-slimy/slimy, smooth/coarse, minute/gross, and viscous/liquid.

Fig 1.2: The Susruta-Samhita, 12th-13th century (*Source: Wikimedia Commons*)

Ayurveda also names three elemental substances, the *doshas* (called *Vata*, *Pitta* and *Kapha*), and states that a balance of the *doshas* results in health, while imbalance results in disease. One Ayurvedic view is that the *doshas* are balanced when they are equal to each other, while another view is that each human possesses a unique combination of the *doshas* which define this person's temperament and characteristics. In either case, it says that each person should modulate their behavior or environment to increase or decrease the *doshas* and maintain their natural state.

1.2 EVOLUTION OF MODERN PHARMACEUTICAL INDUSTRY

a. World

With passage of time, such islands of information that were formed initially, started developing into small enterprises that made the medicines and prescribed them to patients and came to be known as pharmacies. The ones who could expand their business, did so and started making larger batches of medicines, to be stored in containers, ready to dispense to patients when they needed them.

In 1240 Roman emperor Frederic II issued a decree by which the physician's and the apothecary's professions were separated. The first pharmacy in Europe (still working) was opened in 1241 in Trier,

Germany. There are old pharmacies still operating in Dubrovnik, Croatia, located inside the Franciscan monastery, opened in 1317; and in the Town Hall Square of Tallinn, Estonia, dating from at least 1422.

In order to improve quality of medicines that were being made at that time in the 16th and 17th centuries, certain minimum standards were drawn up for the manufacturers to follow. In 1546 the first pharmacopoeia, or collected list of pharmaceutical items with directions for making those preparations, appeared in Nürnberg, Germany. Other pharmacopoeias followed in Basel (1561), Augsburg (1564), and London (1618). The London Pharmacopoeia became mandatory for the whole of England and thus became the first example of a national pharmacopoeia.

In London the Society of Apothecaries (pharmacists) was founded in 1617. King James I authorized the separation of apothecaries from grocers also mandated that only a member of the society could keep an apothecary's shop and make or sell pharmaceutical preparations. In 1841 the Pharmaceutical Society of Great Britain was founded. This society oversaw the education and training of pharmacists to assure a scientific basis for the profession.

Merck began as a small apothecary shop in Darmstadt, Germany by Heinrich Emanuel Merck in 1668 and started larger sizes of production, especially alkaloids around 1827. Similarly, Schering in Germany; Hoffmann-La Roche in Switzerland; Burroughs Wellcome in England; Etienne Poulenc in France; and Abbott, Smith Kline, Parke-Davis, Eli Lilly, Squibb, and Upjohn in the US all started as apothecaries and pharmaceutical suppliers between the early 1830s and late 1890s.

In the same time period, synthetic chemistry was also evolving, especially dyestuffs derived from coal tar. It was only soon discovered that these dyes (and their by-products) had ability to act as medicines, especially as antiseptics initially and later against a wide range of diseases. Researchers soon modified the dyestuffs and their by-products to make them more effective as medicines.

Therefore at the end of the nineteenth century and beginning of twentieth century, when both these groups of businesses came together, that resulted in explosive growth rate of the pharmaceutical industry and we can trace the larger and wider operations of these companies from this time period.

This period also saw developments of biologicals in the form of vaccines etc. that were also a part of the large developing pharmaceutical operations in various countries. Englishman Edward Jenner introduced the first vaccine, against smallpox in 1796. He was followed in 1881 by French microbiologist Louis Pasteur who demonstrated immunization against anthrax. Four years later he also developed a vaccine against rabies. More such preparations followed over the years.

The pharmaceutical research from here onwards, the beginning of the twentieth century, marked a future trajectory away from the historical sources of medicines from plants to more closely rely on synthetic chemistry. Since the by-product of sudden development of large towns and its associated antiquated sanitary standards, infections were widespread and were the main cause of health concerns at that time. Necessarily therefore, the initial efforts for new medicines were directed in this direction and was rewarded by the invention of first anti-infective called Arsphenamine (trade name Salvarsan) in 1910 by Paul Ehrlich, a German scientist. This invention was also significant that it was derived using a scientific approach of synthesizing many chemicals and tested each of them until he found the effective one, incidentally Arsphenamine was 606th compound to be tested.

This was followed later by more such significant discoveries like Penicillin in 1929 by Sir Alexander Fleming. Later many more were introduced including other antibiotics (Streptomycin by Merck, Chlortetracycline by Lederle, Chloramphenicol by Parke-Davis, Erythromycin by Abbott and Lilly, and tetracycline by Pfizer), hormones, vitamins and insulin. Cardiovascular, neurological, and anti-asthmatic diseases also had a fair share of such new medicines.

b. India

In India, the advent of western allopathic medicines came with the coming of western physicians into India. Perhaps the earliest example could be the Portuguese Mestre Joham, accompanying the expedition of Pedro Alvares Carbral in 1500 as the earliest European physician not only in Goa but in all India. Mestre Joham settled in Goa and married a local girl. He was followed by others like Father Joham, Gaspar Pires, Tome Pires, Mestre Jeronimo Dias, Mestre Gil Oria, Cosme Saraiva and Dimas Bosque. The most famous Portuguese physician of the time was Garcia d'Orta who came to India in 1534 when the Portuguese first came to Goa and remained here till his death.

He had already acquired a house and an extensive garden full of medicinal plants when in 1554 he was granted a long lease of a part of an island (Bombay) which he also sublet to other people for additional income. He also supplemented his previous medical knowledge with many more medicinal plants that were new to him in India and was fond of acquiring such knowledge from interactions with Deccanis, Gujaratis, Bengalis, Singalese (Ceylon), Persians, Arabs and Malays when he was assisted by an intelligent Konkani servant girl Antonia. In 1563, Orta wrote his influential book in Portuguese whose title translates as Colloquies on the Simples, Drugs and Materia Medica of India.

A hundred years after Orta, a Dutchman Hendrik Adriaan van Reede tot Drakenstein (1636–1691), became the governor of Dutch territories in Malabar, and himself the son of a chief forester in the Netherlands. van Reede consulted the Vaidyars, the traditional Ayurvedic physicians with an extensive, time-tested knowledge of the medicinal value of plants. His chief helper was a Vaidyar named Itti Achuden. Van Reede's magnum opus, the 12-volume *Hortus Malabaricus*, was published from Amsterdam during the period 1686–1703. It described about 780 species of plants, supported by 794 illustrations.

John Fryer (c. 1650–1733) comes across as the next physician of some prominence who after graduation from Cambridge, joined the East India Company and first came to Iran for two years (1677-1679) and from there came to India, landing up at Surat and Bombay.

Nicholas Manucci (1639 – 1717) from Venice was perhaps the most well-known European doctor who came in direct contact with Mughal royalty. In 1656 Manucci came to Delhi and worked as the Mughal Emperor Shahjahan's son Dara Shikoh's artilleryman. After Dara's murder in 1659, he decided to become a doctor, apparently without any training or knowledge. During 1671–78, Manucci practiced medicine in Lahore and then, during 1678–82, served as physician to Shah Alam, the eldest son of Aurungzeb. While in Bidar during this period, he was also sent by the emperor to treat the wounds of the last living Guru of the Sikhs, Guru Gobind Singh which he had acquired after being attacked by assassins. Along similar lines was the story of Francois Bernier (1620–1688) who had a formal degree, an M.D. from Montpellier. Arriving in India in 1658 or 1659, he served for a while as a surgeon to Dara Shikoh and then to his brother Aurungzeb.

Many other European surgeons came to India like:

Armenian	Sikandar Beg	Suleiman Shikoh, Dara's eldest son in 1658
Dutch	Jacob Minues	Agra in 1663
Dutch	Gelmer Vorburg	Assam
Portuguese	Luis Beicao	Mirza Raja Jai Singh in the Deccan (1664)
Venetian	Angello Legrenzi	Shah Alam at Aurungabad (1679)
Venetian	D'Estremon	Sultan of Golconda (1684)
Frenchman	Cattem	Bengal (1700)
Frenchman	Francois de la Palisse	Mughal court
Frenchman	Claudius Malle	Governor of Allahabad 1666
Armenian	Johannes Petuliet	Nawab of Carnatic 1693

By late 1700 to early 1800s, the practice of western medicine slowly got established as the primary health provider service and it had developed to an extent that the physicians were increasingly finding it difficult to collect and prepare their prescribed medicines. Therefore the time was ripe for opening of slightly larger scale apothecaries (pharmacy shops). The first one was opened in Calcutta in 1811, by a Scottish chemist and druggist called Bathgate. He started dispensing prescriptions and toileteries, later adding photographic department and began manufacturing products such as aerated waters, galenicals and biologicals. The company later opened several branches, including one in Calcutta in 1900 and another in Ballygunge in 1910.

Around 1815 a small apothecary's shop was opened in Calcutta by two British surgeons, John Robinson and James Williamson. A third partner, John Smith, joined them in 1826, and a fourth, Thomson Dowson Stanistreet in 1844. The firm changed its name to Smith, Stanistreet & Co. and gradually built up a substantial pharmaceutical trade. By 1869 it was acquired by Charles Noyce Kernot who was so successful that Silas Burroughs (of Burroughs Wellcome), on his travels through India in 1883, noted that Kernot had made "a very large fortune" from it.

E. J. Lazarus, a Welshman from Carmethen arrived in India around 1839, initially gaining experience in a British pharmacy and in a few years moved to Benares, starting his own firm, the first such firm in Benares. William Treacher established the business of Treacher & Co in Bombay in 1864 (manufacturing and wholesale chemist business), opening a branch in Poona in 1879, and another in the popular hill station of Mahabaleshwar in 1889. Similarly Thomson & Taylor opened English pharmacies in Bombay and Poona in 1872 and David Skinner Kemp came to India in 1855 and, within 10 years, had set up his own business in Bombay. He took on two local partners, and in 1882, the business was converted into a limited company.

A British man, Edward Plomer came to India with the East India Company in the early 1860s and sensing a good business opportunity, decided to open a pharmacy shop to mostly cater to the British population in Shimla and also sold stationary, tobacco and set up a photography studio. In 1869 a Scotsman Tom Bliss joined the firm and four years later in 1873 when the owner offered to sell the business, with the assistance of friends, he acquired the firm. Four years later, in 1877, Bliss bought another pharmacy business in Lahore, again trading under the title E. Plomer & Co. He later opened other branches, in Amritsar and Delhi. J. L. Lyell set up the first British pharmacy business in Mussoorie in 1862. He had earlier founded his first British pharmacy in Allahabad in 1858.

Many enterprising Indians were able to develop their apothecaries (or as they called them 'Medical Halls'). One such was Butto Kristo Paul. Starting in the 1860s in a tiny shop in a small one-storeyed building it had moved to a busy side lane in 1896, and occupied two upper floors of the building, with an elegant sign board. B. K. Paul & Co. It carried out wholesale as well as retail business, and dealt in a wide range of drugs, chemicals and related articles. Many such chemists opened up all over India in late 1800s and early 1900s like Jagat Singh and Brothers in Lahore and Murree, Harnam Das Thakur Das and Sons in Nowshera etc.

The earliest Indian pharmaceutical manufacturing company was Bengal Chemical and Pharmaceutical Works started in 1901 in Calcutta. Later, Alembic Chemical Works was established in 1907 at Baroda where it started manufacturing tincture and alcohol. Sometime later in 1935, Cipla was established in Bombay.

A Pharmaceutical Society of India was formed in 1913 and, in 1920, a new publication — the Indian and Eastern Druggist — for British pharmacists in India was launched. It remained in existence until 1941.

Government of India on 11th August 1930, appointed a committee under the chairmanship of Late Col. R. N. Chopra to see into the problems of Pharmacy in India and recommend measures to be taken. This committee published its report in 1931 stating that there was no recognized specialized profession of Pharmacy. No quality standards existed that included Indian medicinal products as well, in addition to European ones. A little while later Prof. Mahadeva Lal Schroff initiated pharmaceutical education at the university level in the Banaras Hindu University. In 1935 United Province Pharmaceutical Association was established which later converted into Indian Pharmaceutical Association. The Indian Journal of Pharmacy was started by Prof. M. L. Schroff in 1939.

From this report, we find the following categories of pharmaceuticals being used at that time:

- Tincture and other Spirit Preparations
- Liquid Extracts
- Solid Extracts
- Alkaloids
- Organic Antimony and Arsenic Compounds
- Vaccines and Sera
- Organic Therapeutic Products
- Proprietary Liquid Preparations
- Proprietary Solid Preparations
- Oleums, Syrups and Oxymels
- Confections, Emplastrum, Glycerine, Pulveres (powders), Unguentums (Ointments)

In 1940 Government brought 'Drugs Bill' to regulate the import, manufacture, sale and distribution of drugs and was finally adopted as 'Drugs Act of 1940'. Next year the first Drugs Technical Advisory Board (D.T.A.B.) under this act was constituted, as was Central Drugs Laboratory in Calcutta.

In 1945 a milestone was created when Drugs Rule under the Drugs Act of 1940 was established, which is still in force although after numerous additions and deletions as per requirement of the times. In the same year Government brought the Pharmacy Bill to standardize the Pharmacy Education in India. In 1948 Pharmacy Act was published, followed by establishment of Pharmacy Council of India next year. Last major milestone was the publication of the First Edition of Indian Pharmacopoeia in 1955.

1.3 CURRENT STATUS

Indian pharmaceutical industry has an annual turnover of about Rs. 2.2 lac crores, out of which little less than half is contributed by exports. Pharmaceutical exports go to all corners of the world with the majority (about half) going to EU and USA. Around 12,000 manufacturers are actively producing APIs (Active Pharmaceutical Ingredient) or Bulk Drugs as well formulations (dosage forms like tablets, capsules, injections etc.). India is producing a wide range of pharmaceuticals like (in order of market share):

- Anti-Infective
- Cardiovascular
- Gastro Intestinal
- Vitamins and Minerals
- Respiratory
- Pain/Analgesic
- Anti-Diabetic

Top ten Indian pharmaceutical companies:

- Sun Pharmaceuticals
- Lupin
- Dr. Reddy's
- Cipla
- Aurobindo
- Cadila
- Glenmark
- Glaxo Smithkline
- Divis Labs
- Torrent

Top ten Indian biotechnology companies:

- Serum Institute of India
- Biocon
- Jubilant Life Sciences
- Syngene International
- Biological E
- Nuziveedu Seeds
- AstraZeneca Pharma India
- Mahyco
- Bharat Biotech International
- GSK India

While India is recognized internationally for its well-developed infrastructure with respect to pharmaceutical industry, (as demonstrated by fast growing exports of pharmaceuticals, medical devices, pharmaceutical machines, biotechnology products etc.), there are various factors that will be having an impact on future growth. Chief among these include:

- Healthcare spending by government
- Number of hospitals and beds
- Healthcare spending by population
- Health insurance penetration
- Affordability and accessibility of medicines
- Penetration into Tier 2 and rural markets
- Development of Generics market
- Development of biotech segment etc.

1.4 FUTURE

The world pharmaceutical industry had total sales in 2017, of USD 1.11 trillion. Out of this USD 150 billion was spent by pharmaceutical companies on research and development. The top pharmaceutical companies in 2018 include:

- Pfizer
- Roche
- Sanofi
- Johnson & Johnson
- Merck
- Novartis
- Abb Vie
- Gilead
- GSK
- Amgen

Pharmaceutical sciences are by themselves quite specialized and involve a very high level of technology in biologicals, sciences and engineering. Still, efforts are ceaseless to improve in various fields within the industry. Some of the areas attracting special attention from researchers and technologists include:

- Discovering new and better molecules to treat various diseases
- Research methods to minimize or replace animal testing
- Increasing use of supercomputers for molecular modelling for research
- Introducing newer and better drug delivery systems to enhance therapeutic effect
- Researching for green chemistry to minimize generation of waste materials and conservation of energy
- Researching for green engineering for better efficiencies
- Adopting automated manufacturing to a greater extent than at present
- Improving manufacturing efficiency using computerized manufacturing execution systems and ERP
- Increasing use of biotechnology to manufacture complex molecules in cost efficient manner

2 PHARMACEUTICAL CAREERS

2.1 PHARMACEUTICAL INDUSTRY

a. MANUFACTURING

i. Production

Pharmaceutical companies must earn their revenues by selling the products being manufactured in their factories. The products may be of their own research or generic but they have to be manufactured and packed to be brought to the sales channels for distribution. It follows therefore that to ensure continuous and reliable supply of products, the manufacturing facilities have to run smoothly and be able to produce the intended products with minimum cost and achieve maximum efficiency in its manufacturing operations, while at the same time achieving all desired compliance and quality standards.

Production of pharmaceuticals may be broadly divided into two major parts:

1. Active Pharmaceutical Ingredients (APIs)
2. Finished Formulations or Dosage Forms

Active Pharmaceutical Ingredients (APIs)

APIs are the core chemicals that have a medicinal effect on our body. These are normally synthesized by a long process of chemical reactions involving multiple stages of reactions. Let us take an example of chemical synthesis of paracetamol, a commonly used painkiller:

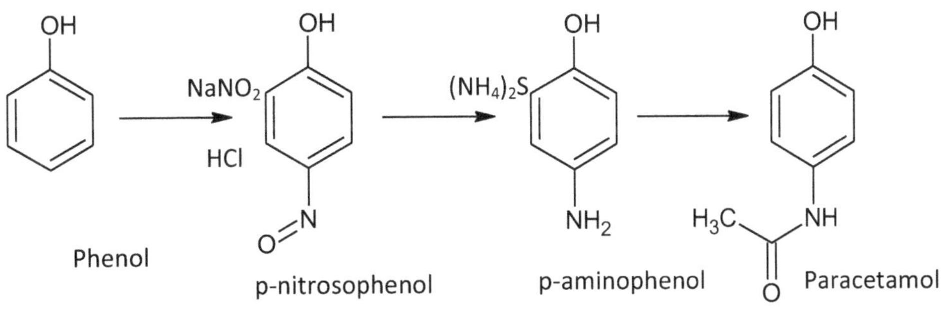

In the earliest adopted process as outlined above, phenol is reacted slowly with sodium nitrite and hydrochloric acid (solution) at around 0°C. This gives para nitrosophenol, which is filtered out. At second step, the para nitrosophenol is reduced to para aminophenol (PAP) by reaction with ammonium sulphite. The second step reaction occurs at around 40°C. PAP as produced above in second step is now acetylated with acetic anhydride to produce Paracetamol in the third stage. This process has been called the Sterling process. Many more processes have since been introduced like the Monsanto process, Mallinckrodt process, Celanese process and so on.

This being an example of a simple manufacturing process, for many other APIs the processes are very long and complex, often involving 10-15 or even more intermediate steps. Such processes also require precise control of temperature, pressure, timing and flow rate thereby requiring chilling plants, boilers, air-conditioners, air compressors, water treatment plans and extensive control instruments. The overall process in all cases however can be described as starting from ordinary chemicals and ending with a pharmaceutical that has a medicinal effect on our body. It is usually in the form of powder, crystalline or amorphous, dense or light, white, cream or any other shades. It is collected under controlled environment (remember it's a pharmaceutical now so regulatory controls come into play) and stored in airtight containers of appropriate material of construction.

Similarly different but related processes exist for APIs derived from herbal sources, animal sources, microbes etc. The actual processes that take place on lab scale, followed by pilot scale and finally industrial scale are far more complex involving automation and control systems of processes, reaction time and temperature/pressure controls and is quite complex.

Type of Manufacturing	Processing Steps				
Chemical Sources	Production of the API starting material	Introduction of the API starting material into process	Production of Intermediate(s)	Isolation and Purification	Physical processing, and packaging
Animal Sources	Collection of organ, fluid, or tissue	Cutting, mixing, and/or initial processing	Introduction of the API starting material into process	Isolation and Purification	Physical processing, and packaging
Herbal Sources	Collection of Plant	Cutting and Initial extractions	Introduction of the API starting material into process	Isolation and Purification	Physical processing, and packaging
Microbial Sources	Establishment of master cell bank and working cell bank	Maintenance of working cell bank	Cell culture and/or fermentation	Isolation and Purification	Physical processing, and packaging

The main reason that we use animal and plant sources for medicinal products is that it is either not possible to synthesize chemically in a laboratory or the process to synthesize is so complex and cumbersome and expensive that its far more practical to extract the same from plant or animal sources, a process which itself is quite specialized and complicated. Before going further to formulations, some commonly used pharmaceuticals are listed that are used today as medicines and are derived from plant or animal sources:

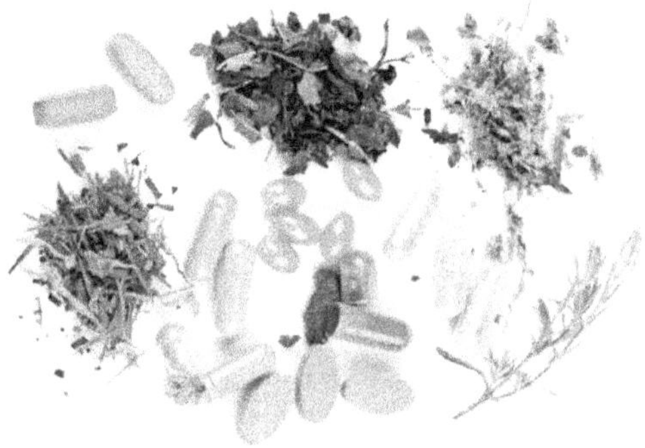 PLANT SOURCES	 ANIMAL SOURCES
Allantoin	Enoxaparin
Atropine	Heparin
Bromelain	Amylase, Lipase
Colchicine	Antithrombin III, human; Factor II; V, VII, IX, X
Curcumin	Lactobacillus acidophilus
Digitoxin	Gelatin
Digoxin	Insulin
Etoposide	Collagen
Hesperidin	Recombinant antihaemophilic factor
Papain	Interferon beta-1a
Quinidine	Epoietin-alfa
Rutin	Lutropin alfa
Sennosides A, B	Monoclonal Antibody based molecules (MaB)
Taxol / Paclitaxel	Vaccines (various)
Teniposide	Somatropin
Valapotriates	Snake Antivenom
Vinblastine	Conjugated Oestrogens
Vincristine	Chondroitin
Paclitaxel	Glucosamine
	Chitin
	Lanolin
	Propolis
	Trypsin

Note: Whole plants or their parts as used in traditional systems of medicine such as Ayurveda, Unani and Siddha have been excluded from this list as they do not constitute orthodox pharmaceutical sector.

Laboratory

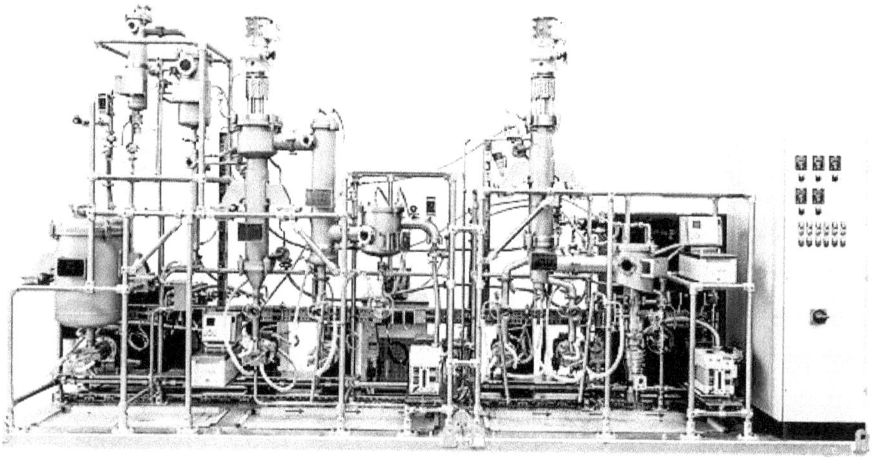

Pilot Plant

Industrial

Finished Formulations or Dosage Forms

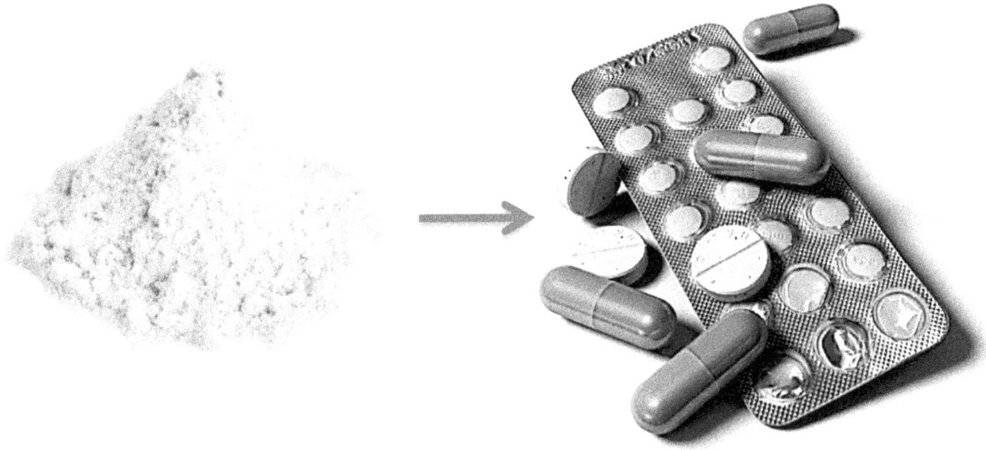

Active Pharmaceutical Ingredient — Finished Formulation or Dosage Form

The dosage forms are prepared from the APIs following a specialized manufacturing process in order to administer medicine to a patient.

The finished formulations are normally available in the following forms:

- Tablets
- Capsules
- Liquid Orals
- Topical Preparations (ointments, creams, gels, lotions etc.)
- Injectables

Besides these commonly used products some specialized dosage forms are also available as Aerosols (liquid and powder), transdermal patches, buccal inserts etc.

Why do we have to convert the API to a dosage form? Why not just administer the powder form of the API itself? These are common question that come to mind when we try rationalizing the need to covert. The truth is that there are numerous reasons why we need to spend a huge sum of money, efforts and time to convert the API into finished dosage forms:

- Masking the taste and odour
- Protection from degradation
- Accurate dosage
- Enhancing absorption in our body
- Controlling where the medicine is absorbed (mouth, stomach, small intestine, large intestine)
- Controlled release medicine (e.g. single dose absorbed evenly over 24 hours rather than immediately)
- Maximizing the effect of medicine

The process to convert the APIs into dosage forms can be achieved by adding excipients to the API and following a manufacturing process. Excipients are those substances that do not have any medicinal effect on our body but are needed to produce a finished dosage form of required characteristics.

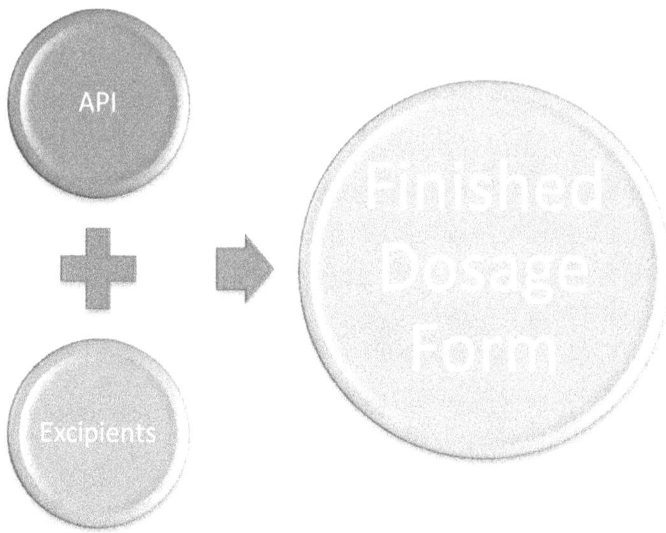

Commonly used ingredients include:

- Solvents
- Binders
- Lubricants
- Suspending agents
- Flavours
- Sweetners
- Colours
- Solubilizers
- Antioxidants etc.

Machines Used for Manufacture of Dosage Forms

Liquid Packing Line

Tabletting Machine

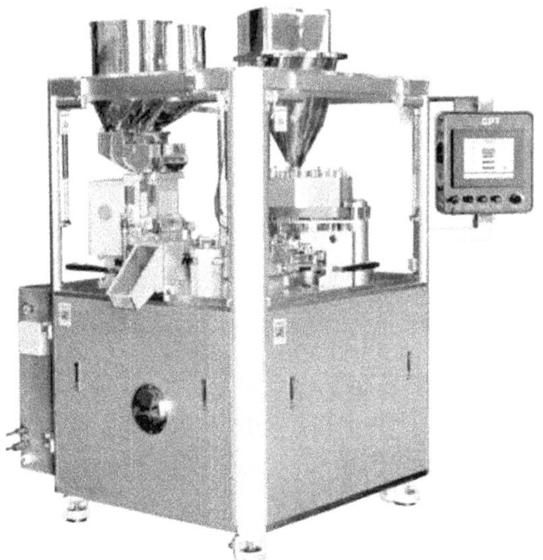

Capsule Filling Machine

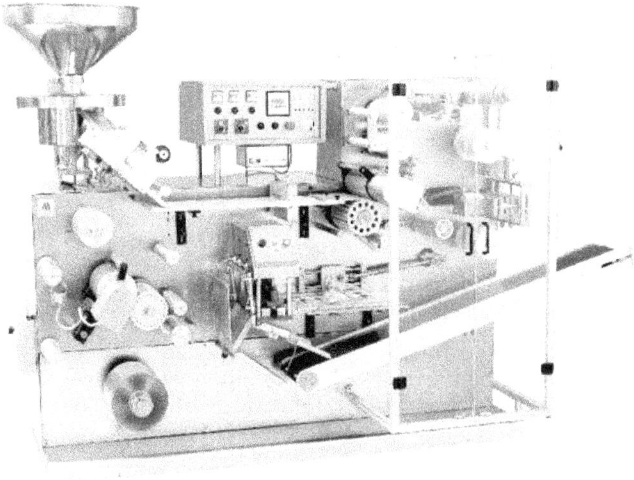

Blister Packing Machine for Tablets/Capsules

Typical work description for a person employed in pharmaceutical manufacturing would include planning production schedule, ensuring receipt of raw materials for production and operating the production machines as assigned from time to time, including ensuring their cleaning and periodic maintenance. The actual production should be efficient and expected yields should be obtained and at the same time high quality should be maintained. Required documentation has to be maintained (paper or digital) to ensure compliance with the laws and regulations in force.

One of the most important aspects of pharmaceutical manufacturing is the concept of Good Manufacturing Practices (GMP). It is a system that defines the overall manufacturing operations in a factory designed to ensure that all activities are performed as per written and approved procedures. This is done to ensure uniformity of quality and quality is assured at every step of the process, rather than finding out the mistakes in the end.

Average annual package of a Production Officer (junior) in a pharmaceutical company in India ranges between 2 lacs for smaller companies to 4-5 lacs for bigger companies.

Average annual package of a Production Manager (GM Production) in a pharmaceutical company in India ranges between 10 lacs for smaller companies to 45-50 lacs for bigger companies.

ii Pharmaceutical Engineering

In a running pharmaceutical plant a lot more work has to be performed that is not directly involved with manufacturing but rather in ensuring the right facility conditions and support services are available for the purpose. This would include maintenance of manufacturing machines and equipment, operations of utilities like steam boiler, chilling and air-conditioning plant, air compressors, vacuum systems, water treatment plants, building and construction maintenance etc.

While actual manufacturing processes will be controlled and supervised by production team, each of those machines will require some utilities like electricity, purified water, compressed air and gasses (e.g. Nitrogen), vacuum, steam, chilled water etc. Pharmaceutical engineers would be responsible that these are adequately provided for and these entire systems are working in a smooth manner. In case there is breakdown in any of these systems, production can come to a halt and it results in tremendous losses for the company. The role of a pharmaceutical engineer is thus critical in a pharmaceutical manufacturing operation.

Some of the utilities are also controlled by local pharmaceutical laws that lay down minimum quality standards of such services like various kinds of waters are defined ranging from ordinary potable water to very high purity water for injection, based on quality standards of such waters. Where required, pure steam has to comply with such statutory requirements of quality and safety. Filtered air with precise particle density of specific sizes in a room may also be defined per specific standards as also the temperature and humidity levels. Appropriate machines are thus needed to control and measure such systems, including HEPA filters (High Efficiency Particulate Air).

Pharmaceutical engineers have to work in close coordination with the manufacturing personnel as well as people from quality control and quality assurance in order to ensure all activities are in compliance with local pharmaceutical manufacturing laws. Indeed, they are often part of joint team for specific projects and some are even working exclusively in quality assurance, quality control and manufacturing operations.

Future work specializations that hold great promise for pharmaceutical engineers include:

Sustainable Manufacturing: It describes manufacturing processes for creation of best quality products that use minimum natural resources, minimizing toxic substance generation and produce minimum waste and greenhouse gases emission. Efforts are being made to reduce energy consumption, increased use of renewable energy, minimizing water consumption in process, waste recycling etc.

Green Chemistry: It may be described as the design of chemical products or processes to reduce or eliminate the use or generation of hazardous substances. Efforts are being made towards waste prevention, safer chemical ingredients, less hazardous synthesis methods, renewable inputs like water/energy, using catalysts, enzymatic rather than chemical synthesis, continuous rather than batch processing, reducing process mass intensity, and using eco-friendly solvents.

Green Engineering: This covers all concepts related to physical assets available in a pharmaceutical facility. This broadly includes sustainable buildings, sustainable energy management, sustainable utilities and sustainable water management.

Operational Excellence: To lower the cost of producing pharmaceuticals, besides lowering the raw material costs, one way is to reduce the manufacturing cost. This can be achieved by increasing productivity with existing machines by increasing their productive time, reducing the number of breakdowns and to reduce the cleaning/changeover times and by optimizing batch cycle times. One of the most prominent and promising way to improve productivity is to include automated manufacturing rather than batch manufacturing. Commonly used method to measure such enhanced productivity is by measuring Overall Equipment Effectiveness (OEE).

Continuous/Automated Manufacturing: Pharmaceutical production, being tightly controlled by laws governing manufacturing of pharmaceuticals, mainly consists of batch production. This means one batch of predetermined size is taken up and goes through various manufacturing steps, each time being subjected to quality tests. After passing such tests only the next step of production can commence. This process greatly reduces the manufacturing efficiency. Therefore efforts are currently being made to switch to continuous manufacturing with automatic systems of quality and process checks. This results in much higher output and hence lowered cost to manufacture.

A Bachelor of Science is the minimum amount of education required to become a pharmaceutical engineer, but a master's or doctoral degree is strongly encouraged.

The preferred educational requirements for the job of a Pharmaceutical engineer include an undergraduate or graduate engineering degree (B.E./B.Tech or M.E./M.Tech) or B. Pharm/M. Pharm with specialization in Pharmaceutical Technology or Pharmaceutics. Some colleges in India are also offering such post graduate specializations in Pharmaceutical Engineering. From engineering background, specializations having interest for pharmaceutical industry include, Chemical, Mechanical, Industrial etc.

HVAC Engineers

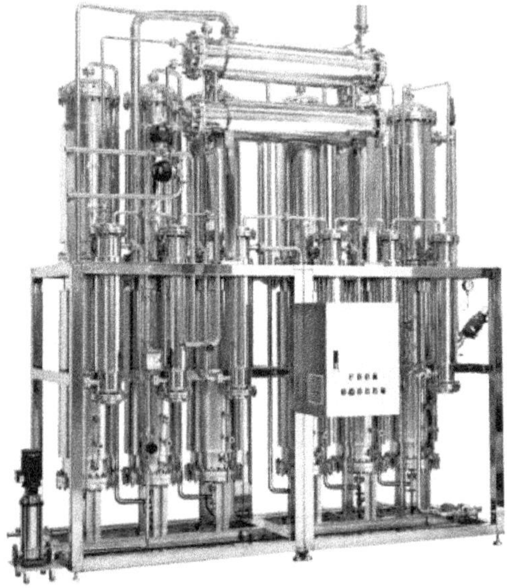
Sterile Water Plant

Boiler

Compressed Air Plant

Typical job profiles in this field may be labelled as:

- Process Engineer
- Engineer (Projects)
- Engineer (Production/Chemical)
- Associate Engineer
- Electrician
- Electronic Technician
- HVAC Supervisor
- HVAC Technician
- Industrial Engineer
- Instrumentation Engineer
- Maintenance Supervisor
- Maintenance Technician

Average annual package of a Service Maintenance Engineer in a pharmaceutical company ranges between 2 lacs for smaller companies to 7-8 lacs for bigger companies. While for senior engineering manager, it ranges between 3-4 lacs to 15 lacs per annum.

iii QUALITY CONTROL

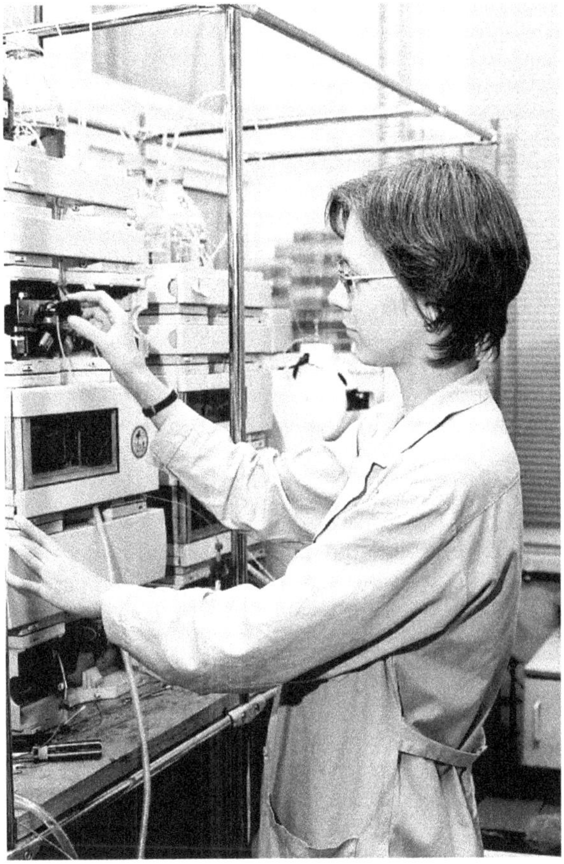

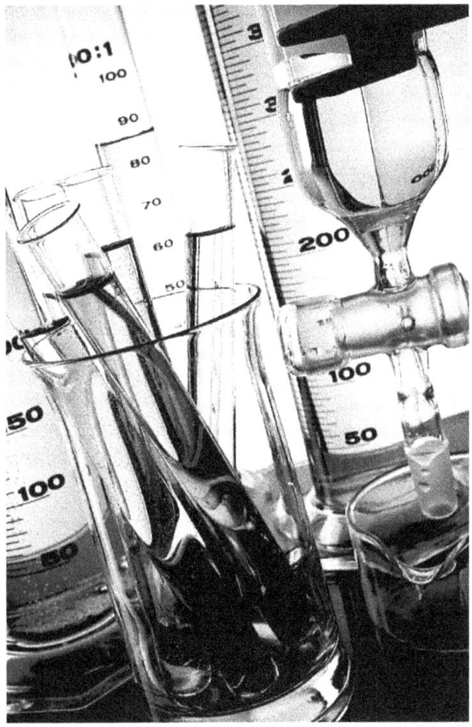

Pharmaceutical products of any type are always critical in nature as the health of the patient directly depends on it. Therefore it is imperative that they are always of highest quality possible. In order to ensure that in any pharmaceutical manufacturing facility all products are of accepted high quality, there is a department of Quality Control. Its function is to ensure the identity, purity and safety of all products made in that facility.

To achieve this, testing laboratories are established that further consist of different types like chemical testing, instrumental testing, microbiological testing and biological testing. To ensure uniform high quality of all pharmaceutical products, most countries (including India) have established standards for various pharmaceutical substances which have to be passed by all products. Such standards are compiled in a book (one or more volumes) called Pharmacopoeia. For example United States Pharmacopoeia, British Pharmacopoeia, Indian Pharmacopoeia, Japanese Pharmacopoeia etc. Each of these pharmacopoeias have legal jurisdiction in their respective countries. The role of the quality control lab is therefore to ensure that the products meet or exceed the standards as laid down by the pharmacopoeias. Quality control department performs the following functions:

Routine

Raw Material Testing	Equipment Cleaning Testing
Packing Materials Testing	Finished Products Testing
In-process Control Testing	Stability Studies

Non Routine

Calibration of equipment and measuring instruments	Investigating test failures such as Out Of Specification (OOS)
Preparation of working standards	Analytical method validation
Analytical method development	

In a typical pharmaceutical manufacturing facility, all the raw and packing material coming in from suppliers are put in a quarantine area from where samples are collected which have to first undergo specified quality control tests. Once they are approved by the quality control lab, they can then be accepted for storage in a warehouse for eventual use in the manufacturing process. Normally, a qualified junior chemist does the testing and which is checked by senior chemist and further approved by the laboratory in-charge. Such records are also maintained and controlled mandatorily as per laws.

Since almost all pharmaceutical manufacturing processes are based on batch production (not continuous), therefore in-process testing is done at various stages of manufacture to ensure all quality parameters are under control. And final finished product testing is done on completion of the manufacturing batch.

Quality control laboratories in most pharmaceutical companies consist of two essential elements, Chemical Analysis section and Instrumental Analysis section for testing of most non-sterile products. However, for sterile products testing Microbiological Analysis section is also required which may have an associated animal house for certain specified tests as prescribed in pharmacopoeia. The Chemical Analysis section houses a large bench area with chemicals and related glassware (test-tubes, beakers, burettes, measuring cylinders, conical flasks etc.) for testing. It also contains fume hoods and robust exhaust and ventilation systems. The Instrumental Analysis section is segregated from the chemical side due to sensitive electronics of the various instruments used for testing like spectrophotometer, HPLC, gas chromatographs etc. Microbiological section houses equipment for microbial contamination, sterility testing and other tests, and houses equipment like BOD Incubator, colony counter, microbial identification systems, microscopes, laminar flow bench etc. It has designated sterile area classified as ISO class 5 (older class 100). Microbiological section also has filtered classified air through use of HEPA filters.

These laboratory sections usually also have shared or separate areas like sample control room, rooms for consumables storage, waste staging, cold storage, document control, purified/sterile water system, compressed air/gases distribution system, chemical weighing, glass washing, sample incubation. The labs also have conveniently located copy rooms, office areas, conference rooms, restrooms etc.

Quality Approval Process - Incoming

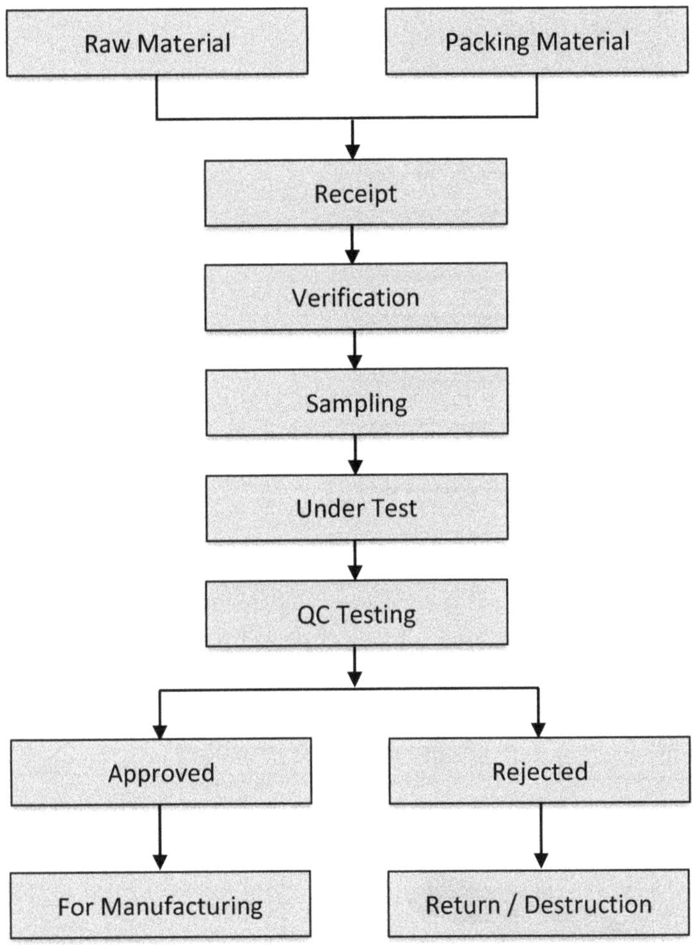

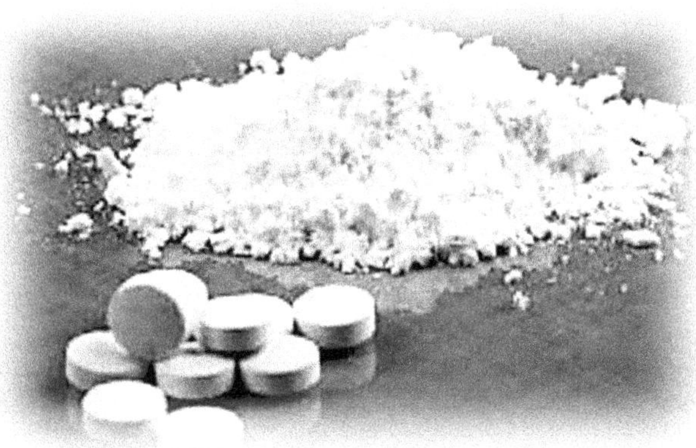

Quality Approval Process – Finished Goods

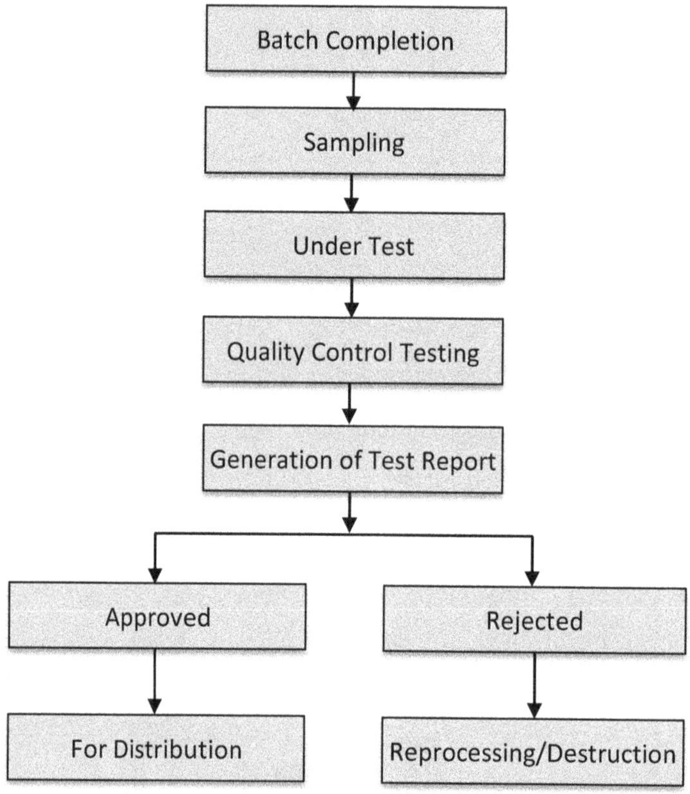

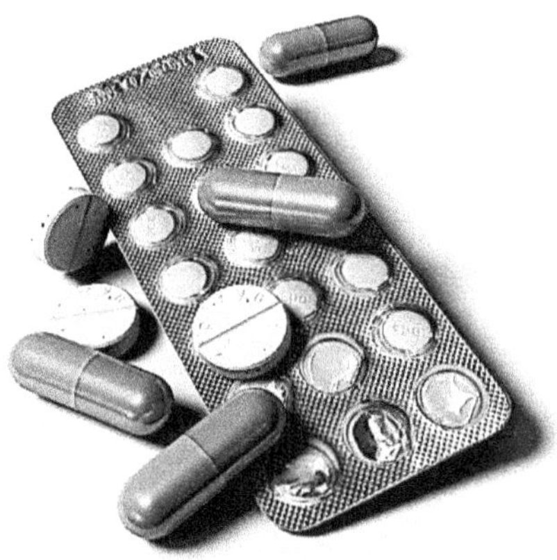

Eligible qualifications for working as an analyst in the pharmaceutical quality control lab include B. Sc, B. Pharm, M. Pharm and PhD, in the order of preference and associated pay scales and growth prospects.

While obvious choices for career are the pharmaceutical companies, there are additional career options like:

- Independent Analytical Labs
- Analytical Research Organizations
- Chemical Research Organizations etc.

Average starting annual salary is around Rs. 1,20,000 to 2,40,000 depending on the company and the candidates' qualification and experience. Top of the line salary for quality control lab manager or director after 10-15 years of experience is around Rs. 6,00,000 to 24,00,000.

iv QUALITY ASSURANCE

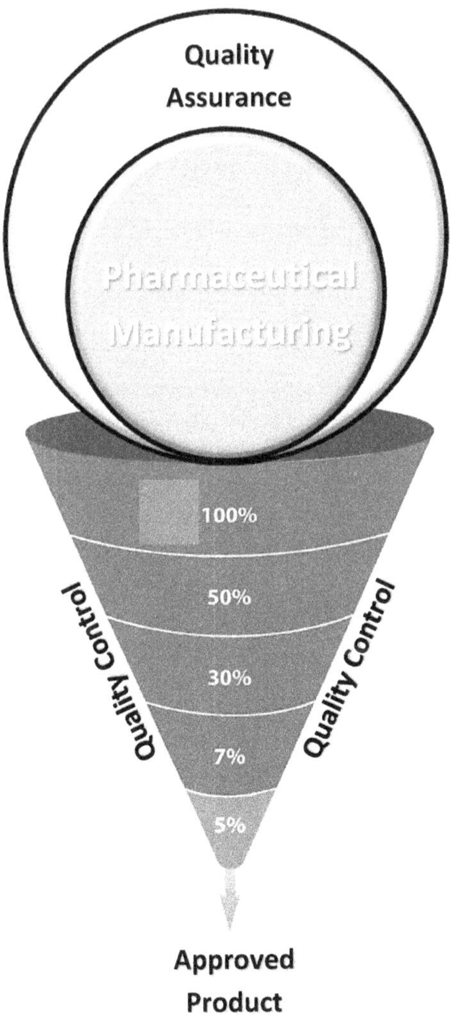

Quality assurance is a way of preventing mistakes and defects during the manufacturing process hence avoiding problems earlier on rather than defect detection and rejection after manufacturing by quality control. As the above figure demonstrates, pharmaceutical manufacturing takes place in an environment of quality assurance so that rejection and resulting wastage is minimized.

Although all personnel in an organization are responsible for quality, the quality assurance department is primarily responsible for conducting quality assurance tasks and providing system that is both effective and efficient.

A good quality assurance department should be staffed by appropriately qualified personnel with good interpersonal skills. The department should operate independently from the other departments and must regularly review quality by performing audits to ensure that the regulations are being followed.

Functions of QA in Pharmaceutical industry

- Raw materials used in the manufacturing are approved and procured from approved vendor
- All data is recorded as per cGMP and is reviewed for accuracy and traceability
- Procedures are in place for performing the activities, operating and calibrating the equipment
- Quality is built into the plant, process and product. It ensures that a robust quality system is in place
- Trainings like induction, on job, scheduled and after any changes are conducted for respective individuals on time
- To prepare and approve quality policy, quality objectives, quality manual and validation master plan
- Periodic monitoring of the quality objectives
- Monitoring all validation and stability activities to ensure they are completed as per the schedule
- Ensures that all changes impacting the product and the established systems are documented and reviewed
- Ensures that all deviations, OOS/OOT and market complaints are logged and investigated to identify the root cause so as to take CAPA to prevent recurrence
- Preparation of annual product quality reports, trending of data, determining product and process performance
- To arrange and conduct the self-inspection, identify gaps
- Preparing, approving and monitoring the implementation of key documents (Quality Policy and Objectives, Quality Manual, Validation Master Plan, etc.).
- Approving an equipment calibration, qualification and maintenance schedule, as well as critical utilities qualification calendar (HVAC, water, gas and power distribution systems, etc.).
- Ensuring that specifications and test procedures for raw materials, packing materials, in-process testing, APIs, stability testing, etc. are all in place.
- Ensuring that planned/unplanned changes or deviations are documented, reviewed and analyzed, and recommending studies, tests or validation activities to be performed.
- Logging and responding to customer complaints, supervising the investigation into the cause of the issue, providing an investigation report to the customer, etc.
- Initiating, documenting and investigating market returns, reprocessing (for API batches) or destruction (for finished batches), and informing regulatory authorities about defects found after distribution.

- Training and leading the internal audit team for each department, interacting with auditors during external, internal and customer inspections, and intimating management of the observations.
- Reviewing and approving manufacturing records and QC testing data before any intermediate, API or finished batch is released, as well as periodic trending of this data.
- Initiating an OOS (out of specification) investigation and reviewing the QC test if any raw material, packaging, intermediate or stability sample does not meet established and approved specification during the latter.
- Qualifying and auditing calibration service providers for tests and calibrations not performed in-house, reviewing and preparing Quality and Technical agreements for other manufacturing sites.

Eligible qualifications for working in pharmaceutical quality assurance department include B. Pharm, M. Pharm and PhD, in the order of preference and associated pay scales and growth prospects.

Choices for career include the pharmaceutical companies quality assurance department.

Average starting annual salary is around Rs. 2,50,000 to 5,00,000 depending on the company and the candidates' qualification and experience. Top of the line salary for quality control lab manager or director after 10-15 years of experience is around Rs. 15,00,000 to 30,00,000.

v Information Technology

Information Technology has pervaded the pharmaceutical industry at all levels, from research to manufacturing to marketing. While a lot has been said about IT in research and in marketing operations, this chapter will focus on IT in pharmaceutical manufacturing.

Most pharmaceutical plants use a paper batch record to track production and provide instruction to operators. At various places on that sheet of paper, the operator must sign off that they have completed a specific task. In a pharmaceutical operation this batch record is as important as the product itself because the product cannot be sold without complete documentation on how it was produced. Electronic paper gradually evolved, as computers became more prevalent in the workplace. With electronic batch records (EBR), all data is stored in the computer system, allowing more data to be stored. The only thing missing from most electronic batch records initially was a signature. Signatures are required to prove those specific tasks have been completed. When the Food and Drug Administration (FDA) ruled on acceptable electronic signatures in August of 1997 the last stumbling block to the paperless plant was removed.

An Electronic Record may be defined as "any combination of text, graphics, data, audio, pictorial or other information represented in digital form that is created, modified, maintained, archived, retrieved, or distributed by a computer system".

An Electronic Signature may be defined as "a computer data compilation of any symbol or series of symbols executed, adopted or authorized by an individual to be the legally binding equivalent of the individual's handwritten signature. An electronic signature is no good until the company of the signer authorizes electronic signatures and recognizes them as legally binding. When a system generates electronic records that can greatly impact product safety and quality, it can be labeled as "high-risk" system. It is however, important to categorize and identify the systems as high or low risk ones. International Society of Pharmaceutical Engineers (ISPE) in a white paper submitted to US FDA have listed some of the high and low risk systems that generate GxP records:

High Risk Systems – Quality Decisions, Change Control, Configuration Management, Security, Procedural Controls etc.

Low Risk Systems – Environmental Monitoring Systems, Operator Training Records, Instrument Qualification Records, Word Processing of SOPs, Instrument Calibration Records etc.

eManufacturing

Standard Operating Procedures are named quite aptly. As the name suggests, these are standards to be adopted for procedures of any specified operation. The purpose of a standard operating procedure is to describe the performance of a controlled process. As most processes encountered in a pharmaceutical facility are routine or repetitive activities, SOPs document such repetitive processes. Indeed, if there is change encountered in the process, there is a separate SOP for change control. Therefore, they define how a task is to be performed to achieve a specified outcome and standardize the way a task is to be performed so as to minimize variation. They are also used for training purposes of the technical staff and fulfill important regulatory requirements. While, traditionally such SOPs were paper based, since last number of years, the transition to electronic SOPs (eSOPS) has started.

Advantages of eSOPs

- Increased efficiency in issuing SOPs. The SOP documentation in-charge no longer needs to replace paper copies in binders spread throughout the lab.
- Assurance that the staff is accessing the most current procedure.
- Search and hyperlink capabilities reduce the time required to find a procedure or attachment.
- The system allows technicians and analysts to access the current version of the regulatory standards on-line, and view the Quality Manual online as well.
- Allows true release and effective dates so that the staff can review and receive training on upcoming procedures before their effective date.
- Far superior access control system available with electronic SOP systems with related security features, not possible with paper based SOP system.

The logical next step forward is the concept of Electronic Manufacturing (eManufacturing). Electronic manufacturing includes the eSOP system discussed above plus coupled seamlessly with Electronic Batch Records (EBR), which in turn is coupled with Enterprise Resource Planning (ERP) sometimes via a Manufacturing Execution System (MES). Laboratory Information Management Systems (LIMS) would also be involved at each of these modules to bring to conclusion a successful, efficient and lean system of eManufacturing.

A batch record is typically a distributed collection of instructions, signatures, and reports written on paper or stored as MS office documents that follows a batch of product through the manufacturing process, creating a historical record of exactly how that batch was produced. The batch record is meant to enable the manufacturer to sell goods into regulated environments, by producing the manufacturing documentation required by regulatory agencies. The batch record can also be used internally for retrospective cost and productivity analyses of manufacturing equipment, personnel, and processes. An electronic manufacturing system is a computerized system that specifies and controls manufacturing, documents all processes and quality information, automates the process of regulatory compliance, provides instant visualization of current manufacturing processes, and facilitates retrospective analysis of batch manufacture.

In a typical pharmaceutical company having paper based documentation system, several hundred forms including batch manufacturing records, validation protocols, GMP drafts, SOP's and Certificate of Analysis reports are typically signed with a wet-ink signature by employees. These people are often located in different parts of the building (sometimes different buildings), which require the forms to be hand-carried from person-to-person. This process is very time consuming and slows down the manufacturing process. Attempting to manage all of these forms on paper also leads to an unnecessary delay in the approval process. After implementing eManufacturing, pharmaceutical companies are able to easily and efficiently sign and authenticate forms. The company is then able to create an all-electronic environment, which can increase its ability to manage documents and streamline the entire approval process. Additionally, by moving forms electronically through email and providing shared access to forms in a database application, the need to physically move documents is completely eliminated. Significant time savings are realized when on completely eliminating moving, storing and retrieving paper. One can complete the approval process in a quarter of the original time.

Benefits of Electronic Batch Records (EBR)

When pharmaceutical manufacturers decide to implement an EBR system, they have to focus on achieving certain quantifiable goals that can offset the cost of implementation and provide a positive return on investment (ROI). These include:

- Reduction of manufacturing errors, exceptions and deviations
- Reduced risk of regulatory non-compliance
- On-line manufacturing process visibility and analysis
- Reduction of manufacturing costs
- Greater retrospective analysis capability
- Instant production of manufacturing history reports required for regulatory submissions and inspections

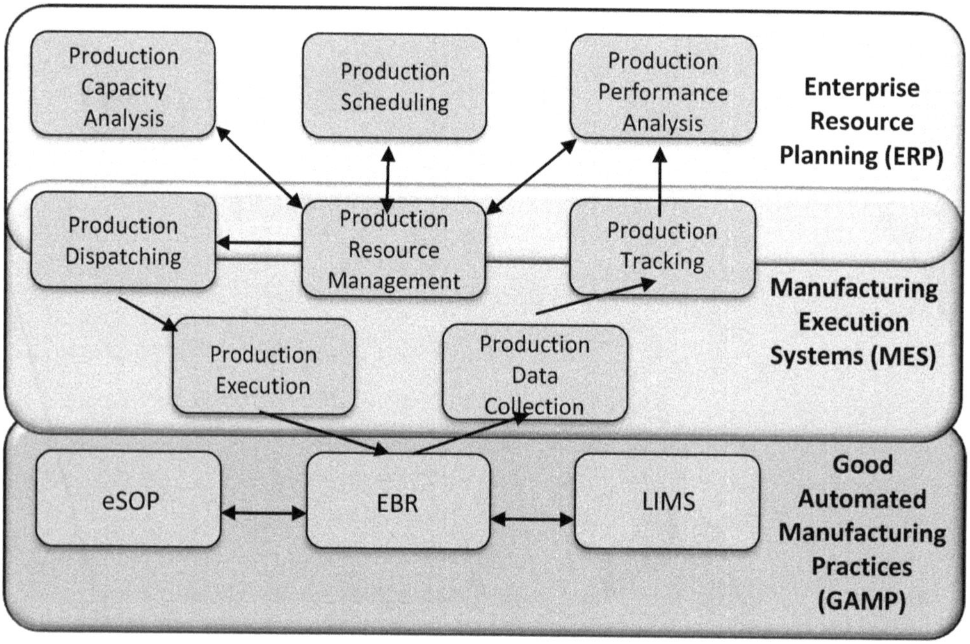

E-manufacturing enables real-time communication between the various islands of information from shop floors, corporate business systems (like ERP) and laboratory information management systems, so that the entire enterprise can act together to achieve ideal quality and cost benefits. Going paperless in manufacturing can also allow pharmaceutical companies to manage the master data across the firm's sphere of operations (that may be spread over a large geographic area). In a recent ISPE communication, it was reported that approximately 96% of workplace errors involve human factors and around 70% of documentation errors involving omission are due to bad design. Human errors are the leading cause of injuries, downtime and reduced productivity in pharmaceutical industry.

Cybersecurity in Pharmaceutical Industry

Since the pharmaceutical industry is so highly regulated, any normal breach or deviation triggers a full scale root cause analysis and corrective and preventive actions (CAPA) to ensure compliance. Therefore in case of an unauthorized breach, the stakes are very high. Not only is the investigation thorough and time consuming but also may result in bringing to a halt all related production activities and these losses can go into very large sums of money. There is a wide range of cybersecurity threats that pharma companies encounter. Some may include relatively harmless hacking of employee data for personal or professional reasons. Most are however malicious in nature. Hackers can tap into and steal personal data of employees to sell on the open market including biometrics, social security, address etc., or Darkweb (web content that use the Internet but require specific software like TOR, configurations, or authorization to access).

Sometimes, stolen hardware also leads directly to a lot of confidential or proprietary information. For example a laptop of a senior management person may be stolen for hardware value alone but on going through the stored information, more threats can materialize. Many top-level organizations provide remote-wiping of hard disc contents if such event happens. Sometimes employees may steal such obsolete servers etc. that are lying unsecured in a facility that may offer such information or IT sub-contractors. Most common however is online hacking to steal data that may include employee data, clinical trials data, research pipeline, financial and commercial data, proprietary manufacturing trade secrets, formulas, manufacturing batch records (to help counterfeiters) and so on. There have instances where hackers have introduced trojans and other malicious code or ransomware which essentially brings all such systems to a halt and can be restarted only if a ransom is paid and the malicious code can be removed by the hackers themselves.

Almost all pharma companies have established some basic defense procedures against such cyber-attacks. Adequate firewalls and procedures are adopted, all software and drivers are regularly updated, distributed data backups are designed and in place to seamlessly connect in case of loss or breach. With the spiraling cost of data handling, storage and security, there is an obvious rise in usage of cloud computing by all companies. With Amazon Web Services (AWS) and Microsoft Azure leading the pack, there are numerous such service providers to service the needs of big and small corporate clients.

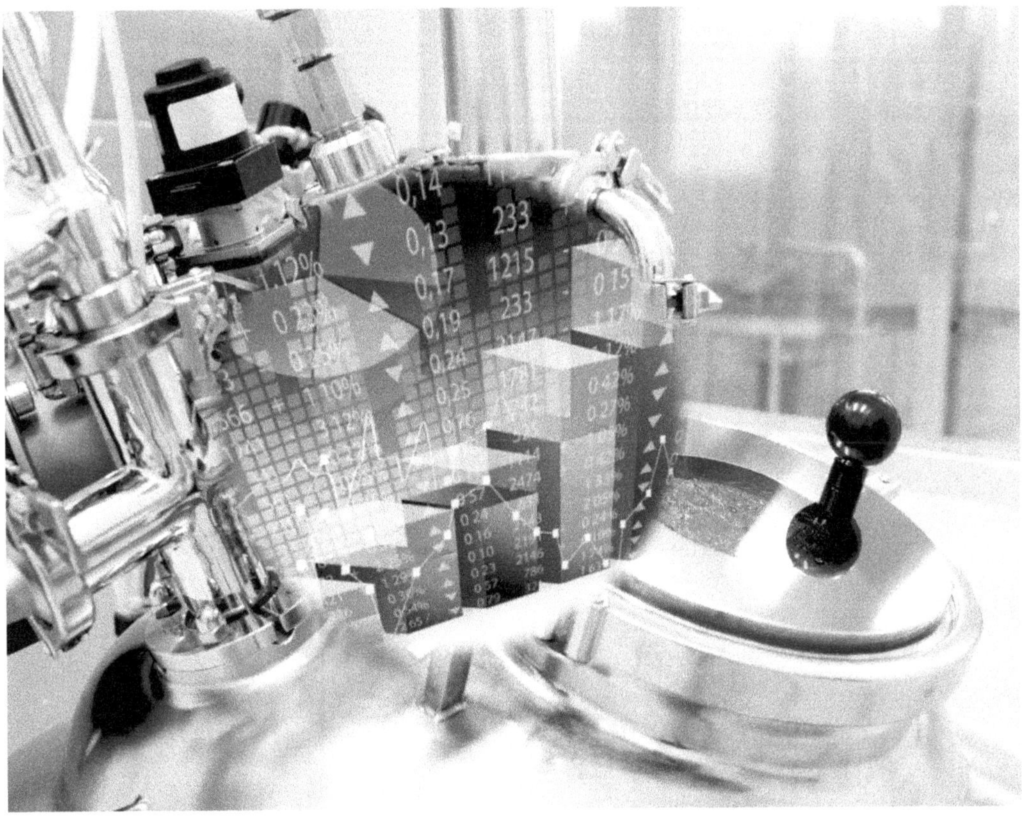

Pharma 4.0

Using the software development numbering model, the development of industry, including the pharmaceutical industry, is portrayed in this manner:

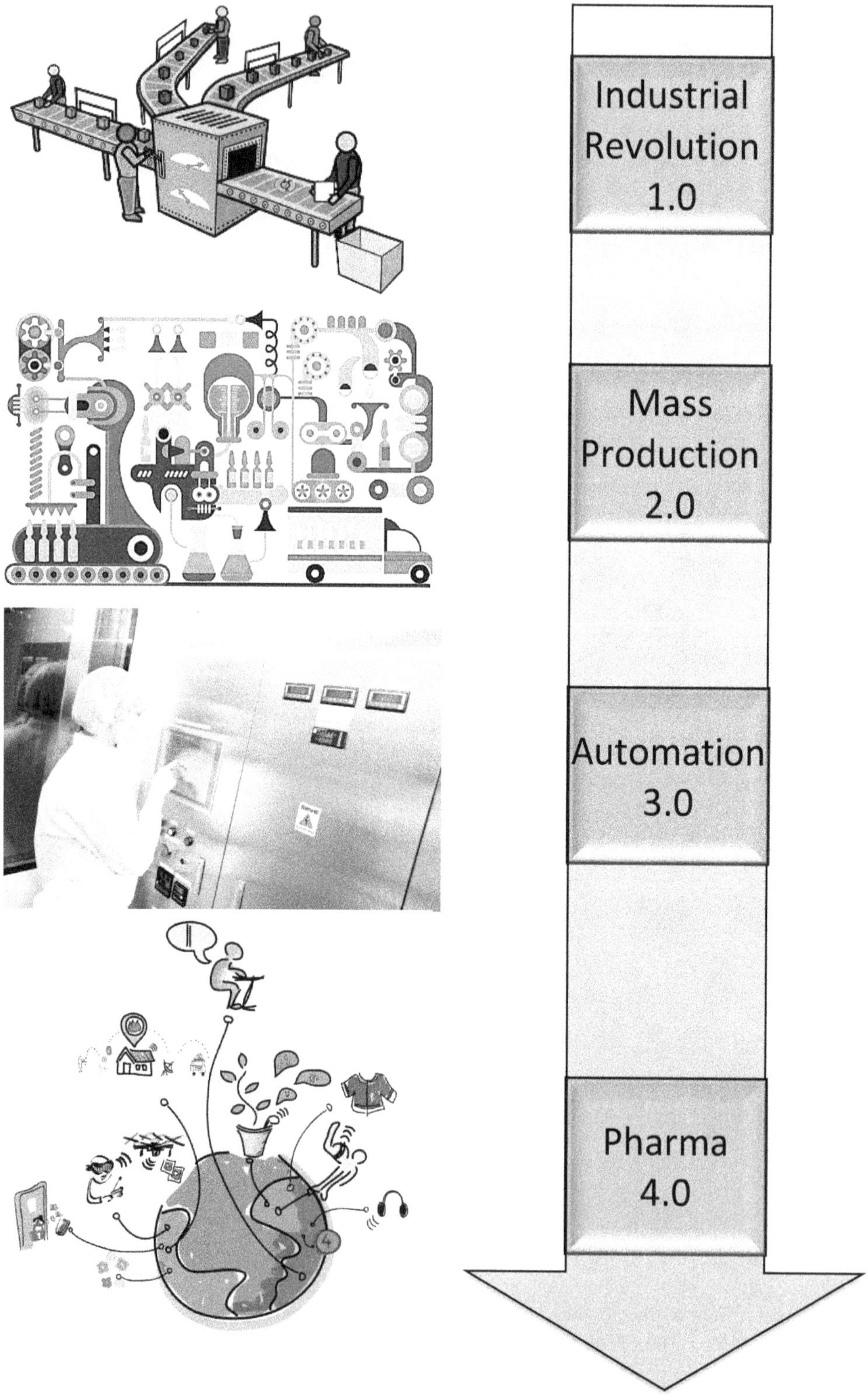
Industrial Revolution 1.0
Mass Production 2.0
Automation 3.0
Pharma 4.0

Pharma industry realized in 2017 that Big Data could dramatically increase the value of data produced during drug development or manufacturing operations. AI technologies took over the imagination in 2018 when it dawned that it could unlock much of the value of Big Data. Now in 2019 is we have most resources in our hands to leverage Big Data, IoT and AI to deploy solutions that fundamentally affect the full drug development lifecycle. Artificial Intelligence (AI) will play a growing role in data analytics.

Current Good Automated Manufacturing Practices (GAMP) aimed to improve quality oversight when they were first introduced, but they are retrospective. They can tell what's gone wrong but not what's about to go wrong, predictively. In Pharma 4.0, by increasing the amount of monitoring throughout the production cycle it offers predictive analysis and insights that offers/implements corrective action on its own if needed. Even now it's beginning to be used and known as process analytical technology (PAT). Emerging technologies can lower costs, speed-up production and improve research and development. Pharmaceutical companies have heightened concerns about traceability, product quality and process validation.

Artificial Intelligence (AI), Internet of Things (IoT), Real World Data (RWD), and Blockchain will fundamentally impact drug product lifecycle. While there are many emerging solutions, there is limited experience in applying these solutions in the real-world.

Technologies like Hadoop, Hive, and Pig process all the big data. Statistics and related programs, like open-source 'R', or proprietary systems like Minitab, SAS or Mathworks are also needed. To interpret the data and create data visualization tools like Microsoft's Power BI and such will also be needed. On the other hand in-depth pharma production knowledge will obviously be needed and its going to be rare to find both the spheres of knowledge within the same individuals. Therefore, a probable team of IT and pharma specialists will work together in a Pharma 4.0 plant.

The skill sets needed therefore for a future in pharma IT sector can be gauged from above. A B. Pharm or M. Pharm degree in addition to a short term diploma in data analytics would be useful. A background in regulatory affairs will be an additional asset due to requirements of software validation at various levels.

Average starting annual salary is around Rs. 2,50,000 to 5,00,000 depending on the company and the candidates' qualification and experience. Top of the line salary after 10-15 years of experience is around Rs. 15,00,000 to 30,00,000.

c. MARKETING AND SALES

Marketing is often defined as the umbrella category that encompasses sale, advertising, publicity, public relations, and promotion. Marketing department by using their strategies make presentations and organize campaigns, group events, conduct surveys for healthcare professionals. They also work with contacts on one-to-one basis. Marketing experts give their opinion after finding out the market need. They continuously visit the doctors to know their requirement, visit the drug stores to know the sales volumes of different products and even to the hospitals to know the disease trends in a particular region. Market professionals poll public opinion and analyze the demographics and buying pattern. In this way, they roughly estimate a yearly need of a definite pharmaceutical product. They play the role of researcher, statistician, social psychologist and sociologist.

i Domestic Marketing

As the name indicates, it is the supply of medicines within the country. Indian Pharmaceutical industry expanded drastically in the last two decades. Today it has more than 10000 registered units with almost 300 large units and other small scale units. Indian domestic market is picking up very well and can touch the target of US $30 billion by 2020. Out of 70% of the domestic demand fulfilled by pharma companies, top 10 companies occupy 30% of the domestic market by sale.

Types of Business in Domestic Market

Indian Pharmaceutical industry portrays a picture of fast development. Indian companies are involved in synthesis of active pharmaceutical ingredient, Formulations, Clinical research requirement of bulk drugs and formulation. In fact, more than 30,000 different pharmaceutical formulations worth $210 million are manufactured and sold in India.

Key Factors Propelling the Sale and Growth of Domestic Market

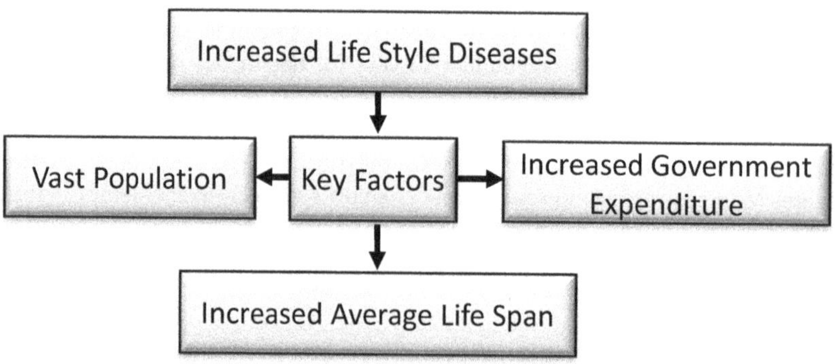

Strategies Adopted

Companies plan various strategies for the purpose of expanding their market presence and maximizing corporate benefits

- Promotion/ launch of new products/ molecules is mostly done through presentations
- As doctors play an important role in medication use so companies use social psychology by highlighting brand value and financial ways to influence doctors by offering gifts, education grants and sponsoring conferences and research
- Domestic market is very price sensitive and both consumers and retailers need good quality product at low price. Pharma companies develop a sound mechanism through marketing executives. Based upon their feedback from service users and competitors and also through inter department co-ordination, the company takes decision regarding the development of a drug.

Marketing of pharmaceuticals in India usually entails two types of sales channels to be pursued:

1. Prescription only medicines that are sold only on prescription of a doctor
2. OTC (Over The Counter) medicines that can be sold without any prescription from a doctor

OTC medicines require marketing efforts more focused on distributors and retailers supported by substantial advertising campaigns on print, broadcast and digital media. This type of sales channel is quite similar to other general FMCG (Fast Moving Consumer Goods) non-pharmaceutical products. Prescription only medicines on the other hand are prohibited by law to be advertised to the general public and are predominantly marketed by personal visits to doctors by medical representatives to present and promote their company's medicines directly to them using detailing guide, medical literature and sometimes supported by sponsoring medical conferences etc. Since this channel is the predominant one and exclusive to the pharmaceutical industry, we shall be explaining this aspect in detail below.

Medical Representatives

Medical or sales representatives in pharmaceutical industry are a key link between pharmaceutical companies and medical or healthcare professionals. Big pharma companies hire huge number of sales representatives. They work strategically to increase the awareness and usages of a company's products. They usually specialize in a particular product or therapeutic area like Pain division, Respiratory division, Cardiovascular Division, Diabetes Division, Ophthalmological division, Gynecological Division, Psychiatric Division, Neuro Division, Dermatological Division, etc.

Hierarchy in Sales and Marketing

The Pharma sales and marketing are highly technical fields and offers excellent opportunities for the pharmacy graduates. Pharmacy professional starts their career in sales and marketing as Medical Representative and go up to the levels of:

- Medical Representative
- Area Sales Manager
- Regional Sales Manager
- Zonal Sales Manager
- Marketing Manager

- Deputy General Manager (DGM)
- General Manager (GM)
- Vice President (VP)
- President

Qualifications

Minimum requirements are for B.Sc or B. Pharm and preferable additional qualifications in sales/marketing (diplomas etc.).

Knowledge and Skill Required

- Communication skills-excellent verbal communication, excellent written communication
- Presentation skills
- Ability to think outside the box and be creative
- Ability to drive and inspire
- Confident
- Quick decision-making ability

Salary of a Medical Representative in a pharma company varies from 2 lacs to 5 lacs per annum depending on type/size of company, area where stationed and years of experience of the candidate. For example the average salary in Pfizer India hovers at around 5 lacs per annum, Dr. Reddy's Labs at 3.5 lacs per annum and Emcure Labs at 2.2 lacs per annum. Other variable factors affecting take home salary include the earned amounts in Bonus, Profit Sharing and Commission which are factors exclusive to marketing department.

Zonal sales manager in a pharma company earns an annual package of 4 lacs to 9 lacs while a National sales manager in a pharma company earns an annual package of 20 lacs to 100 lacs.

Market Research

Market research analysts collect and analyze data to support the marketing of medicines during every stage of the product life cycle, including pre-launch, launch, and when the products become established. They design and conduct market research studies, analyze accumulated data, and communicate findings to management to support business recommendations. MRAs usually work closely with product managers. Only bigger pharmaceutical companies have such division and sometimes they are a part of Product Management division (see below).

Product Management

Degree in Pharmacy with MBA (marketing) after few years of experience in sales and marketing can work as a member of the Product Management Team.

Responsibilities

- Market research
- Give lead to next products to be developed at R & D
- Promotional activities

- Launching and withdrawal of product in market

Qualifications

B. Pharm + MBA (marketing), B. Pharm + marketing experience, MBA (pharmaceutical management) + marketing experience etc.

ii International Marketing

As the world became more connected the marketing became decentralized and crossed national borderlines. The companies always strive to achieve higher growth and profit and to meet these goals, the focus of companies shifted to international sale or marketing. It works in different ways:

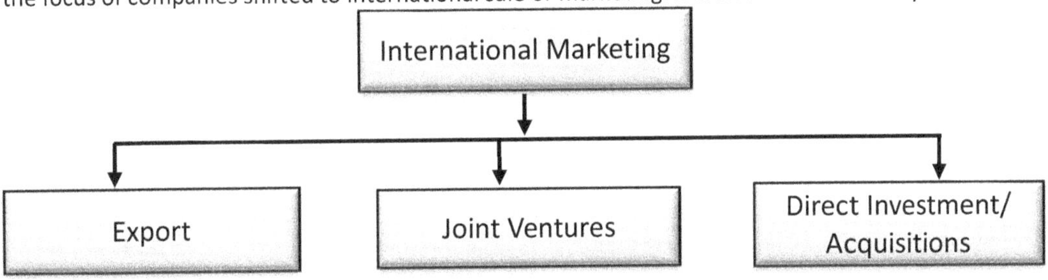

- Exporting - involve supply of medicines directly into foreign markets. Key companies are Sun Pharma, Dr. Reddy's, Biocon, Cipla
- Joint Ventures - These are combined efforts between two or more business entities with the aim of mutual benefit from the economic activity e.g. Novavex + Cadila
- Direct investment/ Acquisitions - Company makes its facility in foreign country and with the aim of manufacturing and marketing a product within overseas market. For example Dr Reddy's - Betapharm Arzneimittel, Matrix Laboratories - Docpharma NV, Ranbaxy Laboratories (Sun) - RPG (Aventis), Jubilant Organosys - Target Research, Torrent - Heumann Pharma and many others

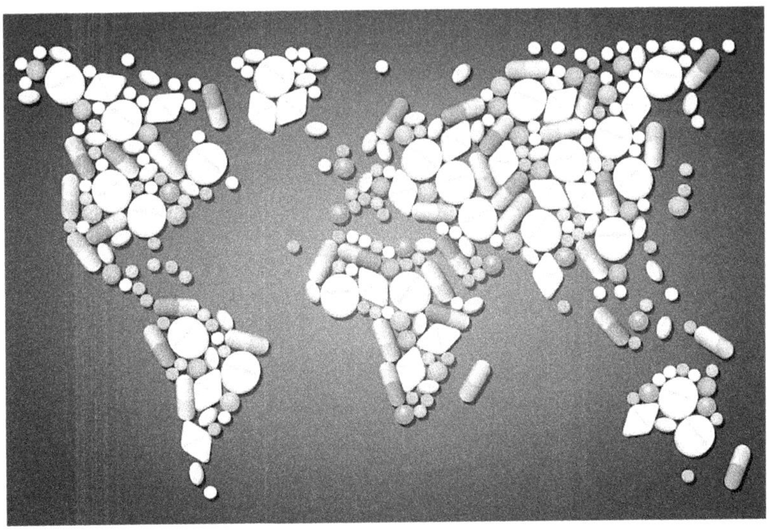

India's pharmaceutical exports grew to USD 17.3 billion in 2017-18. The US is the top destination for Indian pharma exports, followed by the UK. America accounts for about 25 per cent of the India's pharmaceutical exports. The other important destinations include South Africa, Russia, Nigeria, Brazil and Germany. Generic drugs form the largest segment of the Indian pharmaceutical sector, with 75 per cent market share (in terms of revenues).

Key international markets: Indian pharmaceuticals have taken a centre stage and collaborated with global pharma companies to market their products

USA: The largest generic market and the most sought after target for Indian companies involved in the generic business and it drives the growth of export of Indian pharma story

Europe – Primarily UK and Germany are the major export markets for Indian companies. Europe has more than 300 marketing authorizations approved by the Medicines and Healthcare Regulatory Agency (MHRA) for a wide range of products.

Brazil – India showed considerable presence in export to Latin America, South Africa and Russia

At the same time, foreign pharmaceutical companies have also tapped the Indian market through collaborations and acquisitions. Multinationals launched their products by using marketing and distribution strategies of Indian collaborators. For example: Partnership of Pfizer and Glenmark; Novartis and Aurobindo; GSK and Orchid.

Strategy to Increase International Sale

The typical structure of an international division in a pharmaceutical company consists of geographical divisions being broadly classified under two major heads, viz. Regulated Markets and Less Regulated Markets. The regulated markets may comprise of USA, UK, EU, Australia, South Africa (Japan and China do not offer easy access to their pharma markets hence negligible exports presently) and rest of the countries may be classified under less regulated markets. The regulated markets require a much more exhaustive paperwork, documentation, GMP standards and stringent quality checks that less regulated markets and hence type and number of manpower for these divisions will differ slightly. The international division also has higher level of interactions with the Regulatory Affairs division of the company as well finance division that is tasked with international payments and receipts.

Qualifications

While a basic science graduation degree is essential, it is normally not enough to get employed for pharmaceutical exports division. A B.Pharm degree is a definite plus with additional advantages accruing from M.Pharm or MBA degrees. A post-graduate diploma in export management is also a plus as also a dedicated degree of export like those offered by Indian Institute of Foreign Trade (IIFT) like, MBA in Foreign Trade and Certificate Programme in Export Import Management. Some pharmaceutical colleges are also offering integrated five years B.Pharm plus MBA courses like NIPER (Mohali and Hyderabad), Narsee Monjee, Manipal etc.

iii IN-LICENSING

Licensing may be defined as transfer of rights from licensor to licensee to use the intellectual property owned by licensor within specified parameters of geographic area, time period among many others. It may involve purchase of material from licensor by the licensee for direct sale, manufacturing process with component purchase, right to use trademark, technical assistance for manufacturing etc.

Indian pharmaceutical business is of generic drugs i.e. re-engineering of the potential drug molecule through innovation of new processes and launch their own version in the market. After signing the TRIPS agreement (Trade Related Intellectual Property Rights) in 2005, Indian pharma companies faced challenges because of not having strong R&D for new drug development. Though Indian companies increased their budget in R&D manifold but because of the small size of Indian pharma companies and very high cost of development of new drugs, the companies could not launch their own drug molecules. Indian companies will take time to come out with their own patented drug molecules. The market for new generation drug where the multinationals holds the patent is more than 5000 crore. So to remain successful in the domestic market, the domestic companies are applying the strategy of in-licensing with multinational companies to launch their patented novel medications in India at reasonable prices. This gives them advantages of access to new molecules that they themselves are not allowed to manufacture (due to patents) or do not have the capability to do so or wish to take advantage of technical capabilities of an already established big pharma company and maybe using its trademark as well. Advantages of in-licensing include:

- First to market to capture large section of market as big advantage over future competitors
- Less time required to launch with availability of technical and marketing data already available
- Less capital outlay as compared to development of own product
- Using past experience of licensor in marketing the product in other markets
- Improving in-house expertise to promote novel products, first time in India
- Gaining prestige in India as innovator with new and better products with international backing
- Gaining prestige outside India as a preferred partner for MNCs to launch their products in India without own presence
- Tapping new markets with minimum investment – improving Return on Investment (RoI)

So drug companies purchase the rights to market the drug. As these products have approvals for marketing in developed countries so the regulatory procedures are easier and faster in India as they directly undergo a bio-equivalence study and a Phase-III (drug test in patients) trials. Companies such as Sun pharma Laboratories, Wockhardt Ltd, Cipla Ltd, Torrent Pharmaceuticals Ltd, Dr Reddy's Laboratories Ltd, Nicholas Piramal India Ltd, Elder Pharmaceuticals Ltd and USV Ltd have already signed in-licensing agreements with foreign drug makers. Both the partners get mutual benefits and establish themselves.

iv OUT-LICENSING

Out-licensing scenario in India is a little less populated due to the fact that research molecules coming out for commercialization are few and far between. Therefore Indian pharma innovator companies are increasingly willing to out-license those new products that have just entered phase 2 clinical trials and thus avoid the most costly phase 3 clinical trials.

Out-licensing strategy has attained significant importance these days. It gives permission to one company to use intellectual property rights of the other company. Suppose a small company investigates a drug molecule and generates clinical data through clinical trials, but have limited resources to market the drug. At this point, out-licensing of their molecules to global innovator companies through technology collaboration can ease the accessibility of experimental drug globally. Domestic pharma companies are entitled to royalties on the sales of the drug and could also retain the rights for the drug in certain markets. Besides reducing the burden of costs, this strategy is also effective in terms of generating revenues from the pipeline at an earlier stage. Indian companies are able to strike out-licensing deals with global giants. For example:

- Sun pharma out-licensed its new investigational drug Tildrakizumab for Psoriasis to Almiral, a European regional leader in dermatological products; Almiral will conduct larger clinical global studies of the drug and commercialize the product in Europe. Sun received upfront payment of 50 million dollar
- Glenmark took the lead when it signed a landmark agreement with Forest Laboratories, US for its molecule for asthma 'Oglemilast'®
- Indian biotechnology company Biocon entered in partnership pact with Lupin to commercialize Enbrel® biosimilar.

c. RESEARCH AND DEVELOPMENT

i. Chemistry

Chemistry plays a vital role in pharmaceutical science and is one of the most important of all the scientific disciplines. To thoroughly understand the synthesis and action of a drug on the human body, we require in-depth knowledge of its chemical structure and the impact of this structure on the behaviour of the drug in the body. For better clarity, chemistry is the study of/determines everything from synthesis, purity, formulation, dosage, absorption to elimination of the drug from the body. Hence, a strong grasp of the chemistry is the basis of drug design and discovery.

Types of drugs

Natural -Natural products have pharmacological activity that can be useful in treatment of various kinds of diseases. After centuries of empirical use of herbal preparation, the first isolation of active principle alkaloids such as morphine, strychnine, quinine in the early 19th century marked a new era in the use of medicinal plants and modern Phytochemical research.

The major challenge is that drug is commonly isolated in small amounts from natural sources and could not meet the growing demand of vast population so the focus shifted to semi synthetic and purely synthetic approaches.

Semi synthetic: By this technique the existing natural products are modified to improve or alter their activities. The natural products are used as starting point in the chemical synthesis and then synthetic analogs are prepared with improved efficacy, potency, safety and purity e.g first semi-synthetic pure drug aspirin based on a natural product salicin was isolated from *Salix alba* introduced by Bayer in 1899, Paclitaxel from *Taxus brevifolia* for lung, ovarian and breast cancer. Antibiotics e.g.Ampicillins, Amoxycillins from naturally isolated 6 aminopenicillanic acid.

Synthetic –Synthetic organic chemistry became an exceptional important discipline in discovery of drug molecules e.g synthesis of paracetamol, ibuprofen through synthetic routes in the laboratory. The popularity of the synthetic products increased due to its production control, cost, time schedule, quality control.

Drug Research: The innovation in research pharmaceutical companies brings the new pharmaceuticals to the market. The process of optimizing the lead molecule into a candidate drug is complex, usually the longest (minimum 12 years) and most expensive (>1 billion dollar) stage in the drug discovery process.

Approaches of Drug Synthesis

Traditional approach

The conventional drug design methods include random screening of chemicals found in nature or synthesized in laboratories. The drugs were discovered through trial and error testing of chemical substance on animals or cultured cells. Medicinal chemists relied primarily on data from *in vivo* testing. Therapeutic effects were noticed through accidental effects e.g accidental discovery of first naturally occurring antibiotic penicillin or observed side effects of Minoxidil i.e. the transformation of an antihypertensive drug to a drug which stimulates hair growth. The major problem with this method is long design cycle.

Modern day approach

A drug-discovery program includes structure based design and typically starts with the identification of suitable drug target. It requires years of scientific study to determine the biochemistry behind a disease, for which pharmaceutical intervention is possible. The result is the determination of specific receptors (targets) that must be modulated to alter their activity by some means. Drug discovery and design requires interdisciplinary efforts of molecular biologist, biochemist, microbiologist and computer scientist along with chemist. Information technology and computational methods have speeded up the drug discovery process.

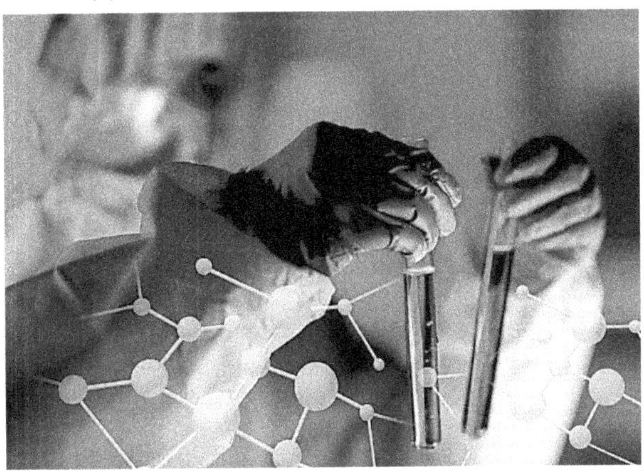

Drug research is divided into 3 parts

Drug discovery: It involves the search of active compounds that can fit into a specific cavity target both geometrically and chemically. Target can be protein, enzyme, particular cell or a pathway. These compounds serve as a lead molecule for the generation of more active compounds. For example there are 300 drug target genes or binding sites for antihypertensive drugs where drugs can bind and activate them. Pharmaceutical innovation and synthesis of drugs depends upon binding and activation of these sites. Hundreds of compounds representing multiple drug classes have been synthesized and approved for treatment of hypertension. Design of the molecules according to different target sites is always complementary in shape and charge to the target. For example:

- Inhibition of enzymes (ACE –Angiotensin converting enzyme) - **Captopril**
- Calcium channel blockers (block the entry of calcium into muscle walls) - **Nifedipine**
- Diuretics - help the kidneys to remove excess salt and water from the body tissues and blood - **Furosemide**
- Receptor blockers (x and B) - **Propranolol, Atenolol**
- Direct action on smooth muscles - **Hydralazine**

Other Approaches

Synthesis of Libraries

i) **In house libraries:** The medicinal chemist synthesize small samples of new molecules during their day-to-day research in academic institutions or research companies. Over the course of years and decades of research, a compound library steadily grows. A library reflects the areas of research that have contributed to the collection.

ii) **Uses of in silico approaches-In silico approaches (computer-assisted discovery)** have expanded these chemical libraries rapidly. A research company can have libraries with 1-2 million substances.

Library Screening:

The library may consist of traditional compounds with potentially high activity molecules, smaller fragments of less activity, or even virtual molecules tested through molecular modelling simulations. The active compounds discovered through a screen are called ***hits***

Filtering Hits to Leads

If a screening process is successful, a number of hits will be identifed. The number of hits varies depending on the target. It could be as high as 5–10% or as small as 0.1% of the tested library.

Virtual Screening: In a virtual screen, computerized molecular models of both the target and library member are aligned to determine potential complementary intermolecular interactions. Molecules with a high level of complementarity, indicates potential strong binding.

Drug development: Lead compound identification i.e search for likely to be a drug candidate from these hits marks the transition from drug discovery to development. Use of High throughput screening (HTS), advances in robotics,data handling has simplified the process of library screening. The success rate though this development phase is extremely low: <1% of candidate drugs eventually end up in the pharmacy. Lead Screening further subjected to lead optimization

Lead optimisation – involves synthesis and characterization and in vitro, in vivo in silico techniques. Established spectroscopic and analytic methods are used to ascertain the purity and integrity of the synthesized derivatives, including Fourier transform infrared (FTIR) spectroscopy, ^{1}H-nuclear magnetic resonance (NMR), ^{13}C NMR, and mass spectroscopy.

Drug design: The design of biologically active molecules with complementary structural features for the receptor active sites are designed on the basis of physicochemical properties and molecular interactions.

Role of Chemical Research in Generic Pharma industry

Research and development of Active pharmaceutical ingredient is critical for success and competitiveness for generic industry in global scenario. Traditionally India is a favoured destination for sourcing low-cost, good quality API for manufacturing pharmaceutical formulations.
But the patent expiry of innovative drugs and the increasing demand for generic medicines, which are made from APIs has given impetus to the growth of the Chemical industry.

Areas of research: Chemical research plays an important role in the development and optimisation of:

- New synthetic routes /schemes and manufacturing procedures for already known medicines.
- New salts/polymorphs
- New use of the formulation
- Upgrade process of existing products
- Development of existing solid state forms

Approaches to API synthesis

- Analysis of original drug just after launch
- Improvement of the basic patent procedure
- Different chemistry with the common intermediates with basic patent approach
- Quite different innovative approach
- The selected synthetic route is improved and upgraded during its development.

The development of any such process requires an interdisciplinary approach and experts in organic synthesis, medicinal, chemistry, chemical technology and analytical chemistry. In this phase of research and development, experiments are carried out on a milligram or gram scale and then researchers create the vision with virtual projection of process feasibility on the industrial scale, often in tonnes. Bringing new synthetic scheme and process optimisation of API synthesis reduce the cost factor.

Role of chemist

Modern medicinal chemist plays a crucial role in the early phases of drug discovery. The major responsibilities are:

- To frame hypothesis and sets objective for the new drug because of his knowledge of pharmacology and biochemistry.
- To synthesize, purify and characterize new chemicals after HITS are identified and decides on analogs to be prepared.
- To explore the structure activity relationship in an effort to get the maximum activity and reduced toxicity.
- To decide the appropriate animal model to carry out the in vivo activity.

Skills Required

- Thorough knowledge of organic and Medicinal chemistry
- Understanding of biology that relates to the target disease
- Knowledge of the literature that is relevant to target disease
- Knowledge of the factors which influence ADME
- Pharmacological test used for screening compounds in vivo
- Strong interpersonal skills to interact with scientists from other disciplines as drug discovery is a collaborative approach of various fields

Job opportunities for a medicinal chemist

- Chemical research and development
- Analytical research and development
- Industrial bulk drug manufacturing
- Quality control
- Government drug testing laboratories

ii CLINICAL

India cherishes a very significant position in the global pharmaceuticals market. A vast population of 1.2 billion, wide variety of diseases and patient pool attract pharmaceutical companies to this country for conducting clinical research (Clinical trials, BA/BE studies). Besides large and diverse patient pool, we also have a large pool of pharmacists, clinicians and doctors who are experienced to steer the pharmaceutical industry to a higher level.

Clinical Research Programme: After testing of new drugs in the laboratory and in animals, the most promising experimental treatments are moved into clinical trials. During the clinical research, NCE is first time administered to human beings. The study is conducted in phases. Drug developers submit an Investigational New Drug (IND) application to FDA with the following data

- Animal study data and toxicity data: animal study data is submitted in order to obtain preliminary efficacy, toxicity and pharmacokinetic information
- Manufacturing information
- Clinical protocols (study plans) for studies to be conducted
- Information about the investigator

Designing Clinical Trials

A specific study plan called protocol is designed which states questions and objectives related to a medical product. Before a clinical trial begins, the protocol is reviewed with respect to the following criterion

- Who qualifies to participate (selection criteria)
- How many people will be part of the study
- How long the study will last
- Whether there will be a control group and other ways to limit research bias
- How the drug will be given to patients and at what dosage
- What assessments will be conducted, when, and what data will be collected
- How the data will be reviewed and analyzed

Clinical trials are often conducted in four phases.

Phase 1 Trial

Experimental drug is tested in a small group of people (20-100 healthy volunteers) for the first time. The study evaluates treatment's safety, safe dosage range, bio-availability information and identifies side effects.

Phase II Trials

To check the effectiveness of drug on a larger number of people (more than hundred) with disease condition and to further evaluate its safety, efficacy and side effects.

Phase III Trials

Experimental study drug is given to large group of people for monitoring of its efficacy and adverse effects if any. The information will allow the experimental drug to be used safely.

Phase IV Trials

Post-marketing studies, which are conducted after a treatment is approved. It provides additional information including the treatment or drug's risks, benefits.

Clinical Trials for Generic Drugs: Availability of the generic products in the market has gained serious public consideration regarding their safety and efficacy with respect to the innovator products. Bioavailability/Bioequivalence studies are conducted to establish therapeutic activity of a particular drug by comparison of the test drug with innovator or reference drug. It saves a lot of time required for the drug discovery as well as the huge cost for the developments of the drug molecules by the Pharmaceutical companies.

BA/BE Study: BA/BE study has to be carried out in a CDSCO approved CRO (Contract Research Organization) under the guidance of Ethics Committee. To initiate any study the CRO have to follow the following steps.

Agreement

An agreement of CDA (Confidential Non-disclosure agreement) and Research service agreement (financial agreement) between the CRO and Sponsor have to be signed.

Protocol

The CRO prepares the protocol in consultation with Clinical Pharmacologist (MBBS, MD) and Study Coordinator as per regulatory requirements and in agreement with the sponsor. The details of the IP (Investigational Products) of both Test and Reference drug and API are provided by the manufacturing company.

Ethics Committee Approval

The CRO (Bioequivalence Study Centre) will submit the protocol in its standard format to Ethics Committee for approval.

Clinical Study (Period I and Period II)

After the approval from ethics committee, the CRO carries the clinical study as per the approved protocol and SOP.

Clinical Phase: Blood samples are withdrawn after single dose exposure of the test and reference products to the volunteers as per the time points specified in the approved protocol. The blood samples withdrawn from the volunteers is centrifuged to separate drug plasma and then stored in deep freezer (-20°C)

Bio analytical phase: Bioanalytical methods are used to measure analyte in plasma, blood, urine, saliva and faeces etc.These samples contain the analyte at low concentration in a large mix of proteins, salts, minerals, lipids, and other small and large molecules.Liquid chromatography-tandem mass spectrometry (LC/MS/MS) is the most commonly used technique which uses mass as a means of detection for measuring pharmaceutical concentrations in such samples.

Documentation, Data Management and Archiving: Evaluation of pharmacokinetic parameters e.g. time taken to reach maximum concentration (Tmax and Cmax), $t_{1/2}$(time taken by half of the drug to be removed by biological system) etc is done. Further statistical analysis is done to prove bio equivalency. Based on the evaluation, report is prepared.

Responsibilities

- Designing trials by assisting the investigators and sponsors in preparation of clinical trial
- protocol manual, its review and approval
- Ensures compliance with all applicable government and sponsor regulations, laws and policies related to the conduct of trials involving investigational or marketed drugs
- Ensures the accuracy and integrity of products prior to their delivery to trial subject
- To educate the participants regarding research study
- Monitor different phases of trials
- To dispense investigational drugs and materials issued by the Investigational Drug Service for research studies
- To maintain records to meet sponsor requirements

Job Profile

- Evaluate clinical pharmacology and biopharmaceutics data for Investigational New Drug (IND)
- Create new analytical methods that can support and accelerate the evaluation of new drug products.
- Identify issues with the safety and effectiveness of marketed drugs through latest available information in literature
- Use and develop new statistical and mathematical methods to enhance drug evaluation

iii BOTANICAL

Use of plant products as supplements for food originates from a long tradition where the herbal infusions, digestives, juices, elixirs, and extracts are consumed to maintain health. Botanicals are plant-based products also known as herbal medicines, dietary herbal supplements, natural and organic foods, phytomedicines. All the parts of plants including roots, bark, leaves, seeds and flowers are used either as medicines or to promote health and well-being. Prior to the advances in synthetic chemistry and the discovery of antimicrobials in the late 19th and early 20th centuries, majority of the population relied on traditional medicines.

The use of herbal supplements and drugs is again gaining attention worldwide owing to its natural origin and lesser side effects or dissatisfaction with the results of synthetic drugs. Botanical drugs, simply defined as clinically validated pharmaceuticals of plant origin, typically contain a multi-component composition derived from herbal practices. Herbs are often used in health care as adjunct therapy to conventional treatment as there is lack of scientific support or limited data for the cure of the disease. The major challenge is the standardization of biological materials from natural sources. The quantum and quality of the safety and efficacy data on traditional medicine are far from sufficient to meet the criteria needed to support its use world-wide.

Therefore there is a strong need for research and development to establish efficacy, dosage and toxicity of traditional medicines and plant products along with clinical efficacy to develop them as sustainable consumer products

Pharmacognosy, a major branch in Pharmaceutical Sciences is recognized as a vital branch of drug development processes. It focuses on scientific investigation and research on medicinal plants for one or more biological activity. Research in this field could bring a new sphere and incredible revolution by reforming, reshaping the herbal medicines to challenges of the 21st century. Phytomedicines can become an equivalent effective, economical and safe treatment. There are two distinct phases of botanical research

Phase One

- The survey of folkloric knowledge pertaining to medicinal plants
- Selection of the plant material with anecdotal claims
- Botanical identity
- Determination of whether its production can be renewable and sustainable

- Preparation of decoctions/extractions as per traditional use
- Phytochemical screening to validate the medicinal claims scientifically

Phase Two

- Isolation, identification and characterization of the biologically active compounds or lead compound and conversion of standardized extract into modern medicines. The compounds are characterized through emerging approaches of rational drug design and the intellectual cooperation of medicinal chemists.

The second phase consists of formulation and its preclinical evaluation of efficacy, dosage and toxicity by using suitable animal models. The final phase will be adequate clinical trials, manufacturing (large scale production of plant material and extract preparation) and to commercialize the product. Plants extract, either as pure compounds or as standardized extracts, provide unlimited opportunities for new drug discoveries It is evident from research that plants have the ability to synthesize a wide variety of chemical compounds and are prolific source to provide new and important leads against various pharmacological targets that are used to perform important biological functions.

Plant Therapeutics

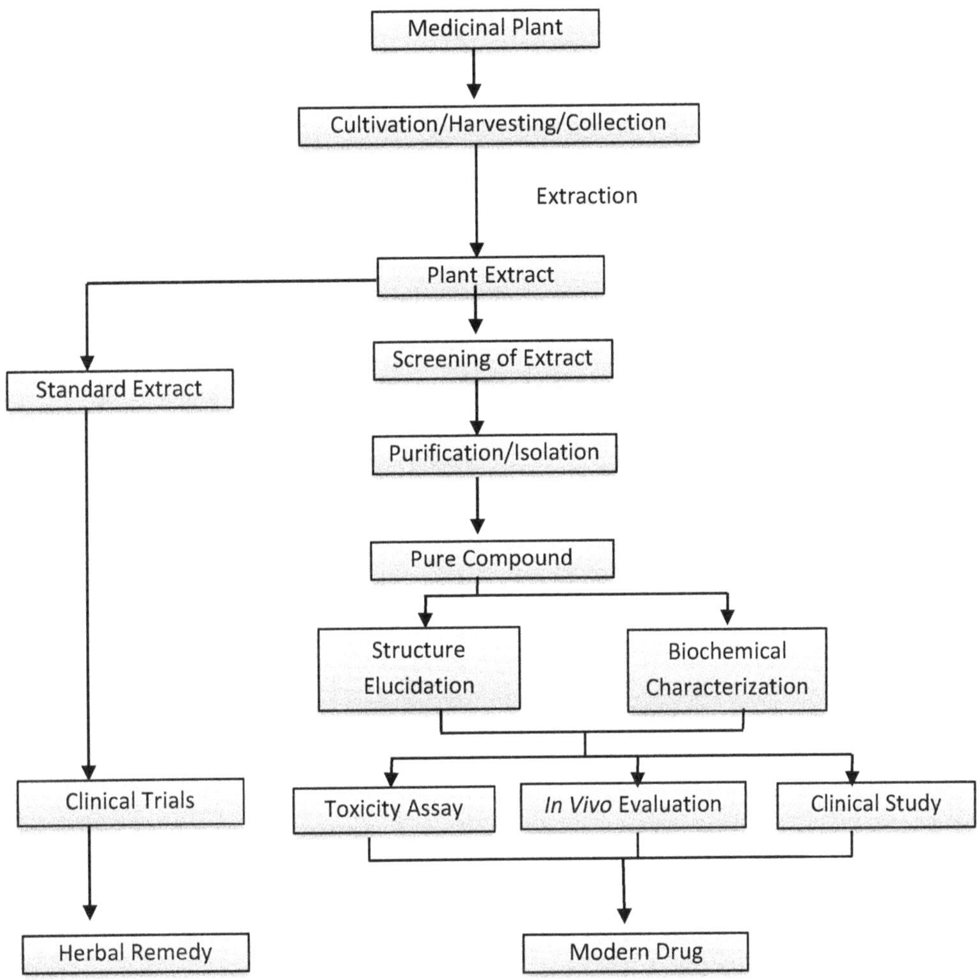

Approximately 25% of the modern medications are developed from plants and research on plants yielded some major drugs as shown in Table

Table: Some major plant products and their indications

Plant Source	Botanical Name	Plant component	Indication
Willow tree	*Salix spp*	Asprin	Analgesic, Anti-pyretic Cardiovascular
Belladonna or deadly nightshade	*Atropa belladona*	Atropine	Anti-cholinergic Pupil dilation
Grecian foxglove	*Digitalis lanata*	Digoxin	Cardiotonic
Velvet bean	*Mucuna deeringiana*	(L)-Dopa	Anti-parkinsonism
Yam plant	*Dioscorea deltoidea*	Diosgenin	Anti-fertility
Opium poppy	*Papaver somniferum*	Morphine Codeine	Analgesic Anti-tussive
Autumn crocus or meadow saffron	*Colchinum autumnale*	Colchicine	Anti-tumour Anti-gout
Cinchona	*Cinchona ledgeriana*	Quinine	Anti-malarial
Madagascar periwinkle	*Catharanthus roseus*	Vincristine Vinblastine	Anti-tumour
Green snowdrop	*Galanthus woronowiis*	Galanthamine	Alzheimer's
Mayapple or American mandrake	*Podophyllum peltatum*	Podophyllotoxin Etoposide	Anti-cancer
Happy tree	*Campotheca accuminata*	Camptothecin	Anti-cancer
Sweet wormwood	*Artemesia annua*	Artemisinin	Anti-malaria
Pacific yew	*Taxus brevifolia*	Taxol	anticancer
Chinese cucumber	*Tricosanthes kirlowii*	Tricosanthin	Anti-cancer
Indian coleus	*Coleus forskolii*	Forskolin	Glaucoma, Impotence
Bhang	*Cannabis sativa*	Nabilone	Antiemetic in chemotherapy
Milk thistle	*Silybium marianum*	Silymarin	Hepatic disorders
Maidenhair tree	*Gingko biloba*	Ginkgolides	Stimulation of peripheral circulation
Purple cornflower	*Echinacea spp.*	Flavonoid, Phenol and polysaccharides	Immunostimulant
Garlic	*Allium sativum*	Allicin	Cholesterol reducing
Korean ginseng	*Panax ginseng*	Ginsenosides	Tonic
St John's wort	*Hypericum perforatum*	Hyperforin	Anti-depressant
Ma-Huang	*Ephedra spp*	Ephedrine and pseudoephedrine	CNS stimulant, appetite suppressant
Garden valerian	*Valeriana officinalis*	Valerine	Calmative, Sleep inducing

Natural compounds could provide excellent models to produce novel drugs. Pharmacognosy is used by pharmaceutical companies to screen, characterize and produce new drugs for the treatment of human disease. Often, naturally occurring drugs cannot be mass produced, so they must be studied in order to develop synthetic analogues. An ideal coordination between various fields is crucial to the development of Phytomedicines. Current research in drug discovery from medicinal plants involves a multifaceted approach combining Traditional knowledge with botanical, computational, phyto chemical, biological, molecular techniques and Pharmaceutical technology approaches. These modifications through different approaches can transform a crude plant extract into a powerful drug.

The research laboratories involved in phytomedicines research showed some outstanding success over the years. Consequently, several promising new chemical entities of plant origin are in clinical trial phase. Scientist at CDRI, Lucknow developed commercial standardised drugs which originates from traditional system e.g. Promind a brain tonic from *B. monniera* (brahmi booti), gugulipid a hypolipidaemic drug from gum guggulu, antimalarial from Chinese plant Artemisnin.

With the vision on plant based research a number of institutions are set up by Council of Scientific and Industrial Research. These institutions are on the forefront of plant sciences research for the past six decades and emerged as institutes of National importance.

- CSIR- National Botanical Research Institute (CSIR-NBRI)
- CDRI Lucknow
- Regional research laboratory Jammu
- Central institute of medicinal and aromatic plant (CIAMP Lucknow) is a plant research laboratory of CSIR
- Regional Research Laboratory Jorhat
- Central food Technology Research Institute Bangalore
- National research centre of plant Biotechnology

In order to promote medicinal plants research, The Government of India has set up National research plant board (NRPB) under Ministry of AYUSH (Ayurveda, Yoga & Naturopathy, Unani, Siddha & Homoeopathy). The mission is to promote research and development and to explore and unfold the rich plant repository of Indian flora. This will bring a paradigm shift in use of plant based medicines.

Prominent Ayurvedic companies in India:

- Dabur
- Himalaya
- Zandu
- Charak
- Baidyanath
- Sandu
- Arya Vaidya Sala
- Vicco Labs
- Patanjali Ayurved
- Surya Herbal
- Hamdard Labs

Botanical research may be conducted by modern pharmaceutical companies also who may look for leads for a modern molecule from plant material as source.

iv DOSAGE FORM DESIGN

Turning a New Chemical Entity (NCE) into a medication is called dosage form design. Medicines are very rarely drugs alone but require additives to insert them into dosage forms and this introduces the concept of formulation.

Although there is a broad range of dosage forms but generally dosage forms are classified depending upon the specific delivery methods: oral drugs, injectable or parental drugs, topical/transdermal drugs, inhaled drugs, and mucosal drugs. The key consideration in choosing the ideal dosage form for a drug is finding an ideal delivery method that serves as the optimal vehicle for both metabolic purposes and for maintaining efficacy of the drug for its journey from production to administration.

Purpose of formulating different dosage forms

In order to provide the safe and appropriate dose of a drug to the patient, drug substances are formulated into different dosage forms. For example:

- To protect the drug substance from destructive influence of gastric acid after oral administration (enteric coated)
- To conceal the bitter, obnoxious or salty taste or odour of the drug substance (capsules, coated tablets, flavoured syrup)
- To provide liquid preparations of the substances that are insoluble or unstable in the desired vehicle (suspensions)
- To provide clear liquid dosage form of the substances (syrups, solutions)
- To provide rate controlled drug action(various controlled release tablets, capsules, and suspensions)
- To provide optimal drug action from topical administration sites (ointments, creams, transdermal patches and ophthalmic, ear, and nasal preparations)
- To provide for insertion intone of the body orifice (rectal or vaginal suppositories)
- To provide placement of drugs directly into bloodstream or body tissues (Injections)
- To provide for optimal drug action through inhalation therapy (Inhalants and inhalation aerosols)

Formulation Development

Different dosage forms require different pharmaceutical technologies and usually present different technical challenges for formulation development. Pharmaceutical technology is the multidisciplinary science of preparing pharmaceutical dosage forms. Pharmaceutical technology requires deep understanding of physicochemical properties of drug substances and excipients, processes technology and equipment and conceptual knowledge of absorption, distribution and metabolism.

Characteristics of Good Formulation

The principal objective of dosage form design is to achieve a predictable therapeutic response to a drug included in a formulation which is capable of large scale manufacture with reproducible product quality. To ensure product quality, numerous features are required

- Must be manufacturable consistently
- chemical and physical stable throughout the manufacturing process and product shelf life

- Bioavailable (*i.e.,* it must contain the exact amount of API in each dose that can be readily absorbed by the human body)
- suitable preservation against microbial contamination
- acceptability to users including both prescriber and patient

Key Steps involved in Formulation development

Conventionally formulations are manufactured to meet quality control tests outlined in product specifications. In case of a batch failing to comply with these test. Recently the concept of Quality by design has brought revolution in the formulation of drug development and is increasingly becoming an important and widely used technique for efficient pharmaceutical product development. It is a joint exercise of marketing, clinical research dept and pharmaceutical tech development which aims and ensures design and development of a quality product.

Quality by design (QbD) is a systematic approach to pharmaceutical development that begins with predefined objectives with emphasis on product understanding and process control.

Different Elements of pharmaceutical development

- **QTPP**: Target the product profile (defining an objective)
- Design and development of product
- Developing the manufacturing process
- **CQA:** Determination of critical quality attributes (CQAs)
- **Risk assessment**: Link raw material attributes and process parameters to CQAs and perform risk assessment
- **Design Space**: Development of experimental design
- **Control Strategy**: Design and implement a control strategy

QTPP (Quality Target Product Profile): It is a tool for setting the strategy for the design and development of drug. It defines the expectations in the final product that will be achieved to ensure the desired quality, taking into account safety and efficacy of the drug product.QTPP is widely used in development planning, clinical and commercial decision making, regulatory agency interactions, and risk management. The QTPP guides formulation scientists to establish formulation strategies and keeps the formulation effort focused and efficient i.e.planning with the end goal in mind. The QTPP summarizes

- Clinical objective of dosage form, route of administration, delivery systems
- Dosage strength(s)
- Container closure system
- Therapeutic moiety release or delivery and attributes affecting pharmacokinetic characteristics (e.g., dissolution, bioequivalence) appropriate to the drug product dosage form being developed
- Drug product quality criteria (e.g., sterility, purity, stability and drug release) appropriate for the intended marketed product. For example:

Target	QTPP	Justification
Tablet	Dosage form	Pharmaceutical equivalence requirement. Same dosage form
Immediate dosage design without coating	Dosage design	Immediate release design to meet label claim
Oral	Route of Administration	Same route
20 mg	Dosage Strength	Pharmaceutical equivalence-same strength
Immediate Release T_{max} 2.5 hrs	Pharmacokinetics	Bioequivalence
24 months shelf life at room temperature	Stability	Equivalent or better

Product development: The objectives of the product development program using QbD is to identify attributes that drug product should possess to exert intended therapeutic response.

Critical Quality Attributes: CQAs are generally associated with raw materials (drug substance, excipients), intermediates (in process materials), and drug products. Properties included in CQA are:

Form	Parameter	Critical quality attributes
Drug Substance	Physico chemical	Description Identification Particle size Bulk density Polyymorphic forms Water content
Excipient	Physico chemical	Concentration Particle size Bulk density Tap density Hygroscopicity Stability Manufacturability
In Process Material		Water content Hardness Friabilty Disintegration time
Drug Product		Description Identification Assay Impurities Polymorphic forms Tablets/capsules Disintegration Dissolution Hardness/Friability Uniformity

		Water Content Degradation Product Residual Solvents **Oral Liquidss** Rheological Properties Particle size distribution pH **Parentral products** Antimicrobial preservative content pH Antioxiddant content Particle size distribution Testing of delivery system Sterility Clarity
Stability Data		Solid-state stability, Solution-state stability, Physical stability, Chemical stability, Microbiological stability
Container Closure System		

Pharmaceutical formulation is a stage of drug development during which the physicochemical properties of Active Pharmaceutical Ingredients (APIs) are characterized to produce a bioavailable, stable and optimal dosage form for a specific administration route.

During preformulation studies the following parameters are evaluated:

- Solubility in different media and solvents
- Dissolution of the active pharmaceutical ingredient (API)
- Accelerated Stability Services under various conditions
- Solid state properties (polymorphs, particle size, particle shape etc.)
- Formulation Services and Capabilities
- Formulation development of new chemical entities (NCE)
- Optimization of existing formulations
- Process development for selected dosage

CQA differs depending on the type of process, dosage form, and type of method to be developed hence thorough knowledge of real time data to working scientists is important

Development of experimental design: Pharmaceutical development scientists have begun making use of and process simulation to support process development and optimization of manufacturing process. Different mathematical models are available for design of experiment.

Process Selection: Process development and formulation design cannot be separated because a formulation cannot become a product without a prescribed process.

Manufacturing processes of pharmaceuticals contains a series of unit operations to produce the desired quality products. Major contributors of Process selection are:

- Critical Material Attributes
- Identification of Critical Process Parameters (CPPs)

Material attributes are physicochemical or microbiological properties or characteristics of input materials e.g choice of right excipients. All the formulation and process parameters are examined, typically by employing a statistical design-of-experiments (DoE) approach. DOE is a structured, organized method using computer-aided process design (CAPD) for determining the relationship between factors affecting a process and the output of that process. The impact of each parameter is assessed on the final product. The output of the process depends on the process parameters and input material attributes. The aim is to facilitate effective formulation.

Process parameters include type of equipment settings, operating and environmental conditions (time, temperature, pressure, pH, speed and moisture).

Based upon the parameters, formulation composition and process is finalized and optimized.

Responsibilities

- Design, development, optimization and scale up of different formulations
- Perform hands-on characterization studies on drug substance candidates, excipients compatibility studies, temperature sensitivity, O_2 sensitivity, light sensitivity, moisture uptake, particle size distribution, bulk density, tap density, solid state properties, powder/blend uniformity, thermal properties, etc.
- Perform hands-on unit operations for pharmaceutical formulation development of different dosage forms.
- Prepare laboratory prototype formulations and conduct systematic experiments
- Develop the requirements for procurement of equipment/instrumentation necessary to perform pre-formulation/formulation activities.
- Write procedures and execute qualifications for equipment and instrumentation.
- Write and review technical reports

Job Hierarchy

- Vice president
- Associate Director
- Group Leader
- Senior scientist
- Scientist
- Research Associate

v ANALYTICAL

Pharmaceuticals would serve their intent only if they are administered in an appropriate amount and purity. Traditionally viewed as a service department, the analytical department has now become a significant partner in the drug development process. During the drug development process, key decisions are based upon data obtained from analytical methods. The Analytical research and development is responsible for developing methods of analysis for each stage of drug discovery, drug development, drug product development and commercial manufacturing i.e. starting from chemical compounds materials, intermediates, Active pharmaceutical ingredient or bulk drug, drug formulations, impurities and degradation products, biological samples containing the drugs and their metabolites and stability testing of drug substances and their drug products. Analytical method and product development go hand in hand during the entire life cycle of any pharmaceutical product.

The pharmaceutical analyst develops specific, sensitive and well-validated analytical procedures to ensure accurate and reliable data at each stage of the development process. For this, various chemical and instrumental methods were developed at regular intervals which are involved in the estimation of active substance, related compounds, degradation compounds and metabolites. The improvements of the analytical method development and analytical instruments have reduced the time and cost of analysis and enhanced precision and accuracy. The accurate and precise data generated through analysis ensures that the drug substance and drug product meet the established identity, purity as well as bioavailability requirements as per the regulatory guidelines. Analytical method development finally results in official or Pharmacopoeial test methods. Consequently, quality control laboratories use these methods to check the efficacy, identity, purity, safety as well as performance of drug products to comply with quality established by Health regulatory authorities.

Analytical Research

Analytical Chemistry has undergone a quantum improvement in last few decades. With increased demand of accurate and quicker results, numerous chemical or instrumental methods are developed and validated for characterization of drug substances and drug products.

Structure elucidation and Characterization of chemical compounds: Structure elucidation can be carried in two ways

1. Identify the structure of known compounds as described in literature
2. Elucidate the molecular structure of unknown organic compounds

Information is generated through various analytical, chemical, physical and spectral techniques to determine the structure of a compound. The physical and chemical tests give a comprehensive idea of functional group in the molecule and spectroscopic data shows the behaviour of the compounds. Both the techniques supplement each other.

Purification: Chromatographic techniques/crystallization techniques/preparative HPLC are used to separate the compounds from their mixture.

Spectroscopic methods: Chromatographic or spectroscopic methods referred as fingerprints are used as standards for identification. The fingerprinting can be obtained by CHN, chiral testing, UV , HPLC, GC, TLC, IR and Mass spectrophotometer.

Physical Characterization: Crystal structure and Polymorphism: Crystal structure significantly influences drug solubility, bioequivalence and stability. Many analytical techniques are used to identify the polymorphic forms. The most important one is the X-ray diffraction (single crystal and powder).

Other methods are: Spectroscopy (FTIR, Raman and solid-state NMR), Thermal analysis (DSC and TGA) and Light Microscopy

Identification of API: Analytical methods reveals that the api meets the specifications either according to the monographs given in Pharmacopoeia (USP,EuR,IP) or developed methods according to ICH guidelines.

Assay: the % age purity or the assay of the API directly relates to the requirement of known dose. Assay or purity of an analyte can be determined using chemical techniques e.g. Titrimetry, electroconductivity or instrumental techniques e.g. HPLC, LC,Gas Chromatography or HPTLC etc.

Impurities Identification: Impurity profiling relates to the quality and safety profile of the drug. Impurities are unwanted chemicals that remain with the Active Pharmaceutical Ingredients or develop during formulation development or upon ageing of both drug and drug products. Primarily, impurities are detected by chromatographic methods, mainly thin-layer chromatography (TLC) and/or HPLC. Then Identification or structural elucidation of impurities is done using methods described earlier in this section. Impurity standards are synthesized with the proposed structures and used as reference.

Water content: Presence of water shows high impact on the physical and chemical stability the active pharmaceutical ingredient and is an important parameter in determining the quality, activity, potency, efficacy and shelf life of the drug product. Presence of moisture impacts the hardness, dissolution, friability, impurity profile, crystal structure in solid formulations and leads to microbial growth in semi solid dosage forms. A number of analytical methods e.g. Loss on drying, Karl Fischer titration, Near Infrared are used for determination of water content in Pharmaceutical formulations

Particle Size Distribution: Determination of particle size has become a critical parameter in the manufacture of pharmaceutical product. PSD is a significant attribute which could alter the drug product quality parameters like flow-ability of powders, blend uniformity, dissolution and could impact the bioavailability of drugs. Established Analytical techniques from optical microscopy to laser diffraction and dynamic light scattering gives quantitative data on particle shape and size distribution

Residual Solvents: Generally solvents are used during product development e.g granulation, coating or other manufacturing steps. These solvents need to be analyzed in the final dosage due to their toxicity potential. Gas chromatography is the most commonly used technique

QbD approach for method development: In order to eliminate the limitations of high degree of variability encountered at each stage during method development, the systematic QbD-based approach has slowly been becoming the focus area of analytical scientists i.e. "Analytical QbD (AQbD)".In AQbD analytical method is considered as a process and output is quality data

Recognition of Analytical target profile

a) Selection of target analytes (API and impurities)
b) Assortment of analytical technique (HPTLC, GC, HPLC, Ion Chromatography etc.)
c) Choice of method requirements for the desired concentration range

Critical Process Parameters: CPP influence the accuracy and precision of the method. Some critical method attributes are:

1. Physical and chemical properties of the drug substance and impurities such as polarity, charged functional groups, solubility, pH value, boiling point and solution stability
2. Selection of buffers used in mobile phase, pH of the mobile phase, diluents, column selection and elution method in HPLC, GC
3. Injection temperature, flow of gas, sample diluents in GC
4. Mobile phase in TLC

Design of experiments: Method is designed and selected taking into account different critical process parameters. Risk assessment is done to screen out factors that have direct influence on the analytical method. Designed experiment can be efficiently used for method optimization.

Prerequisite for method development

1. Qualified and calibrated instruments
2. Documented methods
3. Reliable reference standards
4. Qualified analyst
5. Sample selection and integrity

Responsibilities

- Developing and validating methods for testing of drug substances, drug products, related or degradation products and metabolites.
- Developing and validating methods for new or existing drug products, for stability Programmes
- Developing and validating test methods used in cleaning validation exercises.
- Preparing analytical method development, validation and test reports
- Transfer of analytical methods to quality control units.

Job Profile

- Analytical Method development and Validation for various formulations, API, Intermediates, elemental impurities and other raw materials using variety of analytical techniques such as UV, IR, HPLC,GC etc
- Preparation of Specifications, Standard test Procedures and Various Protocols for equipment calibration, Analytical method development and their validation to assess precision, accuracy, specificity, linearity, range limit of detection, limit of quantization and ruggedness.
- Development/preparation of complete specifications for raw materials, APIs, finished products, intermediates, excipients along with co-ordination with formulation development.
- Inclusion of in-house tests for strict control of pharmacopoeial materials and products.
- Stability study of APIs and formulations as per ICH guidelines.

vi PROCESS ENGINEERING

Process engineering has emerged as a separate specialized field within the pharmaceutical production operations. While a process has been designed and approved (validated) for a given product, it makes good business sense to continuously improve it along various parameters and to also ensure its integration into the manufacturing infrastructure available. A process engineer therefore ensures that a given process is the most efficient one being adopted.

Major roles played by Process Engineering in pharmaceutical manufacturing include:

- Ensure uniformly high level of quality irrespective of the speed of output
- Optimizing batch sizes and cycle times
- Identifying and removing bottlenecks to improve output
- Improving process yields to gain productivity
- Reducing waste generation and introduction of green manufacturing initiatives
- Increased automation of manufacturing processes to increase output, including through continuous manufacturing and Process Analytical Technology (PAT)
- Measuring continuously and improving Overall Equipment Effectiveness (OEE) for highter efficiencies
- Implementing predictive and preventive maintenance procedures to reduce machine downtime and improve efficiencies
- To ensure uninterrupted compliance at all times and hence prevent production losses due to non-compliance resulting in batch recall/shutdown/reprocessing

Sadly, this part of manufacturing is not taught in pharmaceutical manufacturing subjects and is a rather borrowed concept from the field of Industrial Engineering. Nevertheless, its needed and can be absorbed by observation in real world working and learning on cross subject domain.

B. Pharm or M. Pharm is a fairly good degree to enter this specialized field after a few years of experience in pharmaceutical production. Such pharmacy grads and post-grads have a distinct advantage over chemical or industrial engineers who will lack the product knowledge. And experience of 4-5 years in production will serve as a good base from where to start this specialized work area.

d. REGULATORY AFFAIRS

As the name suggests, it has all to do with regulations. A pharmaceutical company has to be in complete and continuous compliance with the relevant regulations at all times and it is the job of the regulatory affairs department to ensure this. As pharmaceuticals are so crucial for human health, the regulations controlling them are also extremely strict and exacting hence making the job of complying with them very difficult.

Regulatory Affairs (RA) department works with regulatory authorities and different departments within the company in order to meet regulatory commitments. RA also ensures the maintenance of the marketing licence and leads life cycle extension activities such as broadening the indication of the drug, change of formulation, changes in the dosage etc.

The RA department is tasked with reviewing internal policies relating to the manufacture, testing, marketing, and reliability of products to ensure that they are safe to use and work as intended. The RA department must keep abreast of legislative developments in the countries or regions in which a company distributes its products or services. Using this knowledge, they examine all aspects of production, from discovery to distribution, to ensure compliance with regulatory statutes. Depending on the size and scope of the business, the RA department may need to maintain a complete understanding of different regulatory processes of state, national, and/or international bodies.

The RA department assists in the implementation of international and domestic regulatory strategies. They help with the preparation, coordination, and compiling of applications to foreign and domestic regulatory agencies. They respond to common enquiries from customers and regulatory agencies.

They are required to participate in customer complaint reviews to ensure global regulatory compliance and need to address all complaints and file all necessary paperwork.

They may need to research certain problems and inform management when they troubleshoot and fix them. Regulatory affairs specialist is responsible for implementing training guidelines and training all member of the team on important regulations. They also need to generate ideas and implementation plans for organizations in regards to basic regulatory compliance.

Most of the mid and large cap Indian pharmaceutical companies have a well-defined RA department and is ususally divided into departments like Audit and Records, Developed Markets (like USA, Europe etc.), developing markets (like middle east, Africa, South America etc.) and domestic Indian RA department. They work in close coordination with quality assurance, production and facility management, in addition to marketing and medical department as well.

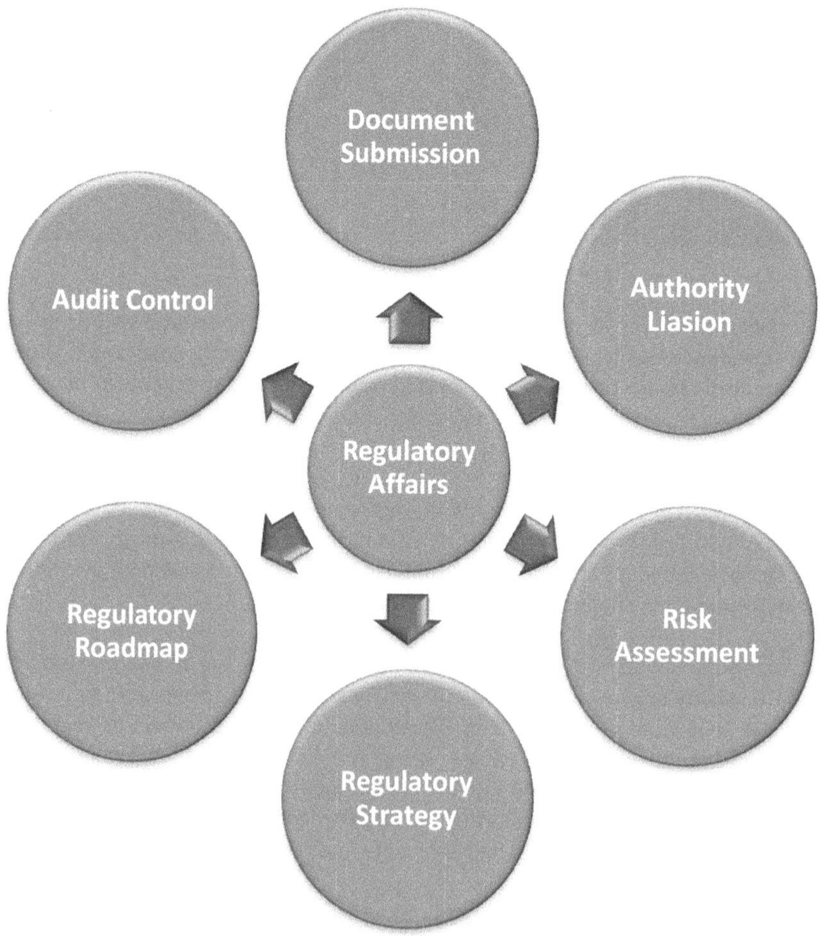

Qualifications

It varies by industry to the job profile. In general, maximum individuals would be M. Pharm (any field, but especially M. Pharm in regulatory affairs). You would also find MSc Chemistry in the API industry RA, Engineers in medical devices, MSc Biotechnology in the biotech companies and B. Pharm/B.Sc in RA support roles.

Skills Required

Good written and oral communication skills
Strong scientific background

Job Description

The Regulatory Affairs department is an important part of the organizational structure of pharmaceutical companies. Internally it liaises at the interphase of drug development, manufacturing, marketing and clinical research. Externally it is the key interface between the company and the regulatory authorities. This is a job with challenging work environment. Major responsibilities are:

- To be aware of the changes in the regulatory environment
- Keeping oneself up-to-date with changes in guidelines and policies by the health authorities
- Advising the company on safety aspects of the customers and patients
- Responding in time to queries from health authorities or hospitals or internal teams like product development, sales, analytical testing, and business development
- Reviewing development records, manufacturing records, analytical reports, stability data, clinical testing reports, literature references.
- Preparing and submitting dossiers to health authority e.g. marketing authorization application (MAA) in EU and new drug application NDA/ANDA in US
- Advise companies on legal matters using their expertise

Average annual salary in the RA department of a pharma company ranges between 4 lacs for entry level jobs to 15-20 lacs for senior most positions, mostly in bigger companies.

e. PHARMACOVIGILANCE

Pharmacovigilance (PV) is the science of collecting information on adverse effects of medicines on our bodies, assessing their full impact and providing actionable data to enable drug safety risk analysis and analysing risk-benefit ratio for preventing harm to patients. While such studies are already a part of clinical trials during research and development of a drug, it is also needed during the entire lifecycle of the drug usage in case any new or unforeseen adverse effects are encountered during normal usage.

Post marketing PV uses tools such as data mining (statistical analysis) and investigation of case reports to identify the relationships between drugs and adverse effects.

Major work areas in this sector include the following:

Adverse Event Reporting

- Individual Case Safety Report
- Coding of Adverse Events
- Seriousness Determination
- Expedited Reporting
- Clinical Trial Reporting
- Spontaneous Reporting
- Aggregate Reporting
- Other Reporting Methods

Risk Management

- Causality Assessment
- Signal Detection
- Risk Management Plans
- Risk/Benefit Profile
- Pharmacoepidemiology
- Pharmacogenetics and Pharmacogenomics

Ecopharmacovigilance

- Risk Identification
- Environmental Data on Medicines
- Environmental Risk Management Plans

Typical work responsibilities include:

- Recording and reporting adverse reactions from healthcare professionals and consumers
- Conducting in-depth interviews with patients and healthcare professionals
- Developing a thorough knowledge of products
- Completing periodic safety update reports on drugs and other treatments
- Writing and reviewing ADR reports and forms
- Noting warning signs of adverse effects of drugs
- Minimising the risk of serious side effects

Key Skills for Pharmacists in PV

- Ability to keep meticulous records
- Attention to detail
- Above par analytical and problem-solving skills
- Ability to interact and communicate effectively with a wide range of people
- A systematic approach to tasks
- Good IT skills
- Good maths skills

Major Regulatory Agencies for PV in India

Agency	**Role of Agency**
Drug Controller General of India (DCGI)	Nodal authority for National Pharmacovigilance
Central Drugs Standard Control Organization (CDSCO)	Operates under supervision of National Pharmacovigilance Advisory Committee
Department of Biotechnology (DBT)	Provides product evaluation and validation through support for clinical trials for health care products
Ministry of Environment and Forests (MOEF)	Provides guidelines for making data entries of information provided by the environmental experts through clinical trials for health care products
Indian Council of Medical Research (ICMR)	Apex body in India for formulation, coordination and promotion of biomedical research
Central Bureau of Narcotics (CBN)	Closely monitors all clinical trials, which require additional narcotics compliances relating to storage, import-export quotas and movement of the investigational drug
National Coordination Center (NCC) for Pharmacovigilance Programme of India	Monitoring, surveillance, collaboration with national health programs and other organizations to increase ADR reporting. Operated by Indian Pharmacopoeia Commission under the Ministry of Health and Family Welfare

Typical Employers

- Pharmaceutical, Biotechnology and Medical Device companies
- Clinical Research Organizations
- KPOs
- Regulatory Agencies like DCG (I) and CDSCO
- Pharmacovigilance units in Medical colleges and Hospitals

Hierarchy in Pharmacovigilance Job

- The entry level job for life science graduate is DSA (Drug Safety Associate). DSAs are mainly involved in case creation, checking for MSI (Minimum safety information – a patient, reporter, suspect drug and an adverse event), reconciliation and follow-up process, data entry of all information available in the document and medical coding.
- Once an individual acquires an experience of 2-3 years and builds up the required skill sets (Medical coding, narrative and scientific writing, good understanding of medical terms and basic understanding of regulatory affairs, ICH-GCP and compliance etc. he can become a DSS (Drug Safety Scientist).
- Individuals having acquired a good narrative writing experience can pursue it on a larger frame, moving from individual cases like writing for PSUR (Periodic Safety Update Report) and PADER (Periodic Adverse Drug Experience Reports) and as well as becoming an aggregate report scientist.
- With an overall of 7-10 years' experience can easily become a team lead or team manager

Pay Scale

Fresher: Rs 3 to 5 lacs pa I After 5 years: Rs 6 to 8 lacs pa I After 10 years: Rs 10 to 20 lacs pa

2.2 ACADEMICS

Academics for pharmaceuticals got recognition in the 19th century when a programme for training chemists was started by Madras Medical College in 1870. This was later converted to a diploma. Similarly, in 1881 a one year training programme was started by the Medical faculty of Bengal. This laid the foundation of pharmacy education in India. The profession gained shape when a well-defined academic curriculum began in 1932 at BHU under the guidance of Professor M.L. Shroff. The subjects included pharmaceutical chemistry, analytical chemistry and pharmacy. Subsequently, graduate programmes began in 1944 in Panjab University and in 1947 in LML College Ahmedabad.

To legalize and organize Pharmaceutical education in India an autonomous body by the name of Pharmacy council of India was established in 1948, under the Ministry of Health. First guidelines were framed and a law was enacted in 1953 to set the minimum qualifications to become a Pharmacist.

With globalization the focus of pharmaceutical education shifted from a technology and product oriented view to clinical pharmacy and R&D. Companies in this field depend upon academicians for innovation in research as the basic research is always carried out in the institutions. This further led to a (surge) in Research Institutes and Universities. Currently we have around 1200 Degree, more than 1100 Diploma and about 260 Pharm. D institutions that enroll more than 200,000 students per year. In this exciting and growing phase of Indian Pharmacy education, a lot of opportunities are available in academics.

Career Path and Required Education

A degree in Pharmacy offers career in academics and research, professionals can start their career as Lecturer/Assistant Professor and go upto the level of Associate Professor/Professor and Principal. The minimum qualification requirements/experience is summarized below:

Post	Qualification	Experience
Lecturer for Diploma in Pharmacy	PCI recognized B. Pharm / M. Pharm / Pharm D I. A person holding MBBS qualification can be considered for the post of Lecturer in the subjects of Anatomy and Physiology, Bio-Chemistry and Clinical Pathology. II. A person holding M.Sc. (Maths) degree shall be eligible for the post of Lecturer (Mathematics) on part time basis. III. A person holding M.Sc. (Zoology) or M.Sc. (Botany) shall be eligible for the post of Lecturer (Biology) on part-time basis. IV. A person holding B.E. (C.S.) or MCA degree shall be eligible for the post of Lecturer (Computer Science) on part-time basis.	3 years professional experience
Lecturer/Assistant Professor for B. Pharm/Pharm D/ Post graduate course	First Class B. Pharm with Master's degree in Pharmacy (M. Pharm) in appropriate branch of specialization in Pharmacy (Qualification must be PCI recognized).	A lecturer will be re-designated as Assistant Professor after 2 years of teaching experience in

in Pharmacy	A PCI recognized Pharm D degree holder shall also be eligible for the posts of Lecturer/ Assistant Professor in pathophysiology, pharmacology and pharmacy practice.	PCI approved/recognized Pharmacy College.
Associate Professor for B. Pharm/Pharm D/ Post graduate course in Pharmacy	First Class B. Pharm with Master's degree in Pharmacy (M. Pharm) in appropriate branch of specialization in Pharmacy (qualification must be PCI recognized) A PCI recognized Pharm.D degree holder shall also be eligible for the posts of Associate Professor in the subjects of pathophysiology, pharmacology and pharmacy practice. Associate Professor shall acquire PCI recognized Ph. D in any of Pharmacy subjects within 7 years to become eligible for the post of Professor.	3 years experience in teaching or research at the level of Assistant Professor or equivalent in PCI approved/recognized Pharmacy College.
Professor for B. Pharm/Pharm D/ Post graduate course in Pharmacy	First Class B. Pharm with Master's degree in Pharmacy (M. Pharm) in appropriate branch of specialization in Pharmacy or Pharm D (Qualifications must be PCI recognized). With Ph. D degree in any of Pharmacy subjects (Ph. D Qualifications must be PCI recognized).	10 years experience in teaching in PCI approved/ recognized Pharmacy College or research experience out of which 5 years must be as Associate Professor in PCI approved/recognized Pharmacy College.
Director/Principal/ Head of Institution	First Class B. Pharm with Master's degree in Pharmacy (M. Pharm) in appropriate branch of specialization in Pharmacy or Pharm D (Qualifications must be PCI recognized). With Ph. D degree in any of Pharmacy subjects (Ph.D. Qualifications must be PCI recognized).	*Essential* 15 years experience in teaching or research out of which 5 years must be as Professor/HOD in a PCI approved/recognized pharmacy college. *Desirable* Administrative experience in a responsible position .

Responsibilities of a Teacher

What soil is to life on the earth, Teachers are to Society

A teacher carries a crucial responsibility of the growth of any profession. A teacher apart from being an educator also contributes to science as a researcher, helps in business development as a consultant and creates social awareness as a community pharmacist. They educate, train and assess the students to produce a competent workforce able to meet the growing demands of the industry and community.

JOB DESCRIPTION

Teaching across universities, both national and international is a highly rewarding and sought-after career. If one has passion for a subject, then there is no better job than academics.

Duties

- Teachers utilize lectures, tutorials, seminars and assignments according to the guidelines provided by Pharmacy council of India.
- Evaluate students on the basis of exams and train students in skills such as critical thinking, problem solving, learning beyond the lectures of classroom
- Empower students for professional challenges either in jobs or research, managing time and prioritize responsibilities.

Globalization led to a rapid growth of generic pharmaceutical business in the Indian market but failed to promote innovation, hence the emphasis of institutes should be on research, creativity and use of technology to develop our own drug molecule. Academic institutes contribute to the society both in service and research. Teachers play a crucial role in promoting research, through projects, for which they receive grants from various funding agencies like Department of science and technology (DST), Indian Council of Medical Research (ICMR), Council of Scientific and Industrial Research (CSIR), University Grants Commission (UGC), Department of Biotechnology (DBT) etc. Teachers also guide and encourage students to explore a variety of perspectives for discovering new drugs and developing new technologies for producing cost effective drugs. Academic conferences play a pivotal role in the growth of a subject by providing a platform to the researchers to share and innovate. Consultancy has been emerging as a promising career for teachers in the industrial sector.

Key skills and strength

- Expert in your field: Teaching in college/universities requires in depth knowledge of the subject and consistent knowledge up gradation

- Presentation skills: Teacher must be confident in delivering his/her lecture.

- Interactive: Students and teachers should interact on same platform. This process of mutual interaction creates a beautiful relationship.

- Teaching ability: should have love for learning and motivation to deepen knowledge and also should have the ability to share the knowledge and skills.

- New teaching strategies: Teachers should convert their lectures format to more or small discussion formats by working in teams, collaborating and communicating with others.

- Research methodology: should have the ability to inculcate research culture in young minds, finding and analyzing information, propose a research idea, and evaluate past research

Pay scale: As per 7th pay commission the pay scale for teachers which includes basic salary and allowances (Gross Pay = Total Pay + D.A. + H.R.A + Med. Allow. + T.A. + Other Allowances) is shown below in Rs.:

Post	6th Pay Commission Scale	7th Pay Commission basic pay	Gross salary per month
Lecturer	15,600 - 39,100 Grade Pay - 6,600	57,700	71,000 - 88,000
Assistant Professor	15,600 - 39,100 Grade Pay - 7,000	68,900	85,000 - 105,000
Associate Professor	37,400 - 67,800 Grade Pay - 9,000	131,400	159,000 - 196,000
Professor	37,400 - 67,800 Grade Pay - 10,000	144,200	175,000 - 215,000

2.3 PHARMACY PRACTICE

It is a term used to describe pharmaceutical care and specific activities through which a pharmacist co-operates with patient and other professionals in designing, implementing and monitoring treatment plan that will improve the health of the patient. Roles of Pharmacy practice is mainly divided into three areas:

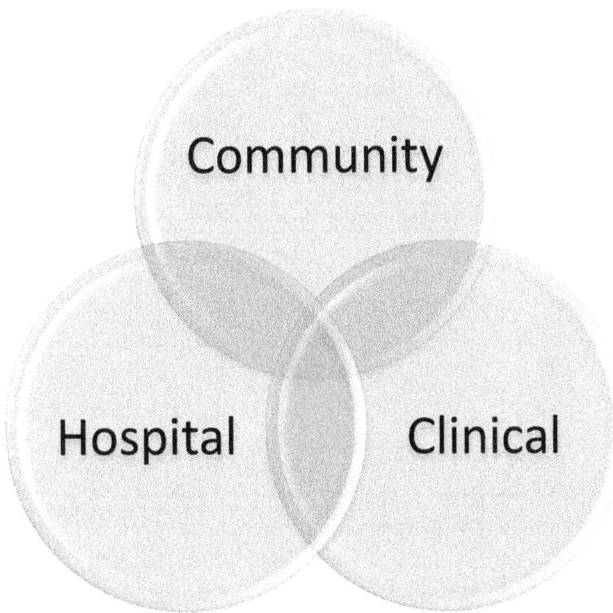

Pharmacy Practice in India

The origin of community pharmacy practice in India can be traced back to British India when allopathic drugs were introduced and were made available through drug stores towards the end of the nineteenth century. During this period, the pharmacy profession remained business oriented and those trained to sell drugs were called drug sellers. The pharmacy practice scenario and especially community pharmacy practice during pre-independence era was highly unregulated and there were no restrictions on the practice of pharmacy in India. The practice of prescribing and dispensing was normally a function performed by doctors. In addition, most doctors trained their clinic assistants to dispense medicines and assist in the compounding of medicinal preparations. The assistants were popularly known as "compounders"

After the enforcement of Pharmacy Act 1948, pharmacist registration certificate became mandatory.

Career Prospects

Pharmacists are integral members of the healthcare team. They are responsible for medication therapy management through appropriate implementation of medication usage, diet and lifestyle choices especially for patients with chronic diseases such as diabetes, asthma and high blood pressure. Community pharmacists often considered the first line of healthcare, play an important role in patient counselling. They are specialized in variety of areas of pharmacy practice, including paediatrics, critical care, cardiology, surgery, psycho pharmacy, neurology, infectious disease, drug information etc.

Job Responsibilities

- Checks the patient's record before dispensing the prescription
- Provide basic drug information in terms of appropriate drug usage, administration, dosage, side effects, storage, and drug-drug and drug-food interactions.
- Counsel the patient for proper selection of over the counter drugs or advising for referral to medical Practitioners
- Take part in health awareness Campaigns on health related or drug related topics e.g. awareness regarding Tuberculosis, HIV
- Provides domiciliary or home services to patients who cannot visit the pharmacy

Hospital Pharmacist

Pharmaceutical care by a physician along with the technical expertise of hospital Pharmacist is the ultimate and best way of achieving better patient care.

Job Responsibilities

- Pharmacists in hospitals manage procurement, storage, preservation of medicines
- Dispense, distributes and monitor patient's medication.
- Work closely with physicians, nurses and other health professionals to ensure that appropriate treatment is being given.
- Advise patients on side effect, compatibility, rational drug use
- Serves as a member of policy making committee of hospital e.g. use of antibiotic, infection controlling committee etc.

Educational Requirements

Pharm. D (6 years program) - 5 years is academics + 1 Year internship in hospital/ Pharm. D (Post Baccalaureate) (Three years program)-2 years study + 1 year internship in the hospital/M. Pharm (Hospital Pharmacy).

Pharmacoeconomics

Drug use evaluation is one of the important fields in health care as resources for healthcare are not easily accessible and affordable to many patients. Doctors always want to give best healthcare benefits and payers want to manage rising costs. Pharmacists combine the objective of both and implement the principles of economics to evaluate most cost-effective therapy. Rising health expenditure has caused a strong demand for pharmacists to involve with government agencies, insurance agencies, managed health care organizations, professional health care associations, hospital administration departments, health care consulting organizations, pharmaceutical companies and international organizations for policy making in evaluating the affordability and rationale use of drugs.

Qualification: Pharm. D or M. Pharm in Pharmacy Practice

Job Description

Knowledge of evaluation techniques like cost minimization analysis, cost benefit analysis, cost effectiveness analysis etc.

Poison Information Center (PIC)

It is a medical facility that is able to provide immediate, free, and expert treatment advice and assistance over the telephone in case of exposure to poisonous or hazardous substances. A Special Information Center (PIC) is set up to inform people about how to respond to potential poisoning. The pharmacist uses his clinical knowledge to provide answer and recommend appropriate treatment.

In India, the National Poisons Information Centre (NPIC) was established in February, 1995 in the Department of Pharmacology at the All India Institute of Medical Sciences, New Delhi. The centre provides toxicological information and advice on the management of poisoned patients adapted to the level of the enquirer.

A wide variety of chemicals are designed for diverse uses in day today life. Though their benefits are enormous, yet they are associated with great risks if misused. The probability of ingestion of these substances/products either accidentally or intentionally has increased manifold. Acute poisoning is one of the commonest emergencies throughout the world. To ensure chemical safety, a framework for prevention and management of eventualities if any, is provided by the Poisons Control Programme of which Poisons Information Centre is an integral part.

Job Responsibilities

- To maintain databases of poisons and appropriate emergency treatment.
- To answer questions about potential poisons in addition to providing treatment advice about pesticides, bites and stings, food poisoning and fumes etc.

Drug Information Center: World is experiencing a drug and health information explosion. The need of the hour is to provide accurate, unbiased and up-to-date drug information. The educational qualification of the pharmacist makes him the most reliable person of the health care team to perform this duty of dissemination of drug information.

Skills Required

- Expertise in retrieving information from books, journals, newsletters, abstracting services, and computerized information systems
- evaluating, and disseminating drug information
- to handle most requests involving drug formulation, stability, incompatibility, conditions of storage, dosages, methods of administration, drug interactions, contraindications, side effects and toxicity, as well as appropriate therapeutic use

Job Responsibilities

To retrieve and provide accurate drug information

National health programmers (NHP)

National Health Programme is based on the health promotion concept and strategy. Government develops programmes which provide healthcare assistance with a vision of national development. Health promotion helps people to increase the control over their own health by identifying their problems and accordingly making choices and taking decisions conducive to health. Pharmacist is involved in direct public health and patient care through their active participation in increasing community awareness regarding National Health Programmers e.g. Communicable diseases, Mission Indradhanush, Pradhan Mantri Swasthya Suraksha Yogna (PMSSY), Tobaco control programme etc .

Managed Care Organizations—MCO is a health care company often gives health services plan with an aim to provide cost effective pharmaceutical care. It is a group of doctors, pharmacists, other health care providers and hospitals. Pharmacists serve as medication expert in MCO and collaborate with other health professionals.
Skills

- Knowledge of managed care policies and procedures
- Highly efficient in prescription filling, drug benefit design
- Innovative ways to provide drug therapy
- Aware of diagnostic or lab services of MCO

Job Responsibilities

Assessing and evaluating each prescription before giving medication, development of drug formularies, patient consultation to reduce unnecessary doctor visits and hospitalization

Clinical Research Organizations: CRO provide clinical trial and other research support services for the pharmaceutical, biotechnology and medical device industry. Studies carried out in human beings following testing in laboratories and animals for investigational drugs that are developed with an aim of clinical outcome. Studies are carried out under strict scientific and ethical guidelines in 4 phases:

Phase I - 20-25 healthy volunteers to assess safety
Phase II - 100 patients to test effectiveness
Phase III - Large study to test effectiveness and safety in 1000 patients
Phase IV - In general population after new drug is approved

Required Qualification

Graduate in Pharmacy but Pharm. D course along with knowledge of development process also develops skills of interacting with patients which adds a significant dimension to the role of pharmacist in clinical trials

Job Responsibilities

- To provides drug information to physicians nurses and other health care professionals regarding investigational drug and design clinical trial
- To ensure that trials are conducted as per the protocol and procedures comply with guidelines
- Maintain records and SOP and ensure quality check
- Report any incidence or adverse drug effect
- Conducts training to ensure that staff remains skilled and update.
- Assists in submitting documents and obtaining approvals from regulatory authorities like DCGI.

Pharmacist employed on permanent basis in central government hospitals like ESIC and AIIMS, Railways, and states like Delhi withdraw respectable salary. However pharmacists working in most state governments and also contract workers get much less. Sometimes pharmacists working on contract are made permanent but usually permanent recruitment is done on basis of competitive exams.

Eligibility for government pharmacist job is diploma in pharmacy or bachelors in pharmacy. Registration as pharmacist in Pharmacy Council of state is required. Usually as per pharmacist recruitment notifications, couple of years experience in dispensing is required. Pharmacist job profile include dispensing drugs as per prescription and maintaining store records and inventory.

Salary of Government Pharmacist: Starting Salary for Pharmacist in Central Government Hospitals located all over India, Railway and Delhi Pharmacists is about Rs. 45,000 per month for first two years and about 56,000 per month after two years.

2.4 DRUG CONTROL DEPARTMENT

It is the responsibility of the National governments to establish regulatory authorities. Many rules and regulations are enforced for the manufacture, trade, distribution and use of medicines. In other words, these regulations prevent the entry of irrational, substandard, harmful and counterfeit medicines to reach the market and protect the quality, safety and efficacy of drugs.

Drug Control Agencies

Drugs are necessary for prevention of disease, to restore health and to save life. Therefore it is the duty of the national governments to ensure that the consumers receive quality drugs at reasonable price. Before independence, India was largely dependent on import of drugs. As a result, the Indian market received substandard, adulterated drugs. In 1927, council of states urged the provincial governments to control indiscriminate use of drugs by controlling the sale of such drugs. A committee was constituted under the chairmanship of Colonel R.N. Chopra. In 1931, the Committee recommended to make a central legislation for control of drugs. As a result, Drug and cosmetic law was passed in 1940.To give effect to this law, rules and regulations were framed in 1945. Various legal enactments to regulate import, manufacture and sale of drugs are summarized in Figure below:

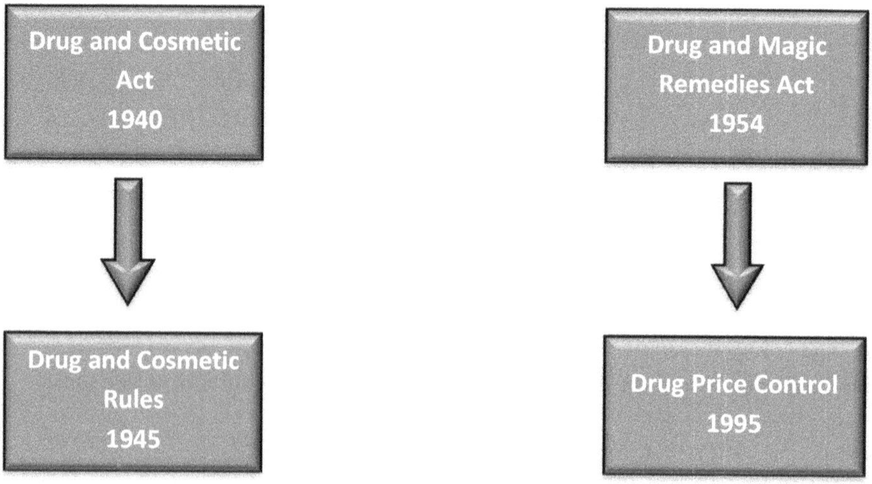

Indian Drug Regulatory System

The drug approval process involves the co-ordination of different departments under different ministries (table). The Ministry of Health and Family Welfare examines pharmaceutical issues within the larger context of public health while the focus of the Ministry of Chemicals and Fertilizers is on industrial policy. However, other ministries also play a role in the regulation process. These include the Ministry of Environment and Forests, Ministry of Finance, Ministry of Commerce and the Ministry of Science and Technology.

Ministries and Government Agencies Involved in the Approval of Drugs

Ministry of Health and Family Welfare	Ministry of Chemical and Fertilizers	Ministry of Commerce	Ministry of Environment
Directorate General of Health Services (DGHS) Indian Council of Medical Research (ICMR)	Department of Pharmaceuticals	Patent Office	Environment Clearance
Central Drug Standard Control Organisation (CDSCO), headed by DCGI (Drug control General of India) Statutory committee Advisory committee	National Pharmaceutical Pricing Authority (NPPA)	Controller General of Patents	
State drug control departments			

Drug Control Organizations

In Indian regulatory system, organizations for drugs control exist at two levels, *viz,* Central Government level and State Government level

The Central Drug Control Standard Organization (CDSCO)

The national regulatory authority of India is CDSCO under the aegis of Ministry of family and health welfare. It is headed by DCGI.

Major Functions of CDSCO

The Central Authorities are responsible for Approval of New drugs, Clinical Trials in the country, laying down the standards for Drugs, Control over the quality of imported Drugs, Coordination of the activities of State Drug Control Organisations and providing expert advice with a view of bring about the uniformity in the enforcement of the Drugs and Cosmetics Act. Approval of licenses of specified categories of Drugs such as blood and blood products, I. V. Fluids, Vaccine and Sera comes under the authority of DCGI.

Affiliated Institutes with CDSCO

Drug Technical Advisory Board (DTAB)—To advise the central government and the state Governments on technical matters

Drug Consultative Committee- Advisory committee to central Government, State Government and drug technical advisory board on any matter tending to secure uniformity of the drug and cosmetic act throughout India

Central Drugs Laboratory – These central laboratories provide quality and effective analytical services for pharmaceuticals and ensure public health by excellence in testing of drugs, cosmetics and medical devices. There are seven National laboratories 5 central and 2 regional which are engaged in the research and analysis of drugs. The organisational chart of state drug control authority is shown in Fig.

The organisational structure of CDSCO

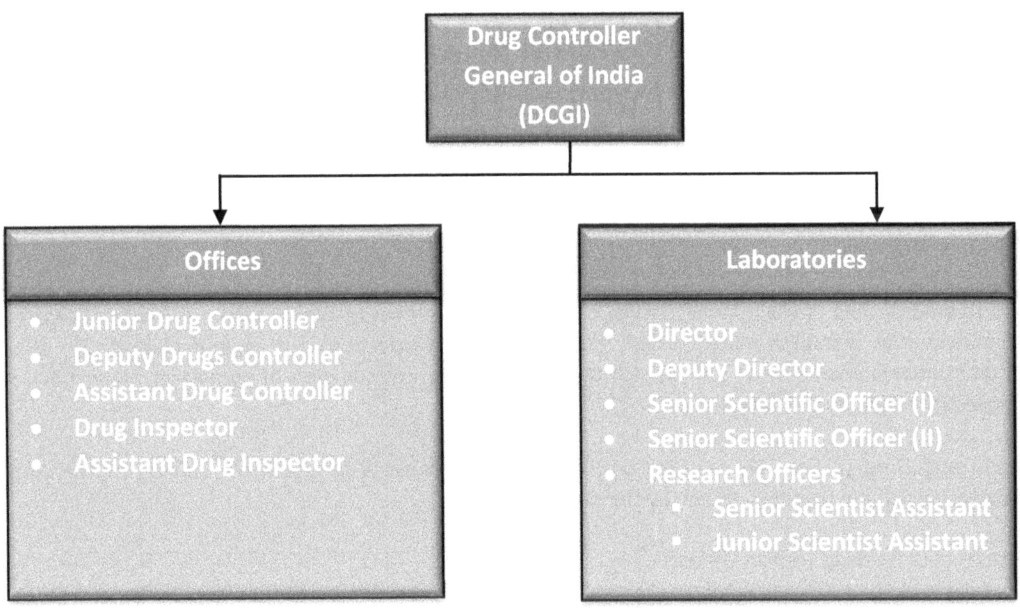

Autonomous Institutions

Indian Pharmacopoeia Commission

Indian Pharmacopoeia Commission is an Autonomous Institution under the Ministry of Health and Family Welfare, Govt. of India dedicated for setting of standards for drugs, pharmaceuticals and healthcare devices/ technologies etc. besides providing Reference Substances and Training

The State Drug Control Department

Under the Drug and Cosmetics Act, the regulation of manufacture, sale and distribution of Drugs in the country is primarily the concern of the State authorities under Food and Drug administration (FDA). It constitutes the following divisions:

- Enforcement wing
- Drug laboratory
- Food laboratory

The Organisational Chart of State Drug Control Authority is shown in Figure below:

State Drug Control Department

Enforcement	Drug Laboratory	Food Laboratory
• Drug Controller • Deputy Drug Controller • Senior Drug Inspector • Drug Inspector	• Drug Analyst • Assistant Drug Analyst • Scientific Assistant • Technical Assistant • Laboratory Assistant	• Public Analyst • Senior Chemist • Laboratory Technician

Enforcement Wing

Enforcement wing deals with licensing of Drugs / Cosmetics / Blood banks / Medical Devices manufacturing establishments, sales establishments, inspections of manufacturing & sales establishments and draw of samples for test and analysis, investigation of complaints, launching of prosecution against the defaulters etc.

Food and Drug testing laboratories: provide analytical services to check the quality of the drug samples which are routinely drawn by the drug inspector.

Duties of State Drug Control Officers

- Additional Drugs Controller/Joint drug controller(Administrative head)
- Deputy Drugs Controller (licensing authority for Manufacturing)
- Assistant Drugs Controller/senior drug inspector (licensing authority for Sales)
- Drugs Inspector (Inspection of sales and manufacturing establishments)

The National Pharmaceutical Pricing Authority (NPPA)

National pricing Authority was instituted in 1997 under the Department of Chemicals and Petrochemicals to fix or revise the prices of decontrolled bulk drugs and formulations; to implement price control through inclusion and exclusion of drugs in accordance with established guidelines; maintains data on production, exports and imports and market share of pharmaceutical firms; monitors and enforces the availability of medicines; Advise central govt. on policy matters from time to time.

Eligibility and Qualification for Drug Inspector in India

To become a drug inspector in different states of India one has to fulfil eligibility conditions which then allows to appear for drug inspector exam which consists of two papers. One paper tests knowledge of pharmacy subjects and the other paper for general awareness and aptitude.

General eligibility condition for drug Inspector in UPSC and most states is B. Pharm or Medicine with specialization in Clinical Pharmacology/ Microbiology. Additional 18 months experience in manufacturing or testing of Schedule C drugs may also be required by some and certainly desirable as additional qualifiers. If applying for post of drug inspector in states, generally one should be familiar with local language and customs.

The recruitment to the position of drug inspector in Central Drug Standard Control Organisation (CDSCO) is conducted by Union Public Service Commission (UPSC) and in various state drug control departments, by the respective states' Public Service Commission (PSC) and staff selection committee on an annual basis.

Union Public Service Commission	http://www.upsc.gov.in
Andhra Pradesh Public Service Commission	http://www.apspsc.gov.in
Arunachal Pradesh Public Service Commission	http://www.appsc.gov.in/
Assam Public Service Commission	http://www.apsc.nic.in
Bihar Public Service Commission	http://www.bpsc.bih.nic.in
Chhattisgarh Public Service Commission	http://www.psc.cg.gov.in
Goa Public Service Commission	http://www.goapsc.gov.in/
Gujarat Public Service Commission	http://www.gpsc.gujarat.gov.in
Haryana Public Service Commission	http://www.hpsc.gov.in
Himachal Pradesh Public Service Commission	http://www.hp.gov.in/hppsc
Jammu & Kashmir Public Service Commission	http://jkpsc.nic.in/
Jharkhand Public Service Commission	http://www.jpsc.gov.in
Karnataka Public Service Commission	http://kpsc.kar.nic.in/
Kerala Public Service Commission	http://www.keralapsc.gov.in/
Madhya Pradesh Public Service Commission	http://www.mppsc.com
Maharashtra Public Service Commission	http://www.mpsc.gov.in
Manipur Public Service Commission	http://mpscmanipur.gov.in

Meghalaya Public Service Commission	http://mpsc.nic.in/mpsc/
Mizoram Public Service Commission	http://mpsc.mizoram.gov.in/
Nagaland Public Service Commission	http://www.npsc.co.in
Odisha Public Service Commission	http://www.opsc.gov.in/
Public Service Commission, West Bengal	https://www.pscwbonline.gov.in/apps/home/
Punjab Public Service Commission	http://www.ppsc.gov.in
Rajasthan Public Service Commission	http://www.rpsc.rajasthan.gov.in/
Sikkim Public Service Commission	http://www.spscskm.gov.in
Tamil Nadu Public Service Commission	http://www.tnpsc.gov.in
Telangana state Public Service Commission	http://www.tspsc.gov.in/
Tripura Public Service Commission	http://www.tpsc.gov.in
Uttar Pradesh Public Service Commission	http://www.uppsc.org.in
Uttarakhand Public Service Commission	http://www.ukpsc.gov.in

Plan of Drug Inspector Examination and Syllabus of Drug Inspector Exam

The written examination consists of two papers with 250 marks.

Paper	Maximum Marks	No. of objective multiple choice question	Duration of the Examination
Paper-I Pharmacy	200	100	2 Hours
Paper-II General Knowledge	50	50	1 Hour

All question papers are set in English and the same should be answered in English only. There is normally negative marking for wrong answers as well.

The contents and subjects to be tested are the same as a candidate should have studied during their pharmacy courses for Paper I and general knowledge will be of current affairs of national and international importance (also specific to state if appearing for state exams), history, social aspects and culture of India and it's states. News impacting pharmaceutical industry will also be tested.

Gross starting salary for drug inspector range from about Rs. 55,000 to 65,000 per month

2.5 PHARMACEUTICAL TRADE

Pharmaceutical business involves two types of activities

- Industry
- Commerce/Trade

Industry refers to that part of the business activity which involves production of medicines, specifically where the raw material is converted to finished products e.g. Tablets, liquids, capsules, injections etc. Commerce is the activity which is concerned with the distribution of the finished product produced by the industry. It serves as a valuable link between producers and consumers. Trade is the centre of any commercial activity. It refers to buying, selling and exchange of goods or services for money. Dealers or distributors involve in the distribution of goods from production unit to consumers at far off places are called traders. The type of trading is shown in Figure below:

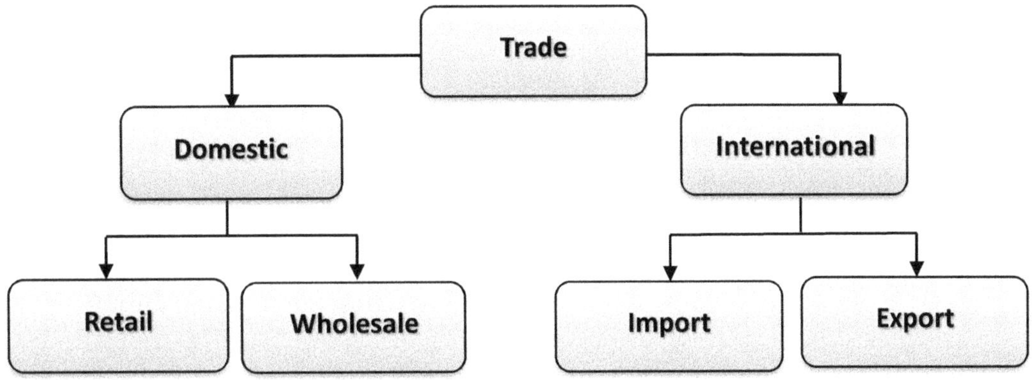

Distribution Channel

Pharmaceutical retailing and distribution is one of the most complex aspects of pharmaceutical business in India. A distribution channel is a set of firms or people that facilitate the movement of products from the point of production to the point of sale i.e.to the end user. It is difficult to directly source the products from manufacturer, so a supply chain is created through multiple layers of supplier, middleman and retailers as shown in figure below:

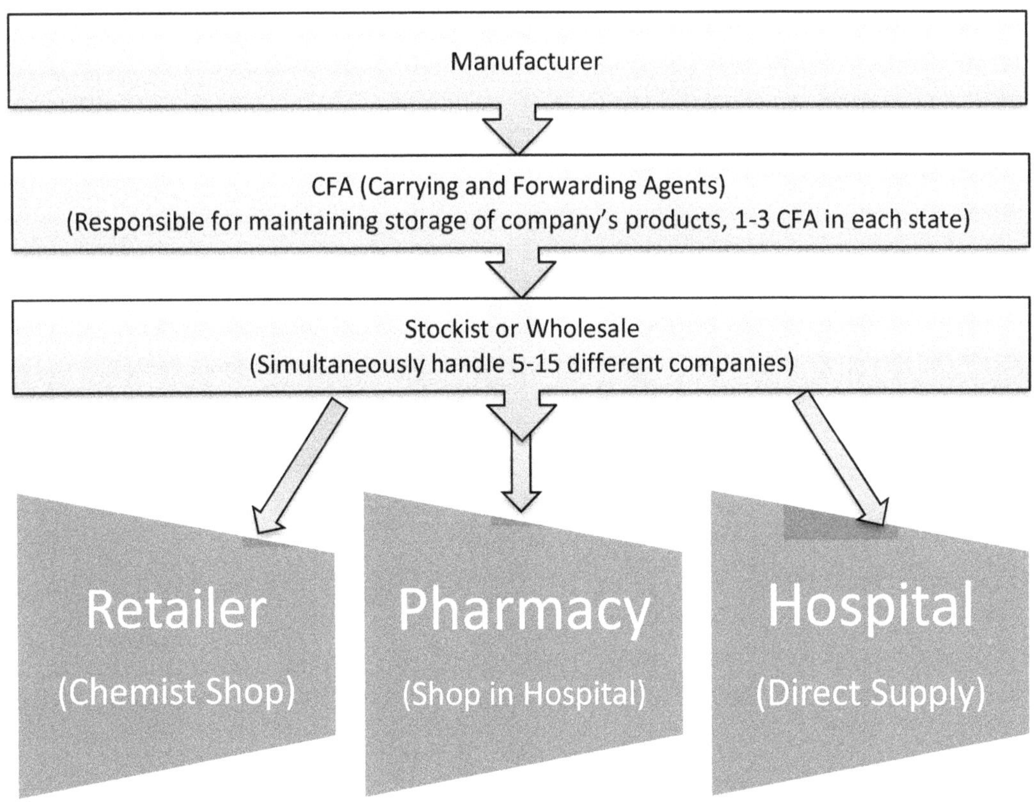

Role of a Retailer: A retailer sells products and/or services to consumers for their personal or family use. Retailers are the final point in distribution channel that links manufactures to consumers. Different retail store formats are shown in figure below:

Stores	Description
Chemist Shop	Near Residential areas
Shop in Hospital	Cater to Patients in Hospital
Pharmacy Chain	Big houses with Franchise-Apollo
In Malls	Pharmacy counters in Supermarkets
Jan Aushadhi	Govt. Retail Stores
E Pharmacy	Online sale of Pharmaceuticals

Licences Required for Retail Pharmacy Shop

The sale of drug by retail must be made in the presence of registered pharmacist approved by the drug department; registered pharmacist is required throughout the working hours.

Requirements for Pharmacists working in the pharmacy

- Should hold a Diploma or degree in Pharmacy
- Must be registered as a pharmacist with the Pharmacy council of the state
- Have undergone adequate practical training
- Have communication skills and capability to give adequate advice to the clients regarding the appropriate use of medicines, illness etc.

Duties of Pharmacist in Retail Pharmacy

- Check the prescription
- Dosage
- Interaction between prescribed medicines
- Advice the patient
- Perform the role of health care provider

Wholesale: In India, 97% of the supply of medicines is through stockists or wholesalers. Companies cannot sell directly to the retail chains or institutions. Due to their strong association i.e. All india organization of chemists and Druggist (AIOCD), companies cannot bypass them. They purchase large quantities of medicines either directly from the manufacturer or from carry and forwarding agents and then supply to retailers, hospitals in small quantities. They also bid for government tenders for institutional supply of the medicines. Their role is to ensure delivery of right medicine at the right time and in the right condition.

Qualifications to be a Wholesaler

The sale of drug by wholesale shall be made either in the presence of registered pharmacist or in the presence of a competent person who shall be a graduate with 1 year experience in dealing in drugs or a person who has passed senior secondary with 4 years experience in dealing in drugs, specially approved by the department of drug control can be a wholesaler.

Generally, wholesalers fall into two categories:

Full line wholesalers: Keep a stock of complete product line of the manufacturer.

Speciality Distributors: Stock speciality medicines and cater to hospitals or physician owned clinics.

2.6 RESEARCH INSTITUTES

Indian higher education system has expanded at a fast pace. Some institutions of India such as National institute of pharmaceutical education and Research (NIPER), Birla institute of Technology and Science (BITS), Government universities like Punjab University, Banaras Hindu University (BHU), Sagar University have been globally acclaimed for their standard of education and research.

Apart from these, several hundred state and private universities offer post graduate courses, research and PhD studies for advanced learning. Colleges may be autonomous, i.e. empowered to examine their own degrees, up to PhD level in some cases, or non-autonomous, in which case their examinations are under the supervision of the university to which they are affiliated. Although, the Government has a network of science and technology laboratories for research and development, the major base of researchers in science and technology remains with the universities. Therefore, university and college teachers need to be supported to meet this requirement. Government strives to promote teaching and research in emerging areas of Pharmaceutical Sciences through funding agencies.

1. Department of Science and Technology (DST)

The Department of Science and Technology plays a pivotal role in promotion of Science & Technology in the country. As an autonomous body, the Science and Engineering Research Board (SERB) is set up for promoting basic research and to provide financial assistance to scientists, academic institutions, R&D laboratories, industrial units and other agencies for research. The Department supports research through a wide variety of schemes specifically designed to meet the requirements of Pharmaceutical field under Pharmaceuticals Research and Development Support Fund (PRDSF). Following are the different fellowship programmes under PRDSF.

- FAST (Fast track scheme for Young Scientists)

  Duration of Project-3 Years: Total Funding-17 lakh

- FIST (Fund for Improvement of Science and Technology Infrastructure)

  It is a new initiative to rebuild Science & Technology infrastructure in the country.

- INSPIRE Fellowship (DST)

  INSPIRE fellowship aims at enhancing research fellowships and nurture talents for scientific research. The fellowship is offered to University 1st Ranker in a particular subject at PG level examination

- INSPIRE Faculty Scheme (DST)

  It provides attractive opportunities to young achievers for developing independent scientific profiles and intends helping them emerge as Science and Technology leaders in the long term. The Scheme offers contractual research positions for 5 years.

- Nano Mission

  The Nano Mission is an umbrella programme for capacity building which focuses on basic research, Infrastrucure development for nano Science and technology development programmes based on nano science applications
- Women Scientists Scheme (WOS-A)

  To provide opportunities to women scientists and technologists for pursuing research in basic or applied sciences A special provision has been made under this Scheme to encourage those women scientists who have had breaks in their careers.
- Women Scientists Scheme (WOS-B)

  This scholarship is to encourage women scientists involved in research and application of innovative solutions for various societal issues at grass root level.
- Women Scientists Scheme (WOS-C)

  This category is mainly focused to provide an opportunity to women scientists for self-employment by utilizing their specialized domain knowledge in areas such as patenting, proof reading, science journalism, technical translation, clinical pathology labs, medical transcription etc.

Website: www.serc-dst.org

2. All India Council for Technical Education: AICTE establishes national level facilities in Engineering & Technology through collaboration between industry and institutions for product development, basic research and consultancy. It promotes technical education through different schemes.

i) Research & Institutional Development Schemes

- Modernization and Removal of Obsolescence Scheme (MODROBS)

The purpose is to enhance functional efficiency of teaching and research through modern infra-structural facilities in laboratories/computer labs

Duration: Rs. 15 lakhs for 2 years

- Research Promotion Schemes (RPS)

Aim is to promote Independent research activity which can lead to growth of knowledge/process in a particular field.

Funding-One time grant of Rs. 5-10 lakhs.

Capacity Building for research – A young faculty (30 years limit), is encouraged to carry out research at Doctoral level in a research institution.

Funding: Rs. 10-12 lakhs

Patentable technology development by a group of faculty members,

Funding: Rs. 20 lakhs.

- Industry-Institute Interaction Schemes

To establish institute-industry liaison by encouraging industrial Research and Development Schemes

Entrepreneurship Development Cells (EDC)

To encourage students to consider self-employment as a career option and provide training in entrepreneurship.

Website: https://www.aicte-india.org/

3. Council of Scientific and Industrial Research (CSIR)

The major functions of CSIR include promotion, guidance and coordination of scientific and industrial research in India

Research Schemes

To promote research work in the field of medicine through Research Fellowships

- Shyama Prasad Mukherjee Fellowship
- Shanti Swarup Bhatnagar Prize
- CSIR Young Scientist Award

Other Science and Technology Promotion Programmes

- CSIR Programme on Youth Leadership in Science
- CSIR Diamond Jubilee Research Interns Award Scheme
- Visiting Associateship Scheme

Website: http://csirhrdg.res.in

4. Department of Scientific and Industrial Research (DSIR)

The activities under the scheme are centered on promoting industrial R&D, development and commercialization of technologies and to encourage R&D

Scheme

The main focus is Technology Promotion, Development and Utilization Programmes

Website: www.dsir.gov.in

5. Indian Council of Medical Research (ICMR)

The primary aim of the ICMR is to promote research in the country in the fields of medicine, public health and allied areas. The Council promotes biomedical research in the country through grants -in-aid given to projects.

- Senior Research Fellowship/Research Associate
- Junior Research Fellowships

Website: www.icmr.nic.in

6. University Grants Commission (UGC)

Major and Minor Research Projects

Main aim is to promote excellence in research in higher education by supporting research programmes of University and College teachers in various disciplines.

Website: ugc.ac.in

7. Department of Biotechnology

A separate Department of Biotechnology (DBT) was set up under the Ministry of Science and Technology in 1986 with a focus on modern biology and biotechnology.

Areas of research support

Animal Biotechnology, industrial biotechnology; Biotechnology of Medicinal and Aromatics plants; Food Biotechnology; Medical Biotechnology (Vaccines, Diagnostics, Drug Development, Plant tissue Culture.

Website: www.dbtindia.gov.in

8. Department of Ayurveda, Yoga and Naturopathy, Unani, Siddha and Homoepathy (AYUSH)

Ayurveda, Yoga & Naturopathy, Unani, Siddha and Homoeopathy (AYUSH) offer a wide range of holistic treatment. These systems of medicine are generally cost effective, valuable and are in practice from centuries.

To strengthen traditional system of medicine and to provide cost effective healthcare, a separate ministry was set up in 2014. Various schemes to promote research in pharmaceuticals are:

Golden Triangle Partnership (GTP): Scheme for validation of traditional Ayurvedic Drugs and development of new drugs.

PTUA Scheme of department of pharmaceuticals: Pharmaceutical technology upgradation assistance scheme for small and medium enterprises

9. Technology Information, Forecasting and Assessment Council (TIFAC)

Objective of the programme is to facilitate commercialization / scaling-up of innovative technologies in terms of novel process / product development and to extend financial support to Indian industries for scaling up technology

Website: www.tifac.org.in

2.7 NON-GOVERNMENTAL ORGANIZATIONS (NGOs)

Non-Governmental Organizations (NGOs) are mostly non-profit organizations that are independent of governments and business organizations that are active in humanitarian, educational, health care, public policy, social, human rights, environmental, and other areas. They are often funded by donations from private citizens, associations/organizations, business organizations and even sometimes governments (through any of their various welfare bodies). Some NGOs do not take formal funding altogether and are run primarily by volunteers. NGOs are diverse groups of organizations engaged in a wide range of activities in different parts of the world. Some may have charitable status, while others may be registered for tax exemption based on recognition of social purposes.
Among the roles played by various NGOs, delivery of healthcare is one of the most important ones. Such NGOs often have a large roster of professionals from the medical as well as the pharmaceutical fields. Some of the roles played by NGOs requiring pharmaceutical knowledge include:

- **Policy Advocacy Groups:** Such NGOs engage in research regarding healthcare delivery in society where access to medicines needs to be improved and based on their findings, try to prevail over the concerned government body to change its policy. For example, it may concern with easing controls to ensure regular delivery of essential medicines (also advising on what type of drugs may be classified as essential medicines), price control mechanisms to ensure affordability of medicines by the majority of people, linking patent protection with high drug prices, suggesting compulsory licensing to ease shortage of drugs, identifying effective measures to combat counterfeit medicines etc.

- **Healthcare Delivery for Weak Economies:** These NGOs are more closely linked with the primary health centres operated predominantly by government bodies and with general public at large and are largely concentrated over a smaller area of activity like a city/village or district. They provide vital inputs of prevalent diseases, population awareness of health and sanitation guidelines to reduce incidence of diseases, helping in procuring low cost and/or generic medicines from local suppliers etc. Pharmacists are also able to provide vital guidelines for storage and handling of essential medicines for localized areas of population.

- **Procurement Services for Government Purchases:** many of the less developed economies of the world, especially in Africa and South America, where there is little pharmaceutical manufacturing activity established in the country, the governments often have to procure these medicines from other countries. Many times, these procurement processes are financed by international aid programs of UN or other big organizations and lay down stringent controls for such processes. In such scenarios, pharmacists in concerned NGOs play an important role in advising and controlling procurement, logistics, warehousing and selection of vendors of such medicines. Pharmacists are also responsible for maintaining optimal levels of inventory based on expiry date of medicines and predicting the quantum of requirements so that wastage is reduced to a minimum.

- **Disaster Relief for Disease Outbreaks:** Currently occurring outbreaks like bird flu, zika virus, dengue, Ebola virus etc. all are cause for alarm for the local population and it is critical to contain the spread of such disease with the highest priority. In addition, the latest medicines must be made available that are most effective with minimal side effects and high physical stability so it avoid getting degraded in un-hygienic environments like hot – humid climates, swamps, stagnant water bodies etc. Pharmacists play a crucial role along with the doctors in ensuring the selection of best medicines for the outbreak.

- **Disaster Relief for Natural Disasters:** In case of a natural disaster, such as an earthquake, tsunami, hurricane, volcanic eruption, or flood, pharmacists play an important role. In addition to the use of antibiotics, optimal use of antimicrobial agents is extremely important to prevent the emergence of more antibiotic resistant bacteria. This is crucial in disaster management as time is of the essence during such mitigation efforts.

- **Disaster Relief for Refugees from War/Terror/Political Events:** Pharmacists are knowledgeable in quality control in any settings (e.g. refugee camps) when it comes to medications to ensure proper health standards and also safety measures, effectiveness of the drug must be ensured to prevent potential adverse drug reactions in order to reduce the amount of casualties. Pharmacists also play an important role in educating the patients and the public. Reducing contamination and infection in a refugee camp is important because the victims are more susceptible to infections due to lack of nutrients and also trauma. Some people are highly traumatized when faced with losing close family members or loved ones during the escape journey or on facing adverse weather conditions in refugee camps (that they are not accustomed to), reject any food and medications being offered as they do not see any use for it. Patient counselling by the pharmacists in such situations is also of critical importance.

- **NGOs Promoting Pharmaceutical Research:** Such kind of NGOs are predominantly composed of highly qualified pharmaceutical scientists and medical researchers having years of experience who are able to guide other research bodies to undertake research in neglected areas where there is perceived need for better medicines. They normally do so by providing funding for approved research projects and hence the research institutes gain a better insight into future areas of research. It should be noted that the aim for discovering/inventing new medical cures is filling the gaps in therapy for certain diseases and not the market potential of such new medicines.

NGOs are considered to be optimal bodies for reaching the poor and providing health care in an efficient and cost-effective way with many national governments not being able to supply sufficient health care, especially in rural areas and not easily accessible by road in far flung areas. In these humanitarian activities, pharmacists need to be recruited by NGO as they serve to ensure the refugees' access to essential medicines. Pharmacists have to choose the best drugs and are responsible to reduce the transmission of infectious diseases and promoting optimal use of antibiotics.

Some of the prominent NGOs include the following:

International Organizations

- The Global Fund to Fight AIDS, Tuberculosis and Malaria - An international financing institution that invests the world's money to save lives.
- Joint United Nations Programme on HIV/AIDS (UNAIDS) - An innovative partnership that leads and inspires the world in achieving universal access to HIV prevention, treatment, care and support.
- World Bank - A vital source of financial and technical assistance to developing countries around the world to fight poverty, including making investments to improve health.
- World Health Organization (WHO) - The directing and coordinating authority for health within the United Nations system, responsible for providing leadership on global health matters, including shaping the health research agenda.
- Médecins Sans Frontières - An international, independent medical humanitarian organization, it provides medical assistance to people affected by conflict, epidemics, disasters, or exclusion from healthcare.
- Pharmaciens Sans Frontières Comité International (PSFCI) – It is the largest humanitarian association in the world specialized in the pharmaceutical sector. Founded in 1985 to retrieve unused drugs from chemists for use in developing countries, PSFCI extended its objectives to help the developing countries set up a local adapted health care system.

Scientific Organizations

- American Association for the Advancement of Science (AAAS) - An international non-profit organization dedicated to advancing science around the world by serving as an educator, leader, spokesperson and professional association.
- American Society of Tropical Medicine and Hygiene (ASTMH) - A worldwide community of researchers, clinicians and professionals dedicated to advancing global health through collaboration, education and career advancement in tropical medicine.
- American Thoracic Society (ATS) - An international society committed to improving global health - particularly regarding tuberculosis diagnosis, treatment and control - and is a forceful advocate for tobacco control and smoking cessation.
- Coalition for Epidemic Preparedness Innovations (CEPI) - A global coalition seeking to outsmart epidemics by developing safe and effective vaccines against known infectious disease threats that could be deployed rapidly to contain outbreaks, before they become global health emergencies. CEPI will initially target the MERS-CoV, Lassa and Nipah viruses.
- Consortium of Universities for Global Health (CUGH) - A consortium of colleges and universities that builds collaborations and exchange of knowledge and experience among interdisciplinary university global health programs working across education, research and service. It is dedicated to creating equity and reducing health disparities, everywhere.
- CRDF Global - An independent nonprofit organization that promotes international scientific and technical collaboration through grants, technical resources, training and services.
- The Global Health Network - A collection of websites and online communities supporting global health researchers by facilitating collaboration and resource sharing.
- Infectious Diseases Society of America (IDSA) - Represents physicians, scientists and other health care professionals who specialize in infectious diseases. IDSA's purpose is to improve the health of individuals, communities, and society by promoting excellence in patient care, education, research, public health, and prevention relating to infectious diseases.

- International Society for Infectious Diseases (ISID) - Supports health professionals, nongovernment organizations and governments around the world in their work to prevent, investigate and manage infectious disease outbreaks when they occur, especially in countries that have limited resources and that disproportionately bear the burden of infectious diseases.
- International Diabetes Federation (IDF) - An umbrella organization of over 200 national diabetes associations in over 160 countries.
- Planetary Health Alliance - A consortium of universities, NGOs and other partners supporting the growth of a rigorous, policy-focused, transdisciplinary field of applied research aimed at understanding and addressing the human health implications of accelerating change in the structure and function of Earth's natural systems.

Advocacy/Policy Organizations

- The Earth Institute - Columbia University's resource that brings together the people and tools needed to address some of the world's most difficult problems, from climate change and environmental degradation, to poverty, disease and the sustainable use of resources.
- Global Alliance for Chronic Diseases (GACD) - An alliance of research funders to support clear priorities for a coordinated research effort that will address this growing global health crisis.
- Global Health Council - The leading membership organization supporting and connecting advocates, implementers and stakeholders around global health priorities worldwide.
- Global Health Technologies Coalition (GHTC) - A group of more than 30 nonprofit organizations working to increase awareness of the urgent need for technologies that save lives in the developing world.
- Kaiser Family Foundation (KFF) U.S. Global Health Policy - An online gateway for data and information on the U.S. role in global health.

Foundations

- Africare - Addresses African development and policy issues by working in partnership with African people to build sustainable, healthy and productive communities. (Africare merged with the Accordia Global Health Foundation in 2016.)
- Bill and Melinda Gates Foundation - Guided by the belief that every life has equal value, the Bill & Melinda Gates Foundation works to help all people lead healthy, productive lives.
- Foundation for NIH (FNIH) - An independent non-profit organization, we accomplish this by raising private funds and creating public-private partnerships to support the mission of the National Institutes of Health (NIH).
- UN Foundation (UNF) - Links the UN's work with others around the world, mobilizing the energy and expertise of business and non-governmental organizations to help the UN tackle issues including climate change, children's health, peace and security, and poverty eradication.
- Wellcome Trust - A global charitable foundation dedicated to achieving extraordinary improvements in health by supporting the brightest minds.

In India

- All India Drug Action Network (AIDAN)
- Drug Action Forum – Karnataka (DAF-K)
- Low Cost Standard Therapeutics (LOCOST)
- Jan Swasthya Sahoyog (JSS)

- Saathi – CEHAT
- Lawyers Collective
- TEST Foundation
- Citizen Consumer and Civic Action Group (CAG)
- SAMA, Resource Group for Women & Health
- Jananeethi
- Community Health Cell
- Headstreams
- Delhi Society for Promotion of Rational Drug Use
- Voluntary Health Association
- Medico Friend Circle (MFC)
- Cancer Aid Society
- EMPOWER

Composition of typical NGO in Disaster Relief

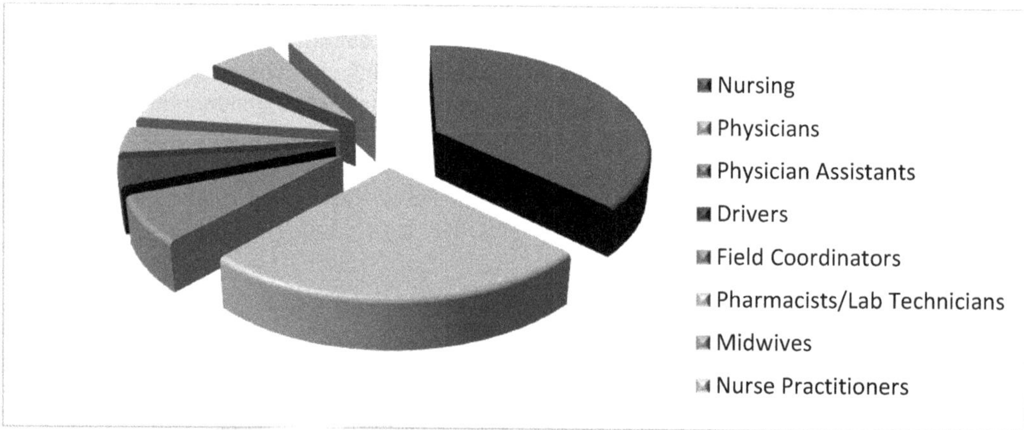

2.8 INTELLECTUAL PROPERTY LAW FIRMS

When pharmaceutical/biotech companies or research institutes or individuals etc. make a new chemical entity or its dosage forms, they expect their efforts and resources to be protected by the governments or laws enacted by them from copying by others. This gives the inventors exclusivity and an obvious advantage which acts as the main incentive to do such research. Such new products, their technologies and other related data may together be described as Intellectual Property.

Research-based pharmaceutical companies that develop new drugs, or modify existing drugs or develop new pharmaceutical equipment or processes, rely on patent system to ensure that they recover the investments incurred for research and development. Pharmaceutical industry may use the information contained in patent documents as crucial input to their R&D work or to find out when a patent is expiring, making possible for the introduction of generics.

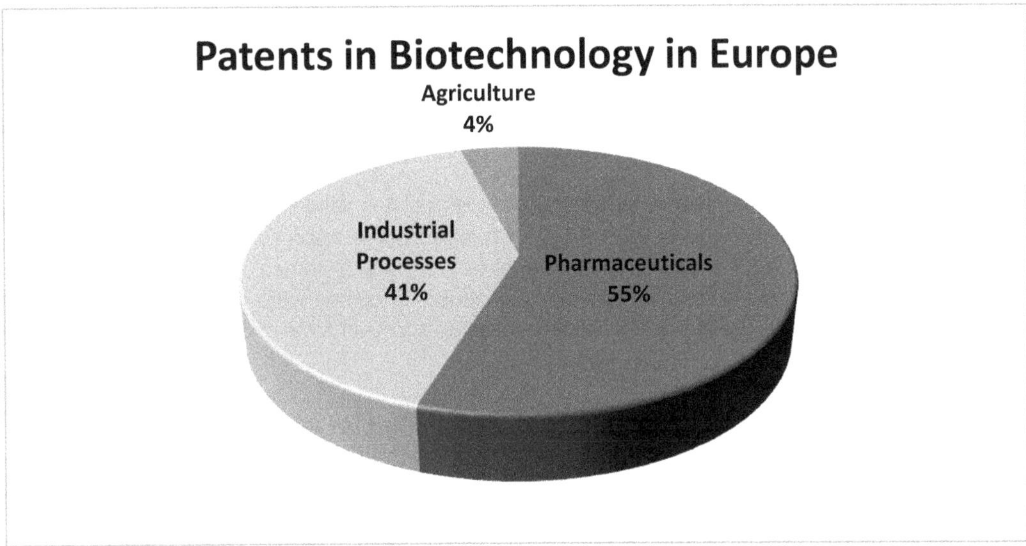

Confidential information, protected as trade secrets, know-how or data relating to new or improved drugs is also valuable. Industrial designs, plant variety protection (for example for high yielding varieties of medicinal plants) and copyright and related rights are also relevant to the pharmaceutical field.

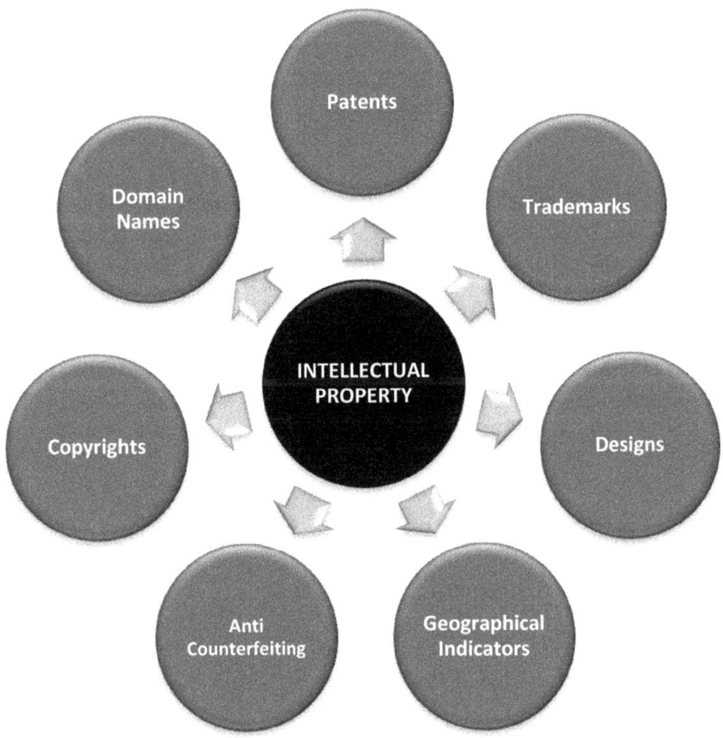

World Intellectual Property Organization (WIPO) defines Patents as "an exclusive right granted by the State for an invention that is new, involves an inventive step (or is non-obvious) and is capable of industrial application (or useful). It provides its owner the exclusive right to prevent others from making, using, offering for sale, selling or importing the patented invention without the owner's permission.

A patent is granted by the national or regional patent office. It is valid for a limited period of time, generally for 20 years from the filing date (or priority date) of the patent application, provided the renewal (or maintenance) fees are paid to keep the patent in force. In some countries, a longer period of protection may be obtained for pharmaceutical products to compensate for the loss of effective period of protection due to delays in obtaining marketing approval from the relevant public health regulatory bodies.

WIPO also defines trademark as "a sign capable of distinguishing the goods or services produced or provided by one enterprise from those of other enterprises. Any distinctive words, letters, numerals, drawings, pictures, shapes, colors, logotypes, labels or combinations that distinguish the origin of goods or services may be considered a trademark. In some countries, advertising slogans are also considered trademarks and may be registered as such at national trademark offices. An increasing number of countries also allow for the registration of less traditional forms of trademarks such as single colors, three-dimensional signs (shapes of products or packaging), audible signs (sounds) or olfactory signs (smells). Aside from the protection of logos and brand names, in some countries, companies in the pharmaceutical industry rely on trademark protection for the distinctive shape or color of pharmaceutical products (such as capsules or tablets) and product packaging."

In the pharmaceutical industry, patentable inventions include new chemical entities (NCE), new products for diagnostics, new dosage forms of known therapeutics, novel combinations of known compounds, manufacturing processes used for a product, manufacturing equipment and new drug delivery systems.

While the patent protection is based on laws enacted by individual countries, therefore paptent application has to be made individually for each country where protection is sought. However, some regional organizations have been set up to offer a single application for a group of regional countries thereby offering substantial savings in time, money and efforts of the patent filing process these include:

African Intellectual Property Organization: http://www.oapi.wipo.net

African Regional Intellectual Property Organization: http://www.aripo.org/

Benelux Trademark Office & Benelux Designs Office: http://www.bmb-bbm.org/ & http://www.bbtm-bbdm.org/

Eurasian Patent Office: http://www.eapo.org/

European Patent Office: http://www.epo.org

Office for Harmonization in the Internal Market: http://oami.eu.int/

Patent Office of the Cooperation Council for the Arab States of the Gulf: http://www.gulf-patent-office.org.sa/

In India, patent laws in force are:

ACT

- The Patents Act 1970
- The Patents (Amendment) Act 1999, 26 March 1999
- The Patents (Amendment) Act 2002, 25 June 2002
- The Patents (Amendment) Act 2005

RULES

- The Patents Rules 2003
- The Patents (Amendment) Rules 2005, dated 28-12-2004
- The Patents (Amendment) Rules 2006, dated 05-05-2006

Indian Patent Rules were amended in 2003, 2005, 2006, 2012, 2013, 2014 and 2016.

The Indian Patent Office is administered by the Office of the Controller General of Patents, Designs & Trade Marks (CGPDTM). This is a subordinate office of the Government of India and administers the Indian law of Patents, Designs and Trade Marks. The patent office is headquartered at Kolkata with branches in Chennai, New Delhi and Mumbai, but the office of the CGPDTM is in Mumbai. The office of the Patent Information System and National Institute for Intellectual Property Management is at Nagpur.

IPRs Granted/Registered (and Disposed) in India

Year	2012-13	2013-14	2014-15	2015-16	2016-17
Patents	4,126 (9,027)	4,227 (11,411)	5,978 (14,316)	6,326 (20,429)	9,847 (30,271)
Designs	7,252 (7,300)	7,178 (7,226)	7,147 (7,218)	7,904 (8,023)	8,276 (8,332)
Trade Marks	44,361 (69,736)	67,876 (1,04,756)	41,583 (83,652)	65,045 (1,16,167)	2,50,070 (2,90,444)
Geographical Indicators	21	22	20	26	34

Individuals or companies or institutes or organizations may file for patents in India through the Registered Patent Agents. Presently there are Over 4,500 Registered Patent Agents in India. One can become a Patent Agent by passing the qualifying exam and having the required eligibility criteria:

- He or she is a citizen of India.
- He or she has completed the age of 21 years.
- He or she has obtained a degree in pharmacy, biotechnology, science or engineering from any university established under law in the territory of India or possesses any other equivalent qualification as prescribed by the Government of India.

The Patent Agent Exam is divided into three parts. Paper I is of 40 objective type questions of one mark each and descriptive type questions of 60 marks. Paper II is a set of two questions (different sets for science and engineering) on drafting of 30 marks each consisting of drafting of specification from given claims and background, drafting of claims from given specification and the rest will be descriptive/interpretative type questions of 40 marks. Third part will be viva-voce based on domain knowledge only. Minimum passing score is minimum of 50% in each part described above and overall 60% aggregate.

Patent agents can work in the following organizations initially and later start their own company:

- Law firms specializing in intellectual property laws
- IPR departments of leading universities and research institutions
- Research based pharmaceutical and biotech companies
- Consulting and technology licensing related firms
- State patent offices

The skills and experience acquired while becoming and practicing as a patent agent may be globally applicable like patent searching, analysis, drafting etc. though a patent agent may or may not be permitted to prosecute in patent offices beyond his / her country. Therefore except for prosecution, a patent agent from India has the potential to be employed in any country.

Salary of patent agent in India varies from 3.0 lakh per annum to 15 lakh per annum.

Some prominent IPR law firms in India:

TIER	LAW FIRM
1	Anand and Anand Kochhar & Co. R K Dewan & Co Remfry & Sagar
2	Chadha & Chadha IP Inttl Advocare Khaitan & Co. Saikrishna & Associates Singh & Singh Law Firm LLP W.S. Kane & Co
3	AZB & Partners IndusLaw Khurana & Khurana, Advocates and IP Attorneys Krishna & Saurastri Associates LLP Lall Lahiri & Salhotra Luthra & Luthra Law Offices Majmudar & Partners Nishith Desai Associates Obhan & Associates S.S. Rana & Co. Singhania & Partners LLP United Overseas Trade Mark Company

4	ALMT Legal Advaita Legal Cyril Amarchand Mangaldas Gagrats Jafa & Javali K & S Partners L.R. Swami Co LakshmiKumaran & Sridharan Royzz & Co. Attorneys at Law SKS Law Associates Samvad Partners Scriboard Singh & Associates

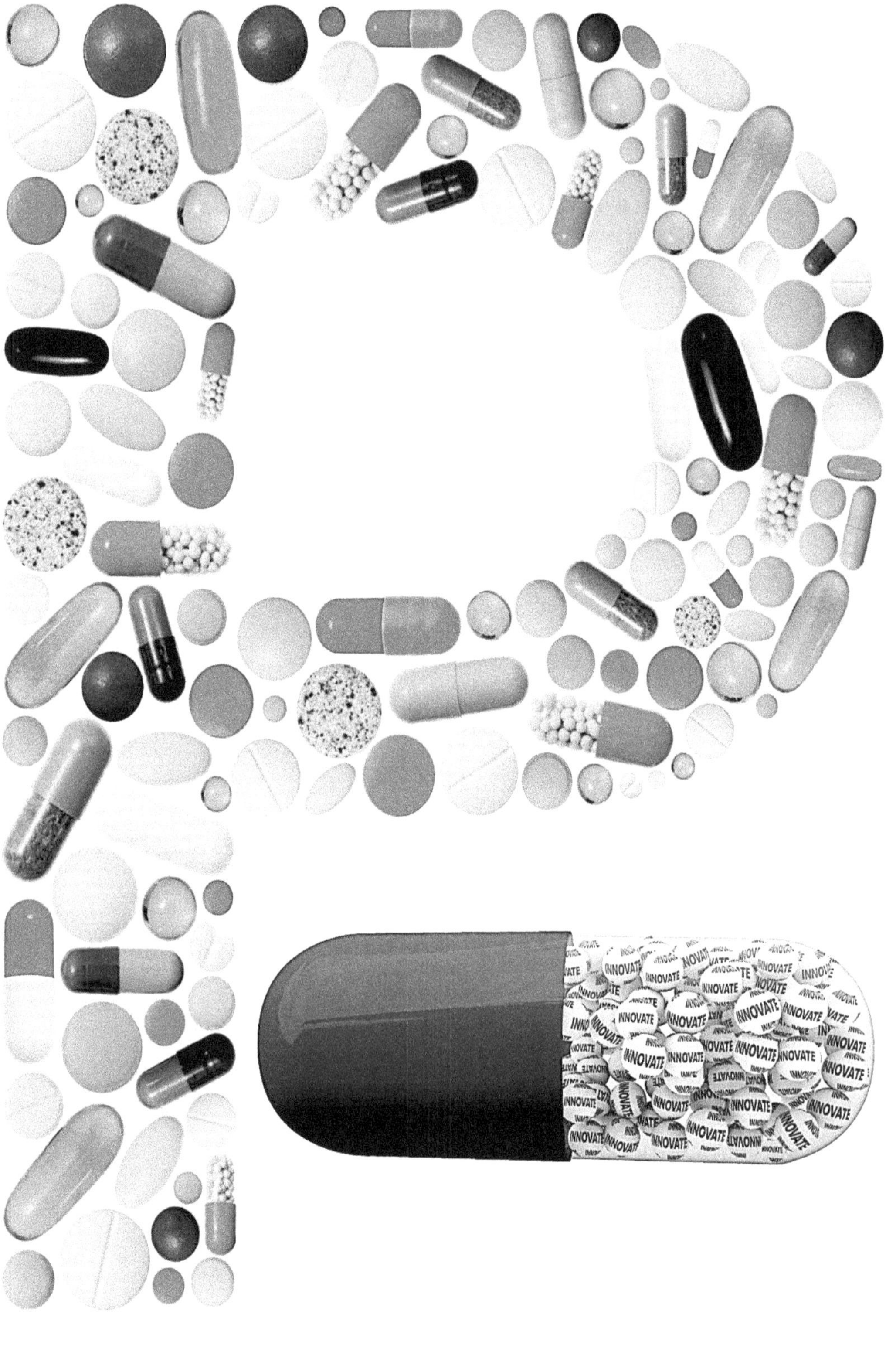

3 PHARMACEUTICAL EDUCATION

3.1 SCHOOL SCIENCE STREAMS

Mostly it has been observed that students make a decision to choose their line of work (in a rough manner) in class 10 in India. That's because a choice between humanities, commerce and science is forced upon them to select for class 11. The ideal way to choose would be to let the child decide depending on his/her choice and also strongly guided and supported by their parents who should do further research for areas of study that is not familiar for themselves.

It is also a fact that those students opting for science are predominantly looking at a career in engineering if they like physics or in medicine if they like biology. Due to the societal structure in place in India largely, a large proportion of students also opt for science knowing well that they may change their stream at college time since science is considered more 'in demand' or at least perceived that way, although this trend is thankfully changing gradually.

Due to negligence by the pharmaceutical professionals of the industry/academics to promote awareness of the profession of pharmacy, hardly anyone is aware of the field of pharmacy. While most of the people have fallen ill atleast sometimes, they are well aware of the role of doctors and hospitals but the role of the medicine they eat is not realized. Few recognize the immense wealth of knowledge that is generated for making those medicines and the great effort and resources needed to discover and manufacture them.

As we shall see later in this chapter irrespective of the minimum requirements of subjects needed to get admission to a pharmacy course, one should at the very least have the subjects of Chemistry, Biology, Physics and Maths (in order of their importance later during the pharmacy course), besides the compulsory subject of English.

The reasoning is quite simple. In simplistic terms, pharmacy can be said to be a healthy mix of engineering and medical fields. Engineering knowledge will enable us to discover and manufacture the medicines and medical knowledge will enable us to know how that medicine will act inside our body. Therefore chemistry, physics and maths will lay the foundation for our engineering knowledge and biology will do that for our medical knowledge.

Students who wish to seek out more information on pharmaceutical studies, should visit some pharmacy colleges in their neighborhood, ask from their network if someone belongs to this field or visit a pharmaceutical company office/factory for first-hand information. Online resources are of course already available.

3.2 PHARMACY COLLEGE ADMISSION

In this competitive world, choosing a right career is the most critical decision in life. Job opportunities and financial concerns often determine the choice of a career. There are wide varieties of options available other than conventional education options of medicine, engineering and commerce etc.

With the aim of serving mankind and continuously working for a healthier life, Indian pharmaceutical industry has made available high quality drugs at affordable price to the world and has become a global destination for Pharmaceutical industries. Indian pharmaceutical market has been valued at about 10,000 crores and is showing positive growth at a steady rate of 10-12% annually. The rapidly expanding field is giving lot of opportunities to explore and becoming the career by choice.

The programmes in Pharmacy fall under the following categories:

Diploma in Pharmacy (D. Pharm) - It is the minimum qualification to become a registered Pharmacist.

Eligibility - Class XII with Physics, Chemistry and Biology or mathematics. Admission is based on the marks in XII or entrance exam conducted by some universities/college. Pass from open school education system of the central/state government institutions from 2015

Duration of the course - The duration of the course is two academic years in colleges approved by PCI under section 12A

Fees - Government institutions – Rs. 12,000 - 15,000/semester, Private institutions – Rs. 70,000 - 80,000/annum

Subjects Taught During the Course

Part 1

1. Pharmaceutics 1
2. Pharmaceutical chemistry 1
3. Pharmacognosy
4. Biochemistry and clinical Pathology
5. Human Anatomy & Physiology
6. Health education and clinical pharmacy

Part 2

1. Pharmaceutics II
2. Pharmaceutical chemistry II
3. Pharmacology and Toxicology
4. Pharmaceutical Jurisprudence
5. Drug store and Business Management
6. Hospital and Clinical Pharmacy

Practical Training - In addition to academic course, 500 hours of practical training spread over a period of not less than 3 months is mandatory. Training can be done in Hospitals/Dispensaries of State or Central Government. Students learn the reading, translation of the prescription, storage conditions of the drugs, dispensing of the prescription.

Employment Areas - Health centres, hospitals, pharmacy shops, Sales and marketing

Bachelor of Pharmacy (B. Pharm)

Minimum Qualification: Class XII with Physics, Chemistry, and Biology or Mathematics or Biotechnology or Computer Science as optional subjects. Admission is based upon either on the percentage of marks in class XII or according to the rank in National Eligibility cum Entrance Test (NEET) exam. Some institutes conduct their own test Lateral Entry Entrance Test (LEET) exam for direct admission into second year.

Qualification - A pass course in diploma in Pharmacy from an institution approved by Pharmacy council of India

Duration - 4 years

Training - A Practical training of 150 hours either in pharma practice or in pharma or allied industry after completion of B. Pharm 2nd year.

Subjects Taught During the Course

Semester 1: Human Anatomy and Physiology I, Pharmaceutical Analysis, Pharmaceutics I, Pharmaceutical Inorganic Chemistry, Communication skills, Remedial Biology/ Remedial Mathematics

Semester 2: Human Anatomy and Physiology II, Pharmaceutical Organic Chemistry I, Biochemistry Pathophysiology, Computer Applications in Pharmacy, Environmental sciences

Semester 3: Pharmaceutical Organic Chemistry II, Physical Pharmacy I, Pharmaceutical Microbiology, Pharmaceutical Engineering

Semester 4: Pharmaceutical Organic Chemistry III, Medicinal Chemistry I, Physical Pharmacy II, Pharmacology I, Pharmacognosy and Phytochemistry

Semester 5: Medicinal Chemistry II, Industrial Pharmacy, Pharmacology II, Pharmacognosy and Phytochemistry II, Pharmaceutical Jurisprudence

Semester 6: Medicinal Chemistry III, Pharmacology III, Herbal Drug Technology, Biopharmaceutics and Pharmacokinetics, Pharmaceutical Biotechnology, Quality Assurance

Semester 7: Instrumental Methods of Analysis, Industrial Pharmacy II, Pharmacy Practice, Novel Drug Delivery System

Semester 8: Biostatistics and Research Methodology, Social and Preventive Pharmacy.

Any two subjects out of the following (Electives)

Pharma Marketing Management, Pharmaceutical Regulatory Science, Pharmacovigilance, Quality Control and Standardization of Herbals, Computer Aided Drug Design, Cell and Molecular Biology Cosmetic Science, Experimental Pharmacology, Advanced Instrumentation Techniques, Dietary Supplements and Nutraceuticals.

Fees = Government Institutions – Rs. 22,000 – 25,000/semester, Private institutions – Rs. 80,000 – 1,00,000/annum

3.3 DOCTOR OF PHARMACY (PHARM D)

The best way of achieving good patient care is by combining the medical expertise of the physician with technical expertise of the community pharmacist e.g. support for drug therapy, clinical studies, research activities and other data mining activities. The existing Pharmacy course in India is more industry oriented (product focus) than clinically oriented (patient focus). To fill this void and with the aim of providing a pharmacy service which is in direct contact with patient and becomes part of integrated healthcare System , a new course was introduced by Pharmacy Council of India in 2008 with the approval from ministry of Health and Family welfare. The other reason was to bring pharmacy degree at par with the basic degree in pharmacy in various countries across the world where Pharm D (Latin – Pharmaciae Doctor which means Doctor of Pharmacy) is a prerequisite for licensing to exercise the profession of pharmacist.

Course Duration

The Pharm D program is a Postgraduate Professional Doctorate of 6 years.
During this 6 years program, 5 years is academic session and sixth year is completely bound to internship in hospital.

Pharm. D (Post Baccalaureate) is a three years program including two years study and one year internship in the hospital.

Eligibility

- Candidates who have passed 10 + 2 with English as one of the subjects and Physics, Chemistry as compulsory subjects along with one of the following subject – Mathematics or Biology or P.C.M.B or P.C.B. with 50% in aggregate or equivalent qualification from a recognized board and a qualified diploma in Pharmacy from any Pharm. D. College recognized by Pharmacy Council of India (PCI).

- Candidates who have passed D. Pharm course with 40% in aggregate from institutions approved by Pharmacy Council of India U/S 12 of Pharmacy Act, 1948, are only eligible to be admitted to first year Pharm. D course.

Difference Between B. Pharm and Pharm. D Course

Parameter	B. Pharm	Pharm. D
Type of course	It stands for Bachelor of Pharmacy. It is an undergraduate level Bachelor's Degree course	Pharm D stands for Doctor of Pharmacy. It is an integrated Post Graduate Doctorate Degree program.
Course Duration	Course duration is 4 years. All four years consists of academic program only. Internship is not a part of this program	Course duration is 6 years. Academic period lasts for 5 years. 1 year is dedicated towards internship
Degree and title obtained after course completion	After completing this course, successful candidates will get Bachelor's Degree in Pharmacy.	After completing this course, successful graduates will get title of Doctor (Dr).
Course content and structure	It is a research and industry oriented course. It focuses on drug manufacturing, research, quality control and general pharmacy studies.	It focuses on fundamental concepts of pharmacy, clinical pharmacy, healthcare studies, pharmacy practice and pharmaceutical care.
Course formats	One format of this course is available (Four year Degree program).	In India, two formats of Pharm D courses are available- Pharm D (6 years long course) and Pharm D (Post Baccalaureate) course (3 years long). B Pharmacy graduates may pursue 3 years long Post Baccalaureate Pharm D program after graduation.
Job profiles and prospects	Candidate can work in medical shops, Colleges, pharmaceutical companies and research firms. Job profiles available are- pharmacist, teacher/instructor, shop owner, marketer and research professional.	After Pharm D, candidate can find work in Hospitals, Clinical research organizations and pharmacy colleges. Job profiles available are- pharmacist, healthcare professional, consultant, research professional and clinical scientist
Scope abroad	Though it has decent work scope in India, it is not so widely accepted in developed countries (Pharm D is the minimum qualification there).	Good work scope abroad. Pharm D is the minimum degree required to practice as a pharmacist in many developed countries.

Role of Pharm. D

Patient care requires knowledge, skills and attitude. After completion of the course, candidate develops and acquire competencies to provide pharmaceutical or patient care services, drug and poison information services, patient counseling, identify drug-drug interactions, monitor adverse drug reactions, carry out therapeutic drug monitoring, help in drug dosage adjustment in special population and renal/hepatic patients, assist/co-ordinate in the conduct of clinical trials, promote rational use of medicines and ultimately contribute to better patient care. Knowledge and skills required for patient care are shown in figure below:

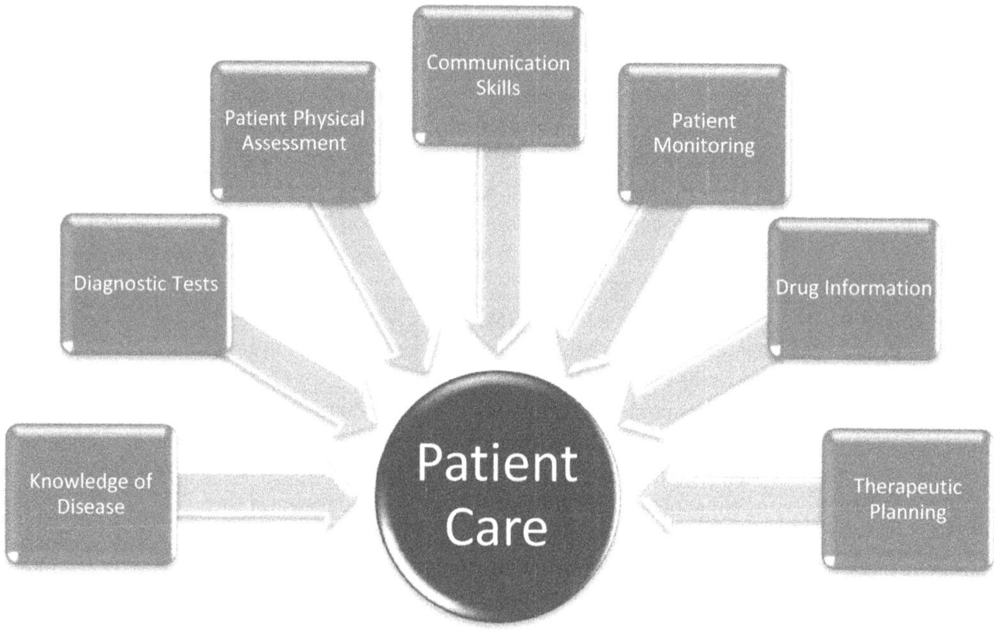

Area of Work

This programme of Pharm D in India is to orient and train pharmacy students towards clinical Pharmacy. Clinical does not only imply to hospital setting or community pharmacy but relates to all the activities where medicines are prescribed and used. Major areas of work are:

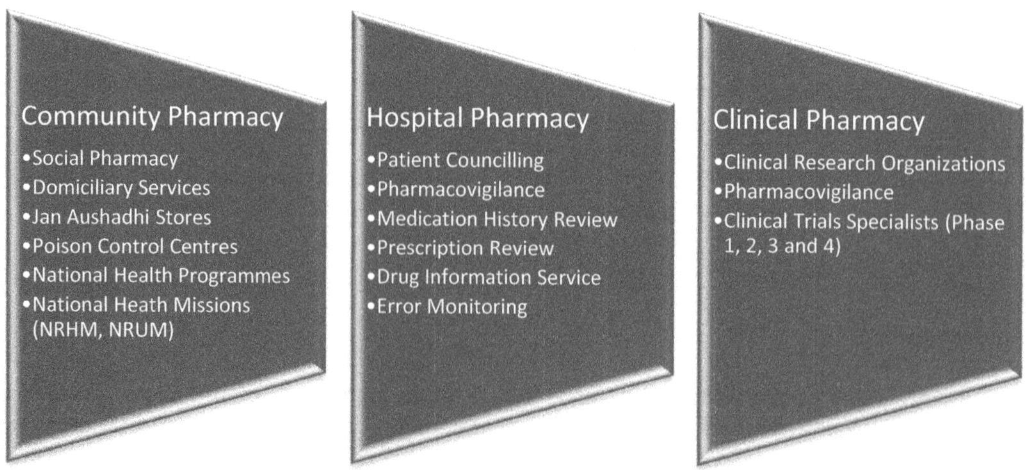

Opportunities in different Countries

Pharm. D is the basic degree to be a registered pharmacist in most of the countries so there are limitations with 4 years course offered in India for those who wish to go abroad. Pharmacy is rated much higher in some developed nations as compared to other professions. A registered pharmacist prescribes the medicines after receiving a diagnosis report from the physician which is not followed in India. Introduction of Pharm D has opened the doors for students who aspire to go abroad as it is treated at par. The criterion for Indian pharmacy students to become registered pharmacist in other countries is shown in table below:

INDIA	USA	UK	AUSTRALIA
B. Pharm / Pharm D	Pharm D	M. Pharm	B. Pharm / M. Pharm
↓	↓	↓	↓
No Exam	NAPLEX / MPJE	GPhC's Exam	KAPS / CAOP
↓	↓	↓	↓
Registered Pharmacist	Registered Pharmacist	Registered Pharmacist	Registered Pharmacist

3.4 POST GRADUATE OPTIONS

The Pharma industry is highly knowledge-based and its steady growth has a positive impact on the Indian economy. It is therefore becomes imperative that the universities play an extremely responsible role in creating quality manpower through superior education system. B. Pharm is a graduate degree bestowed to students who have successfully completed their under graduate study in the field of Pharmacy. After recognizing the professional needs and aspirations of the society, Colleges and Universities offer Post-Graduates courses. Vast number of areas can be explored after graduation which includes

a. MASTER OF PHARMACY (M. PHARM)

M. Pharm is an extension of the graduation course but in a specialized field. It deals with more details and intricacies of drugs and medicines.

The major goals are

- To develop professionally competent manpower of the highest quality to cater to the needs of industry, R & D organizations and educational institutions with a global outlook
- To achieve a deep understanding of the area of specialization through innovation, new technology, new hypothesis and ability to solve new problems
- To develop the skill to work independently on small research projects in specialized areas and other associated fields, this deepens the horizons.

Course

M. Pharm course is of two years duration. Programme is designed to include courses of study, seminars and project/thesis through which a student may develop his/her concepts and intellectual skills. Students have many subjects /specializations options to choose from the list below

- Master of Pharmacy in Pharmaceutical Technology
- Master of Pharmacy in Pharmaceutical Chemistry
- Master of Pharmacognosy
- Master of Pharmacology
- Master of Pharmacy in Pharmaceutical Biotechnology
- Master of Pharmacy in Clinical Pharmacy
- Master of Pharmacy in Pharmaceutical Analysis
- Master of Pharmacy in Pharmaceutical market & Management
- Master of Pharmacy in Quality Assurance
- Master in Pharmacy in Biopharmaceutics
- Master of Pharmacy in Bulk Drugs
- Master of Pharmacy in Drug Regulatory Affairs
- Master of Pharmacy in Industrial Pharmacy
- Masters of Pharmacy in Medicinal Chemistry
- Master of Pharmacy in Pharmaceutical Administration
- Master of Pharmacy in Pharmaceutical Technology & Biopharmaceutics
- Master of Pharmacy in Pharmacy Practice
- Master of Pharmacy in Phytopharmaceuticals & Natural Products
- Master of Pharmacy in Pharmacognosy and Phytochemistry
- Master of Pharmacy in Drug Discovery and Drug Development
- Master of Pharmacy in Medicinal Natural Products

Merits and Demerits of doing M. Pharm

Merits

- Masters in Pharmacy offers specialization in a particular field
- One learns the intricacies of research methodology and helps in developing an analytical mindset
- It provides better practical skills. The course develops communication skills as well as skill for application of knowledge
- M. Pharm is a pre-requisite for higher studies like PhD and Post Doctorate in this field
- Depending on the choice of subject, the student is more specialized and better placed (as compared to simple pharmacy graduate) for achieving superior career prospects with respect to technical areas like manufacturing, engineering, research etc.

Demerits

- If person's interest is in non-technical areas, M. Pharm will not offer any edge over others
- For marketing jobs, M. Pharm is a lesser priority than MBA or marketing post graduate diplomas
- For international trade and licensing, export oriented courses done after B. Pharm offer better value
- For mergers/acquisitions due diligence specialization, MBA or LLB after B. Pharm may be ideal
- Qualifying for UPSC is as easy or tough after B. Pharm or M. Pharm equally. However, it is also true that an M. Pharm will better equip the person during his/her career in pharmaceutical administration/ ministries (state or central).
- Pharmaceutical industry offers among the top number of litigations and hence making a career in a law firm specializing in pharmaceutical cases is better served by LLB rather that M. Pharm

Career Prospects after M. Pharm

There are a number of job opportunities for Pharmacy post graduates in Chemical Industry, Research institutes, Pharmaceutical companies, Universities and Colleges. Various employment areas for different specializations are

Pharmaceutics - Pharmaceutics deals with dosage form of the drug. It is most sought after field in industry.

- Research and Development
- Production / Manufacturing
- Pharmaceutical Engineering
- Project Management
- Quality Control Labs
- Technology Transfer

Pharmaceutical Chemistry - deals with drug design, drug synthesis and characterization of medicinal compounds

- Drug Discovery
- API Synthesis
- Chemical Research Division

- Analytical Research
- Quality control

Pharmacognosy - includes identification, characterization, cultivation, extraction, preparation, quality control, and biological assessment of drugs from natural resources. Area of work is

- Manufacturing of herbal products
- Research and Development of herbal products
- Quality control of herbal products
- Government research institutes

Pharmacology - Study of drug action and their clinical aspects i.e. the effects of drugs on living system. Areas of work are:

- Clinical Research Organizations (CROs)
- Pre-clinical and Clinical Studies
- Clinical Data Management
- Research organizations

Pharmacy Practice - Technical procedures for preparing and dispensing drugs in hospitals and retail settings.

- Clinical Research organizations
- Hospitals
- Community pharmacy
- Drug information centres
- Medical writing
- Pharmacovigilance

Pharmaceutical Marketing - Providing information regarding the drug to healthcare professionals

- Product manager
- Sales and marketing
- Business development

Quality Assurance - A planned and systematic activity implemented in a quality system so that quality requirements of pharmaceutical products are met

- Quality control analyst
- Quality assurance Officers

Regulatory affairs - To ensure that the companies comply with regulations and law pertaining to healthcare sector

- Drug regulatory affairs
- Medical affairs,

- Pharmacovigilance

Pharmaceutical Biotechnology - Focuses on the applications of biotechnology in the field of medicine. Areas of work:

- Biotechnology companies
- Medical coding trainee in various food industry
- Clinical executive

Drug Administration (State Central) = regulates food, drugs, cosmetics, biologics, and blood products

- Drug Department(Central and State)
- Testing Labs
- Pharmacopoeial Commission

Academics

- Teaching jobs in Degree College
- Academic research - Research Associate/Scientist, Biostatician

Research Jobs - Research scientist in

- Department of science and technology
- Department of Biotechnology
- Defence Research and Development Organization
- National institute of Immunology
- Research institutes of Central Council of Scientific and Industrial Research
- National Research Plant Board

Regulatory body jobs

- Pharmacy Council of India
- AICTE

Miscellaneous

IT sector - Medical coding, Transcriptionist, Patient care advisor, Health advisor
Insurance sector - Medical claim processor

M. Pharm Admission Process

Admission to the pharmacy post graduate course can be achieved through two routes:

1. By passing the Graduate Pharmacy Aptitude Test (GPAT) conducted by National Testing Agency (under the Ministry of Human Resource Development MHRD). Most top pharmacy colleges in India base their admission to the M. Pharm programme on GPAT scores.

2. By lateral entry through Self Financing Scheme (SFS) whereby no scholarship will be available (or in some cases like in Nirma University, a reduced stipend is still offered) and without qualifying the GPAT exam

GPAT Website: https://ntagpat.nic.in/ntagpatcms/public/home.aspx

Eligibility

Candidates with bachelor degree in pharmacy are eligible to take GPAT. Those who are in their final year of B. Pharm course are also eligible for appearing in GPAT exam.

Format

The medium of Question Paper shall be in English only. GPAT is an online computer-based test of 3 hours duration with 125 objective type questions. There are 4 marks for a correct answer. There shall be negative marking for wrong answers, for each wrong answer 1 mark shall be deducted.

Scholarship

A GPAT qualified candidate on the basis of their score in GPAT examination is entitled for MHRD fellowship of Rs 12,400/ month for a period of 2 years.

Students who are in receipt of any kind of Scholarship/Stipend or salary etc. are not eligible for grant of MHRD fellowship. Foreign students, sponsored candidates and candidates admitted in PG programmes are not eligible for the fellowship.

Indicative Fee Structure of Some M. Pharm Colleges

S.No	College name	Average Annual Fees (₹)
1.	National Institute of Pharmaceutical Education and Research (NIPER), Mohali	48,300
2.	University Institute of Pharmaceutical Sciences, Chandigarh	48,200
3.	Institute of Chemical Technology (ICT), Mumbai	82,000
4.	Manipal College of Pharmaceutical Sciences, Manipal	3,30,000
5.	Bombay College of Pharmacy, Mumbai	1,30,000
6.	JSS College of Pharmacy, Ooty	2,00,000
7.	Indian Institute of Technology, BHU, Varanasi	30,000
8.	LM College of Pharmacy, Ahmedabad	1,60,000
9.	Maharaja Sayajirao University of Baroda, Vadodara	2,20,000
10.	Birla Institute of Technology, Ranchi	1,60,000
11.	Goa College of Pharmacy, Goa	95,000
12.	Poona college of Pharmacy, Pune	1,20,000
13.	Maharishi Dayanand University, Rohtak	32,000
14.	Jamia Hamdard University, Delhi	1,60,000
15.	KLE College of Pharmacy, Hubli	1,20,000

b. MASTER OF BUSINESS ADMINISTRATION (MBA)

Post-graduation in business administration after a degree in pharmacy will be of immense benefit to the pharmaceutical companies as well as the candidates seeking a career in company management. This usually starts at a higher cadre level and hence the career is fast tracked from beginning itself. Such candidates are usually put in departments of domestic market development, market research, international market development, company strategy development, in-licensing and out-licensing of products/technology etc. With a B. Pharm degree under their belt, such candidates have an edge over other MBA grads who do not have a pharmacy background. One can specialize in any field like HR, Operations, Finance, Marketing, Tech, management etc.

Pharmacy graduates after MBA can work in the following departments of pharmaceutical industry:

- Business Development (Product Management)
- Corporate Strategy Management
- Market Research
- Marketing
- Production Management
- Supply Chain Management
- Procurement, Storage and Distribution
- Market Research and Consultancy (KPO)
- International Business
- Entrepreneurship
- Business Development
- Project Management (Clinical Trial, R & D Technology Transfer etc.)

Top Colleges for MBA in India

Top 10

- Faculty of Management Studies (FMS), Delhi
- Indian Institute of Management (IIM), Ahmedabad
- Indian Institute of Management (IIM), Bangalore
- Indian Institute of Management (IIM), Calcutta
- Indian Institute of Management (IIM), Indore
- Indian Institute of Management (IIM), Kozhikode
- Indian Institute of Management (IIM), Lucknow
- Indian School of Business (ISB), Hyderabad (accepts GMAT)
- Jamnalal Bajaj Institute of Management Studies, Mumbai (accepts CET)
- Xavier's Labour Relations Institute, Jamshedpur (accepts XAT)

Category A++

- Bharathidasan Institute of Management(BIM), Trichy
- Department of Management Studies, IIT Delhi
- Indian Institute of Foreign Trade, Delhi (own test)
- Indian Institute of Management (IIM), Kashipur
- Indian Institute of Management (IIM), Raipur
- Indian Institute of Management (IIM), Ranchi
- Indian Institute of Management (IIM), Rohtak
- Indian Institute of Management (IIM), Shillong
- Indian Institute of Management (IIM), Trichy
- Indian Institute of Management (IIM), Udaipur
- Management Development Institute (MDI), Gurgaon
- Narsee Monjee Institute of Management Studies, Mumbai (accepts NMAT)
- National Institute of Industrial Engineering (NITIE), Mumbai
- SCMHRD, Pune (accepts SNAP)
- SP Jain Institute of Management and Research (SPJIMR), Mumbai
- Shailesh J.Mehta School of Management, IIT Bombay
- Symbiosis Institute of Business Management, Pune (accepts SNAP)
- Tata Institute of Social Sciences, Mumbai (own test)
- Vinod Gupta School of Management, IIT Kharagpur
- Xavier's Institute of Management, Bhubaneshwar (accepts CAT/XAT)

Category: A+

- Department of Industrial and Management Engineering, IIT Kanpur
- Department of Management Studies, IIT Madras
- Department of Management Studies, IIT Roorkee
- Goa Institute of Management, Panaji
- Great Lakes Institute of Management, Chennai
- ICFAI Business School, Hyderabad
- Indian Institute of Forest Management Bhopal

- Institute for Financial Management & Research, Chennai
- Institute of Management Technology (IMT), Ghaziabad
- Institute of Rural Management, Anand
- International Management Institute New Delhi
- K J Somaiya Institute of Management Studies & Research Mumbai
- Lal Bahadur Shastri Institute of Management New Delhi
- Loyola Institute of Business Administration, Chennai
- Management Group- Birla Institute of Technology and Science, Delhi NCR
- Master of Business Economics-University of Delhi
- Master of Finance and Control-University of Delhi
- Mudra Institute of Communications (MICA), Ahmedabad
- Praxis Business School- Kolkata
- SIMSREE(Sydenham), Mumbai (accepts CET)
- Symbiosis Center for Information Technology, Pune (accepts SNAP)
- Symbiosis Institute of Business Management, Bangalore (accepts SNAP)
- Symbiosis institute of Management Studies-for defence personnel, Pune (accepts SNAP)
- T. A. Pai Management Institute Manipal
- University Business School Panjab University Chandigarh
- Welingkar Institute of Management Development and Research-Mumbai

Category: A

- Acharya Institute of Management, Bangalore (Accepts MAT/KMAT/PGCET)
- Alliance Business Academy, Bangalore
- Amity Business School, Noida
- Army Institute of Management, Kolkata (Accepts MAT)
- Birla Institute of Management Technology, Noida
- Department of Management Studies - Christ College, Bangalore
- Department of Management Studies - NIT Durgapur
- Department of Management Studies - NIT Trichy
- EMPI Business School, New Delhi
- FORE School of Management New Delhi
- Faculty of Management Studies - Banaras Hindu University
- Gitam School of International Business, Vizag
- IIRM Jaipur (Only for Rural Management - accepts MAT)
- IMDR, Pune (Accepts CET)
- Indian Institute of Social Welfare and Business Management Kolkata
- Institute for Technology and Management, Navi Mumbai
- Institute of Management Nirma University of Science & Technology Ahmedabad
- Institute of Management Technology Nagpur
- Institute of Management Technology Nagpur
- MANAGE, Hyderabad (Accepts MAT/ICET)
- MHROD - Delhi School of Economics, New Delhi
- MIB, Delhi School of Economics, New Delhi
- N.L.Dalmia Institute of Management Studies and Research
- National Institute of Agricultural Marketing, Jaipur (Accepts NIAMAT)

- National Institute of Bank Management, Pune
- PSG Institute Of Management, Coimbatore (Accepts TANCET)
- Pune University MBA, Pune (Accepts CET)
- SIES College of Management Studies, Navi Mumbai
- Sri Ram College of Commerce - Global Business Operations - New Delhi (Own Test)
- Symbiosis Institite of Media and Communication, Pune (Accepts SNAP)
- Symbiosis Institute of International Business, Pune (Accepts SNAP)
- Symbiosis Institute of Operations Management, Nashik (Accepts SNAP)
- Symbiosis Institute of Telecom Management, Pune (Accepts SNAP)
- Xavier's Institute of Management and Entrepreneurship, Bangalore
- Xavier's Institute of Social Service, Ranchi (Accepts XAT)

Entrance exam abbreviations used:

CAT - Common Admission Test by IIMs
MAT - Management Aptitude Test by AIMA
XAT - MBA Entrance Test by XLRI Jamshedpur
JMET - Joint Management Entrance Test by IITs
SNAP - Symbiosis National Aptitude Test (SNAP)
ATMA - AIMS Test for Management Admission
MAH-CET Maharashtra MBA Common Entrance Test
FMS Delhi University Entrance Test Faculty of Management Studies
IGNOU OPENMAT - Indira Gandhi National Open University Management Admission Test
IBSAT - ICFAI Business School Aptitude Test

Pharmaceutical MBA

A general management degree or diploma may not equip students with the required competencies because many processes that are specific of the Pharma industry are not part of the curriculum. So the requirement of trained professional management manpower is the need of the hour and demands a mindset and focus, which can be best brought about by specialized training. A master of Pharmaceutical MBA is designed to groom Pharmaceutical marketing/management professionals. Course provides theoretical and practical training to help graduates gain a better understanding of pharmaceutical business management functions. The industry does offer a plethora of opportunities to able professionals in this robust growing pharma field. Pharma managers play a pivotal part in the healthcare workforce by influencing the thought process of the medical fraternity as well as patient community. Hence play a substantial role in improving the overall quality of healthcare delivery in India.

Some of the unique subjects taught during Pharmaceutical MBA include:

- Pharmaceutical Marketing Management
- Pharmaceutical Business Environment
- Supply Chain Management in Pharmaceuticals
- Anatomy/ Physiology Pharmacology
- Pharma Distribution Management
- Advertising & Market Research in Pharma Sector
- Sales & Sales Promotion

- Pharmaceutical Product Management
- Pharmaceutical Brand Management
- Fundamentals of R&D Management
- IPR in Pharmaceutical Management
- Manufacturing Practices in Pharma Industry
- Pharma Product Management
- Customer Behaviour
- Macro / Micro Economics

Pharmaceutical MBA is also of two years duration as regular MBA and some of institutions offering such courses include:

- NIPER, Mohali
- MANIPAL, Karnataka
- Jamia Hamdard, New Delhi
- NMIMS, Mumbai
- Padamsree D.Y.Patil College of Ayurved and Research Institute, Mumbai
- Indian Institute of Health Management & Research, Jaipur
- Punjab University, Chandigarh
- MDU, Rohtak
- Indian Institute of Commerce and Trade (IICT), Lucknow
- Institute of Pharmaceutical and Healthcare Management, Kolkata
- Pondicherry University, Pondicherry
- Chitkara University, Patiala

Some colleges also offer an **Integrated M. Pharm + MBA programme**, which is of three years dual degree program. These include Narsee Monjee Institute of Management Studies (NMIMS), Mumbai, Apeejay Stya University, Gurgaon etc.

c. BACHELOR OF LAW (LLB)

Like any other field, pharmaceutical sciences also have to operate within the framework of law of the land. In case of pharmaceutical field, it is especially critical since this is a highly regulated field and small and big infringements are more in number than other less regulated fields. Pharmaceutical companies and government research organizations frequently encounter legal challenges that they must face and hold up against to ensure smooth running of their businesses. Some of the common legal challenges faced include:

- Brand name infringement
- Mislabeling (illegal claims, missing/wrong information, statutory requirements etc.)
- Batch failure (detection by drug inspectors from wholesalers/retailers)
- Quality shortcomings (detection by drug inspectors from wholesalers/retailers)
- Manufacturing documentation control (shortcomings during audit by drug inspectors)
- Export documentation
- Patent infringement
- International disputes (commercial/legal/technical etc.)
- Workplace ethics and safety infringements (biohazard, sterility failure, radioactivity etc.)

Having a law degree, Legum Baccalaureus (Latin) or Bachelor of Law (LLB) combined with a Bachelor of Pharmacy (B. Pharm) is a definite advantage for the pharmaceutical organizations as the intricate world of pharmaceutical jurisprudence combined with the orthodox law field is a potent combination. It offers distinct advantages over either of the two degrees alone and such persons' career prospects are increasing everyday as the size of the pharmaceutical industry is growing exponentially.

While the number of pharmaceutical companies employing lawyers on a permanent basis is limited, law firms specializing in pharmaceutical related litigations are many and this is the potential working places that candidates with law plus pharmacy background must aim for. Therefore, in addition to the legal departments of pharmaceutical companies, one can apply for patent attorney, academia, medication-related litigation, Food and drug administration for various states as well as for CDSCO (Central), medical devices policies and related careers. Also, one can get into regulatory department of pharma companies or in separate regulatory companies that handle approval process of drugs. This is further facilitated by opting for additional PG Drug Regulatory Affairs course.

Course Format

The duration of the LLB course is for three years and the course is divided into six semesters. Bachelor degree (in any field, including pharmacy) is basic academic qualification to apply for LLB course. There is no age limit. The admission for this LLB Course is based on the score of entrance examinations.

One should be aware that increasingly in India, the best rated universities and colleges have been offering an integrated BA – LLB course, after 10+2 which has a duration of 5 years (10 semesters) which is a dual degree course. Admission to these institutes is through separate admission tests like CLAT, AILET, LSAT, SET etc. However pharmacy graduates have no use for these integrated courses as they offer no specialized knowledge of pharmaceutical sciences.

Some of the prominent universities and colleges offering post graduate LLB course include:

- Faculty of Law, Delhi University, New Delhi
- Faculty of Law, Benaras Hindu University, Varanasi
- Jindal Global Law School, OP Jindal Global University, Sonipat
- Department of Law, Panjab University, Chandigarh
- Department of Law, Kurukshetra University, Kurukshetra
- Department of Law, Maharishi Dayanand University, Rohtak
- Rajeev Gandhi School of Intellectual Property Law, IIT Kharagpur, Kharagpur
- Various other state, private and deemed universities in almost all states of India.

LLB Entrance Examination

Most such institutions have their own entrance exams with similar pattern and syllabus.

Syllabus for LLB Entrance Examination

English Language and Comprehension
General Knowledge and Current Affairs
Reasoning and Analytical Abilities
Arithmetic
Legal Awareness and Aptitude

To prepare for such exams, students may consult online guides, last year question papers etc.

d. MASTER OF TECHNOLOGY (M. TECH)

M. Tech. in Pharmaceutical Technology is a 2-year postgraduate course, designed to educate aspiring candidates about the application of scientific knowledge and methods in the field of pharmacy and pharmaceutical industry.

The program essentially involves advanced learning in the concepts and processes involved in the development and manufacturing of products, processes, and components, such as drugs & biologics in the pharmaceuticals industry.

NIPER offers MS (Pharm), M. Pharm M. Tech (Pharm) and MBA (Pharm) course through national level joint entrance examination for admission to its programmes offered at its centres

M. Tech in biotechnology offers the maximum scope after a pharmacy graduation degree as the fields are quite related and this way the students tend to specialize in genetic sciences. There are four different forms of biotechnolgy:

- Blue Biotechnology is the term used to describe the marine or aquatic application of biotechnolgy but its use is relatively rare.
- Red Biotechnology is the term given to the application of biotechnology to medicine and medical processes. Some examples are the designing of organisms to produce antibiotics, and the engineering of genetic cures through genetic manipulations.

- Green Biotechnology is mostly in relation to plants, Phytochemical study, plant yield genetics, etc.
- White Biotechnology is the application of biotechnology to Dairy products, Animal Biotechnology, Bio-process of Dairy products etc.

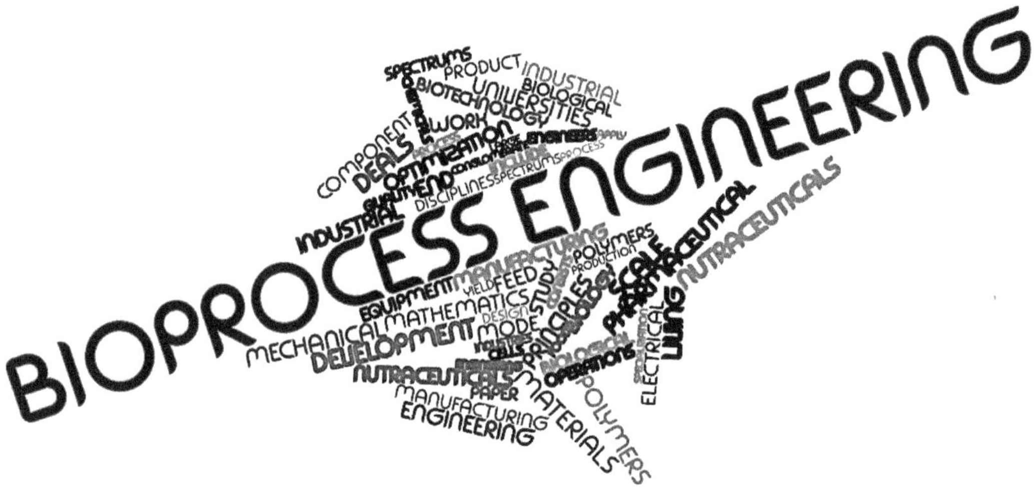

With a lot of work being done in this field of science, a lot of avenues are opening up. Biotech work commonly encountered that is useful for pharmaceutical graduates includes Genetic Engineering, Gene Therapy, Tissue culture, Stem cell techniques, Enzyme engineering and technology, MicroRNA Detection Assays etc. The scope and job opportunity includes:

- Academic Research
- Teaching faculty in Universities
- Industrial Research
- Pharmaceutical companies
- Defense Sector Research
- Blood Banks
- Agricultural Research

M. Sc. in **Cosmetics Technology** is also another rarely mentioned but lucrative career. Pharmacy students already have an established knowledgebase of manufacturing cosmetics and their skin interactions during their undergraduate pharmacy course. Therefore, to further specialize in this field is within the comfort zone of pharmacy graduates.

While Delhi Pharmaceutical Sciences and Research University (DIPSRU), New Delhi offers a four semester (two year) M. Pharm in Cosmeceutics programme, Nirma University (Ahmedabad) and Sandip University (Nasik) offer a two year M. Sc Cosmetic Technology course. In India, there are many leading companies that manufacture cosmetics such as Biotique, Colorbar, Coloressence, Dove, Elle 18, Faces, Himalaya, L'Oreal, Lakme, Lotus, Nivea, Revlon, Ponds, VLCC and many more.

Other M. Tech/M. Sc opportunities are also possible like in Microbiology, Biochemistry, Genetic Engineering etc.

3.5 HIGHER STUDIES (Ph. D, POST DOC)

Starting a PhD is by far the biggest step in student's academic journey. It is the highest academic degree awarded by universities in most countries and fulfills the educational needs of active core Pharmaceutical Sciences professionals.

Purpose: Research requires curious mind, a zeal for learning and an undying passion for work. Design, execution and completion of research project impart fresh knowledge, critical thinking, analyzing ability, developing strong theoretical as well as practical skills and expertise in the field. The acquired knowledge can be applied in developing new technology and discovering new drugs.

Programme: Average tenure for a PhD is three-four years full time course with emphasis on extensive course work for first 6 months followed by years of research work that goes into thesis and then defending it through oral examination i.e. viva. Writing thesis is the ability to present a vast information in a clear manner.

Admission Requirements

- Minimum eligibility - Successful completion of Post-graduation in pharmacy, completed from a recognized university.
- Submission of research proposal-Giving details of the proposed outline of the PhD project, and explaining the methodology one plans to employ.
- For the purpose of encouraging scientific and technological research or to provide a boost to pharmaceutical research in young minds, Government as well as private sector funds research proposals. Candidates are selected based on performance in the CSIR-UGC/ CSIR (JRF)/ NET, GPAT etc. or examinations conducted by the institute and followed by an Interview. Other government research funding agencies are CDRI, DST-INSPIRE, AICTE, ICMR-JRF, DBT-JRF and MHRD etc. Under these schemes, Research fellowships are awarded to candidates through presentation of research proposals.

Fellowship

SRF-CSIR - A stipend of Rs. 25,000/month for first 2 years and Rs. 28,000/month for 3rd year

DST - Rs. 28,000 + HRA

ICMR- SRF - Rs. 28,000 + HRA + Medical as per university norms

Silver Jubilee Research Fellowship - Rs. 35,000/month

Course Work

The purpose of the course work is to expose the research students to pre-requisite of research work followed by working on the Research proposal which includes

- Carrying out a Literature Review
- Conducting original research and compiling the results.
- Publications of research findings in reputed journal

- Attend seminars and conferences on emerging fields of pharmacy
- Writing thesis that presents conclusions.
- Defending thesis in an oral viva voce exam.

Careers

Passion for the area of research may be a difficult ride but a rewarding and fulfilling journey. Though academics is considered as the most obvious and preferred career option after PhD, a doctorate degree can pave the way for a wide range of opportunities in all walks of life ranging from fields of pharmacy especially in research and innovation to investment banking sector. Some specialized fields include:

- Teaching (colleges and Universities)
- Post-Doctoral Research in Universities
- Industrial research and development
- Clinical research organizations
- Medical division of pharmaceutical companies
- Scientific writing
- Inspection and testing institutes
- Sector analysis for investment banking, KPOs
- Think tanks, lobbying firms for pharmaceutical industry etc.

Advantage of Ph. D in Pharmaceutical Industry

✓ They understand how to find answers
✓ They don't fear failure, they learn from it
✓ They know how to deal with negative bosses
✓ They are comfortable with uncertainty
✓ They don't just consume information, they create it
✓ They thrive on both competition and collaboration
✓ They are qualified for any industry position

Challenges - Nothing new comes without problems of rejection, failure, criticism but a scientist and technologist should never be afraid of failures. PhD tests ones' patience but for those who are enthusiastic about expanding their horizon by gaining new perspectives and skills, it is a fulfilling journey.

POST DOC

The aim of the Postdoctoral Research Fellowships is to strengthen research in a specialized field after completion of doctoral studies. It differs from a PhD in the way that the researcher needs to discover a research idea different from that of the advisor. Generally, the duration of the course is 2 years, which can be extended. Many universities in India and abroad offer scholarships for doing a post doc research. To promote research, independent organizations like DST-PDF, DST—PDF/ DBT-IYBA / CSIR.RA/DST and women scientist fellowship, to name a few, also fund research projects. The research proposals are evaluated based on novelty of the idea.

Fellowships

DS Kothari Post-doctoral fellowship by UGC – Rs. 43,800/per month for 1st year, Rs.45,000/- per month for 2nd year, Rs. 46,500/- per month for 3rd year and a contingency of Rs. 1,00,000/annum

Research associates - Rs. 45,000/- per month for first two years and Rs. 55,000/- per month for the third year

Jamia Hamdard Silver Jubilee post doc fellowship – Rs. 60,000/- per month + Rs. 50,000/- per annum contingency

3.6 CAMPUS RECRUITMENT

Laying the Foundation

Getting a job that one desires marks an important turning point in life; it marks the end of the academic efforts and the beginning of a life-long career. It can therefore be called the crowning glory of all the studies and efforts that have gone into your academics. Perhaps this journey can trace its beginning to the first steps that a student takes when he/she walks in to the pharmacy college for the first time. While the early years will be spent understanding the scope of the pharmacy field, the last two years of B. Pharm and the last year of M. Pharm should be spent by devoting some extra time to future career development in addition to the academics.

Such students should make efforts to attend conferences (National/International), Workshops, Scientific sessions etc. as these will expose the students to the outside real world and they will start building up their knowledge base. They will take their first initial steps to grow their professional network among students from other colleges and senior colleagues/alumni who are now having a few years of experience in their respective fields in the pharmaceutical sciences.

They should also develop a habit of reading scientific research articles & review papers from international journals. This will not only keep them updated with the latest innovations and technologies but also develop a good foundation of knowledge. This will also help in understanding manuscript writing styles and drafting research proposals during masters, Ph.D. and post-doctoral studies. They will also understand the concepts of impact factor, citations, referencing etc.

During summer and winter breaks, they should also aim for internships and training programs with pharmaceutical industry, CSIR and privately operated research labs, hospitals etc. These internships are quite hard to get but efforts must be made as such opportunities not only expose the students to real world working, but also create networking opportunities for future and an enhanced awareness of the field and the immense possibilities that are available. Search for references of the companies through parents, relatives, friends, faculty, etc. Take an official certificate and letter of recommendation from your HOD/Principal and contact the companies directly.

Process of Campus Recruitment

Most pharmaceutical companies who decide to participate in any college campus recruitment process, usually have a process in place already that will ask the college authorities to provide the list of top 20 to 50 students opting for campus placements who will then be selected based on their performances.

The colleges will generate such lists based on past performance of a student and their assessment of projected final performance of the students. Depending on the company size/reputation/job openings available, the size of interviewees' batch will be decided by the company. Usually higher the standing of the company, lower will be number of top interviewees shortlisted by the company.

The companies then provide a short 1-2 page description of their business, present openings in which department are being offered, location of job, salary range (variable and not always provided initially) and future growth prospects in their organization. Such info sheets are then distributed among the students by the college by email and/or putting up on notice boards. Once the whole process of applications is completed with all companies and all student applicants, a schedule is made regarding the campus recruitment process henceforth.

While some companies may opt for simple interview process to select suitable candidates, many companies nowadays opt for a three step process for selecting the right candidates for their organization.

- Aptitude Test
- Group Discussion
- Technical and HR Interview

Aptitude Test

The aptitude test is a written test (sometimes conducted online for example by Sun Pharma), normally consisting of three parts, pharmaceutical knowledge domain, quantitative aptitude domain and verbal domain. The pharmaceutical knowledge domain consists of questions that test your studied subjects during your B. Pharm or M. Pharm course and some basic science subjects of class XI and XII as well. Quantitative aptitude domain consists of percentages, speed and distance, arithmetic, time, profit and loss, logical reasoning, puzzles, data interpretation, direction etc. Verbal domain will test your knowledge of reading comprehension, antonyms/synonyms, sentence completion, vocabulary, paragraph completion, fill in the blanks, etc. Overall these tests are not very hard to give or prepare for (2-3 months would be enough) and the idea is to weed out obvious low IQ people rather than selecting top performers.

Group Discussion

This is an elimination round and therefore considered highly competitive. In group discussions a topic is provided on which the students have hold a discussion for about 10 minutes. It is usually not technical in nature so that a lively discussion can take place with opposing viewpoints by different students. Usual topics include current happenings around the world, politics, history, social media etc. A panel of company experts (HR etc.) monitors the discussion. You will be evaluated on your confidence in putting forth your views on the subject , quality of your arguments and any examples that your provide to illustrate your viewpoints. Your ability to interact, listen to others and lead the discussion will largely influence a positive decision on you as a successful candidate. One should practice holding group discussions with friends and family to get the right balance.

Technical and HR Interview

An interview is nothing short of a duel, between the hiring company's expectations and your perceived abilities. While we cannot increase or decrease our abilities at will for an interview (it takes learning, dedication and experience, among others), we can improve our method of projecting our persona so that a favourable response can be achieved. Here are job interview tips to help prepare ourselves for getting interviewed effectively. We should divide our preparation for three phases of this activity; Before, During and After the interview. Proper preparation always helps alleviate some of the stress involved in job interviews and the more we prepare, the more comfortable we will be during the interview. Technical and Human Resources (HR) interviews may be conducted during a single session when the interview panel of the company would be composed of both technical and HR people. By technical it is meant to cover the people from the concerned departments like manufacturing, R&D, marketing, regulatory, clinical etc. Sometimes HR interview may be conducted separately (personally, or telephonic or Skype etc.).

Before the Interview

1. Research: Find out all you can about the company you want to join and use that information during the interview to impress your insight and awareness of the current trends etc. Find out from the placement cell the pharma/related companies visiting the college and make an info-sheet for each of those companies. Mark the dates when they're holding the interviews/written or online tests etc., their official website address, links to their social media channels and a brief description about the company. Find out about the name of the CEO and founder, history, products and services they offer, location and their competitors.

2. Social Media: Create and optimize your social media presence so that for any background search about you, the company will get a more personal and extensive information about us and our personality. While strong political or religious statements or rants are a quick put off for many people, entries for social understanding and responsibility, encouraging anecdotes or inspiring thoughts will always impress, that are almost impossible to squeeze into your interview session.

3. Your Story: Though most interviews start with the same prompt, "tell me about yourself" or "walk me through your resume", we blow it off with boring answers like: I studied science/pharmacy/engineering because I really care about making a difference in the pharmaceutical industry as you can see through my last job at company zzzzzz... You leave out everything that shows why you want this job in the first place. What was your moment of epiphany? How did your childhood influence you? Why does this job excite you? Most people don't answer these questions. They start and end with their professional experience, leaving little to inspire the interviewer. For example, you could start off by saying why since childhood you were fascinated by science and especially the chemistry part where creating new molecules by reacting different ones kept you in wonder. This later matured into specialized field of pharmaceutical chemistry where people can be cured of diseases as a result of those reactions taking place in a laboratory. Since then, over a period of time this journey of self-discovery has led to the interest in powder processing and operations efficiency in pharmaceutical manufacturing. Your Story statement shows that you're a person, not just a professional. It also makes it easy for your interviewer to predict the next chapter of your story. Chances are, we've all had experiences we can connect to where we're trying to go. It's just a matter of selecting the right ones to tell our story.

4. What's Your Weakness: Prepare for the "What's Your Weakness?" question. Most people give a predictable answer like "I'm too much of a perfectionist!" in the process sounding pompous and over-confident. Others give a genuine answer and risk exposing their inherent weakness during the process of selection, falling short of the interviewer's expectations. It's not about admitting your weaknesses. It's about showing how you overcome them. What systems have you put in place? What progress have you made? Include those thoughts to strengthen your answer. For example, a weak statement like: My weakness is that I struggle to complete all pending work in time, a strong statement would be: "I sometimes struggle to complete pending work in time. But I've worked to improve by drafting a time management agenda for daily, weekly and monthly activities to be completed, and make sure to follow up with a recap and clear action items so I know what to do moving forward.

5. Personal Grooming: As the old adage goes, first impression is the last impression, it is imperative to project an image of ourselves as neat, efficient, taking pains to improve appearance and having a pleasant and friendly but professional persona about us. Once we lose the personality advantage by a shabby and unkempt appearance, it's an uphill task from then on for salvaging that job. For males, hair should be neat, short and combed in place (Sikh gentlemen should have neatly tied turban with matching sober colours), freshly ironed well fitted clothes that are sober and not loud or too expensive, sober and simple shoes that are clean. A simple cologne is good but excessive amount may be a put off for many interviewers. No cologne is also ok. Face should be sweat free and a smiling and friendly body language is always an asset. For females, hair should be either well styled and in place if short and tied up in a bun or ponytail/plait if long. Traditional Indian clothes like suits/sarees are acceptable and preferred in industrial areas but should be sober colour, neat and well fitted. Western style attire is also acceptable but should not

be jeans and casual T-shirt but formal trousers/tops with or without jacket. Before an interview, make sure you have appropriate interview attire and everything fits correctly. Get your clothes ready the night before, so you don't have to spend time getting them ready on the day of the interview and polish your shoes.

6. Practice: Practice answering interview questions and practice your responses to the typical job interview questions and answers most employers ask. Think of actual examples you can use to describe your skills. Providing evidence of your successes is a great way to promote your candidacy. Also have a list of your own questions to ask the employer ready.

7. Be On Time: Be on time for the interview. On time means five to ten minutes early. If need be, take some time to reach the interview location ahead of time so you know exactly where you are going and how long it will take to get there.

8. Make sure you're carrying all the important documents (neatly arranged in a file) required for the interview including 3-5 copies of your updated resume, passport, address proof (Aadhar/voter ID/driving license etc.), Class X and XII certificates, certificates of your achievements (academic and extra-curricular)

During the Interview

1. Stay Calm: During the job interview try to relax and stay as calm possible. Take a moment to regroup. Maintain eye contact with the interviewer. Listen to the entire question before you answer and pay attention - you will be embarrassed if you forget the question!

2. Show What You Know: Try to relate what you know about the company when answering questions. When discussing your career accomplishments match them to what the company is looking for. When you have created a list of the qualifications for the job, make a list of your assets and match them to the job requirements. Create a list of up to 10 assets, including skills, certifications, experiences, professional qualifications and abilities, computer skills, and knowledge bases ready to share with the interviewer. Be sure your assets correlate directly with the skills and abilities required by the company. Review your list, and the job requirements, prior to the interview so you're ready to share them during the interview.

3. Look up tips for positive body language and corporate etiquettes and use them during the interview. It's important to appear confident, calm and composed during the interview. Knock on the door and ask before entering and do not sit until you're asked to. Maintain eye contact with the interviewer(s) throughout the interview (it's a sigh of confidence and fearlessness). Do not forget to smile and avoid touching your hair or face during the interview or breaking your knuckles as this makes you seem 'fidgety'.

4. One should not chew gum and the cellphone should be switched off during the interview (or atleast on silent if essential). Also, if you have lots of piercings leave some of your rings at home (earrings only, is a good rule) and cover your tattoos for a conservative image. Bring a breath mint and use it before you enter the building.

5. You don't have to answer every question right away. If you aren't sure, you could ask the interviewer(s) to give you a few seconds to think before answering. Don't be scared to admit if you don't know the answer.
6. Try to stick to English as far as possible, even if you share a regional language with your interviewer. Unfortunately in India, speaking vernacular is considered "backward" by some people and indeed, almost the entire higher education in India is indeed taught in English language, so proficiency and fluency should be cultivated and used in the interview. If you are posed a specific question in another language, it's safe to reply in that language showing your knowledge of that heritage you have acquired but keep it professional and formal, showing all the respect that is due to the interviewer.
7. Your Questions: As the interview comes to a close, one of the final questions you may be asked is "What can I answer for you?" Have interview questions of your own ready to ask. You aren't simply trying to get this job - you are also interviewing the employer to assess whether this company and the position are a good fit for you. Interview questions to ask the employer include:

- How would you describe the responsibilities of the position?
- Who does this position report to? If I am offered the position, can I meet him/her?
- How many people work in this office/department?
- How much travel is expected?
- Is relocation a possibility?
- What is the typical work week? Is overtime expected?
- What are the prospects for growth and advancement?
- How does one advance in the company?
- Would you like a list of references?
- If I am extended a job offer, how soon would you like me to start?
- Are there any other questions I can answer for you?

After the Interview

Follow Up: Always follow-up with a thank you note reiterating your interest in the position. If you interview with multiple people send each one a personal thank you note. Send your thank you note (email is fine) within 24 hours of your interview.

3.7 TOP 50 PHARMACY COLLEGES OF INDIA

SCAN QR CODE TO KNOW THE CURRENT RANKINGS OF PHARMACY COLLEGES IN INDIA OR visit https://www.nirfindia.org

Expectations of Pharmacy Colleges

- Attract the best undergraduate students
- Should be able to provide the equipment, books, knowledge and top faculty for the students
- Should be premier institute for world-class education

Expectations of Pharmacy Students

- Acquire the latest and best education
- Be up-to-date in their field of interest
- Ready to face the outside world on graduating

Expectations of Industry

- Pharmacy graduates should be up-to-date with current international norms
- Should be able to start working with minimum training
- Should be an asset to the industry

	Institute	Courses	Admission Process
1.	Jamia Hamdard Hamdard University Faculty of Pharmacy PO – Hamdard Nagar New Delhi 110062 Tel: 011-26059688 www.jamiahamdard.ac.in	D. Pharm Two years Course	• 10+2 with PCB securing at least 45% marks in the aggregate and also in the aggregate of PCB. • Appeared in the interview conducted by Jamia Hamdard. • Completed the age of 17 years on or before 31 December of the year of taking admission as per PCI norms.
		B. Pharm Regular and SFS Four Years, Eight Semesters	• 10+2 with PCB securing at least 50% marks in aggregate and also in the aggregate of PCB. • Qualified AIPMT (All India Pre Medical Test for MBBS Programme) conducted by CBSE. • Completed the age of 17 years on or before 31 December of the year of taking admission as per PCI norms. • Non AIPMT applicants may be considered on the basis of merit in qualifying examination-cum-interview
		B. Pharm. II Year (Regular and SFS through lateral entry)	• 10+2 with PCB& merit determined by marks obtained in D. Pharm course and/or interview. • Passed Diploma in pharmacy examination of Jamia Hamdard or from any other recognized institution with 50% marks in aggregate.
		M. Pharm • Pharmaceutical Chemistry • Pharmaceutics • Pharmacognosy & Phytochemistry • Pharmacology • Pharmacy Practice • Quality Assurance • Pharmaceutical Biotechnology • Pharmaceutical Analysis	• Passed B. Pharm/B. Pharm (Unani) examination or any other examination recognised by Jamia Hamdard or an institution recognised by Jamia Hamdard and AICTE, securing at least 50% marks in the aggregation of theory papers and practicals. • Qualified GPAT (with valid score card) • Appeared in the Entrance Test conducted by Jamia Hamdard
		Ph.D. • Pharmaceutics	• Passed M. Pharm. from Jamia Hamdard or any other institution recognised by AICTE and Jamia Hamdard in the relevant subject with atleast 55% marks in the aggregate or

		• Pharmacognosy & Phytochemistry • Pharmaceutical Chemistry • Pharmacology	equivalent grade • Candidate having M.Sc. degree in Clinical Research with minimum 55% marks or equivalent grade shall be eligible to be considered for admission to Ph.D. programme in pharmacology subject to the condition that he/she possesses B.Pharm. degree. • The candidates from Bio Science/ Life Science stream with NET-JRF/NET-LS may also apply for different disciplines in Ph.D. in pharmacy. • Appeared in the Entrance Test/Interview or both conducted by Jamia Hamdard.
2.	University Institute of Pharmaceutical Sciences Panjab University Sector 14 Chandigarh – 160014 Tel: 0172 2534101 www.pu.ac.in	B. Pharm Four Years, Eight Semesters	• 50% Marks in 10+2 with English, Physics, Chemistry and one of the following subjects: Biology/Biotechnology/ Mathematics • Admission based on entrance exam P.U. CET-2017 (U.G.)
		M. Pharm • Pharmaceutical Analysis • (Self Finance Course) • Pharmaceutical Chemistry (Regular Course) • Pharmaceutical Quality Assurance (Self Finance Course) • Pharmaceutics (Regular Course) • Pharmacognosy (Regular Course) • Pharmacology (Regular Course)	• B. Pharm. from AICTE/PCI approved Institutions/ Universities with valid GPAT score*. For NRI Category, B. Pharm. with valid GPAT/GRE (General). • Admission to all M. Pharm. Courses is made on the basis of combined merit calculated from aggregate marks obtained in B. Pharm. 4-years Course (30% weightage) and GPAT score (70% weightage). • Category A : Panjab University candidates • Category B : Candidates from institutes other than Panjab University • Note: Any seat(s) remaining unfilled under Category A will be transferred to Category B, and vice-versa. • *The Non-GPAT candidates will also be considered for admission in the Self-Finance courses, only if the seat(s) remain vacant after admitting all GPAT-qualified candidates, provided that their overall percentage of B. Pharm. marks is not less than 60%.
		Ph.D. in Pharmacy • Medicinal Chemistry • Biotechnology • Pharmaceutics • Natural Products • Pharmacy Practice • Pharmaceutical Analysis • Pharmacoinformatics	• GPAT-qualified students are registered from time to time for Ph.D., depending upon the availability of seats under different projects/schemes/fellowships sponsored by different agencies, including industry.

		• Pharmacology & Toxicology • Pharm. Technology (Process Chemistry)	
3.	National Institute of Pharmaceutical Education and Research (NIPER) Sector 67 S.A.S. Nagar – 160062 Punjab Tel: 0172-2292000, 2214682-87 www.niper.ac.in	M.S. (Pharm) • Medicinal Chemistry • Pharmaceutical Analysis • Pharmacology/ Toxicology • Pharmaceutics • Regulatory Toxicology • Natural Products • Traditional Medicine • Biotechnology • Pharmacoinformatics M. Pharm • Pharmacy Practice • Clinical Research • Pharm. Technology (Formulations) M. Tech (Pharm) • Pharm. Technology (Process Chemistry) • Pharm. Technology (Biotechnology) M.B.A. (Pharm) Pharmaceutical Management	• NIPER Joint Entrance Examination (Ahmedabad; Guwahati; Hajipur; Hyderabad; Kolkata; Rae Bareli; S.A.S. Nagar) • Online test shall be conducted at the following centres: • Ahmedabad, Bengaluru, Bhopal, Chennai, Chandigarh, Dehradun, Guwahati, Hyderabad, Jaipur, Kolkata, Lucknow, Mumbai, Nagpur, New Delhi, Thiruvananthapuram, Pune • B. Pharm., M.Sc. (as relevant: Biological Sciences, Organic Chemistry) • The candidate should have passed the qualifying degree with a minimum of 60% marks in aggregate or CGPA of 6.75 on a 10 point scale wherever grades are awarded or equivalent (Percentage of marks or CGPA so calculated will be based on the norms fixed by the concerned University/Institution or aggregate marks or CGPA scored by the candidate for all years of the qualifying degree, in case University/Institution has not prescribed any norm for calculating such percentage or CGPA). • It is mandatory to bring GPAT/GATE/NET score card at the time of counseling/Group Discussion and Interview. • Further GPAT/GATE/NET is an essential qualification for all programme including M.B.A. (Pharm.) except for the following categories of candidates. • Candidates holding B.V.Sc./M.B.B.S./B.A.M.S. degree. • Foreign nationals • Sponsored candidate from public/private sector undertaking, Govt. departments and research and development organizations. • Candidates applying as NRI or their wards [in case of M.B.A.(Pharm.)]
		Ph.D. • Medicinal Chemistry • Biotechnology • Pharmaceutics • Natural Products • Pharmacy Practice	• NIPER Joint Entrance Examination (Ahmedabad; Guwahati; Hajipur; Hyderabad; Kolkata; Raebareli; S.A.S. Nagar) • Online test shall be conducted at the following centres: • Ahmedabad, Bengaluru, Bhopal, Chennai, Chandigarh, Dehradun, Guwahati, Hyderabad, Jaipur, Kolkata, Lucknow, Mumbai, Nagpur, New Delhi, Thiruvananthapuram, Pune

		• Pharmaceutical Analysis • Pharmacoinformatics • Pharmacology & Toxicology • Pharm. Technology (Process Chemistry)	• Based on the performance in the online test, selected candidates will be called for interview • Admission to the Ph.D. Programme will be based on the combined merit obtained by a candidate in the entrance examination and interview. • Limited number of seats will also be available for candidates having their own fellowships from CSIR/ UGC/ ICMR/ DBT/ DST INSPIRE, RGNF etc. in the Department of Medicinal Chemistry; Pharmacology & Toxicology; Pharmaceutics; Biotechnology and Pharmaceutical Technology (Process Chemistry), (Natural Products) etc. Candidates who have appeared for NET-JRF Examination of the CSIR/ UGC/ ICMR/ DBT/DST etc. in the above disciplines but are yet to get the result are also eligible to apply. However, such candidates will be required to produce the proof of having qualified the NET-JRF examination at the time of interview. • Seats are available for Self-Financing Foreign Nationals and Foreign Nationals under various scholarship schemes of the Ministry of Human Resource Development/ Ministry of External Affairs, Government of India. These seats are over and above the available seats mentioned above. Such candidates have to arrange for the clearance from the Ministry of External Affairs, Govt. of India, before they can be admitted, if selected. • Seats are available for candidates sponsored by Government Departments, Research and Development organizations, Public Sector Undertakings/Reputed Pharmaceutical Enterprises. • Candidate should have passed the qualifying degree with a minimum of 60% marks in aggregate or CGPA of 6.75 on a 10 point scale wherever grades are awarded or equivalent as determined by Board of Studies and Research of NIPER (Percentage of marks or CGPA so calculated will be based on the norms fixed by the concerned University / Institution or aggregate marks or CGPA scored by the candidate for all years of the qualifying degree, in case University /Institution has not prescribed any norm for calculating such percentage or CGPA). Passing of GPAT/GATE/NET is an essential qualification except for the following categories of candidates. • Candidates holding M.D; M.V.Sc. • Foreign nationals. • Sponsored candidate from Government Departments, Research and Development organizations, Public Sector Undertakings/Reputed Pharmaceutical Enterprises.
4.	Institute of Chemical Technology N.P. Marg, Matunga (E), MUMBAI-400019	D. Pharm Two years Course	• The candidate should be an Indian National. • Passed the HSC Science with Physics and Chemistry as compulsory subjects along with one of the subject Mathematics or Biology (Botany and Zoology).

	Tel: 022 3361 1111 www.ictmumbai.edu.in		
		B. Pharm Four Years, Eight Semesters	• State Common Entrance Test (CET) for First Year Under Graduate Technical Courses in B. Pharm and Pharm. D admissions. (A) First Year • The candidate should be an Indian National • Passed HSC or its equivalent examination with Physics and Chemistry as compulsory subjects along with one of the Mathematics or Biotechnology or Biology and obtained at least 50% marks (at least 45% marks in case of candidates of Backward class categories and Persons with Disability belonging only to Maharashtra State) in the above subjects taken together. • Obtained Score in CET. • Any other criterion declared by appropriate authority from time to time. (B) Second Year Lateral Entry • The Candidate should be an Indian National. • Passed Diploma Course in Pharmacy with at least 45 % marks (at least 40 % marks in case of candidates of Backward class categories and Persons with disability belonging to Maharashtra State only) from an All India Council for Technical Education or Pharmacy Council of India or Central or State Government approved Institution or its equivalent. • Any other criterion declared by appropriate authority from time to time.
		Pharm. D	• The candidate should be an Indian National. • Passed HSC or its equivalent examination with subjects Physics and Chemistry as compulsory subjects along with one of the Mathematics or Biotechnology or Biology and obtained at least 50 % marks (at least 45 % marks in case of candidates of Backward class categories and Persons with Disability belonging only to Maharashtra State) in the above subjects taken together. Or • Passed Diploma Course in Pharmacy from institutes affiliated to State Board and having approval of competent central authority and State Government and obtained at least 50 % marks (at least 45 % marks in case of candidates of Backward class categories and Persons with Disability belonging only to Maharashtra State); • The candidate should have obtained at least 50% marks in the CET.
		M. Pharm (Regular, 2 years) • Pharmaceutical Chemistry • Pharmaceutics • Medicinal Natural	• The candidate should be an Indian National. • The candidate should have passed the Bachelor's degree in Pharmacy (B. Pharm.) of the ICT or any UGC recognized University/ Institute, with 60% marks in aggregate or equivalent CGPA. [55% marks in aggregate or equivalent CGPA for the backward class

		Products M. Tech (Regular, 2 years) M. Tech (Sponsored, 3 years) • Pharmaceutical Biotechnology	candidate] • Obtained score in Graduates Pharmacy Aptitude Test (GPAT) conducted by All India Council for Technical Education. • For sponsored candidates, minimum of two years of full time work experience in a registered firm/ company/ industry/ educational and/ or research institute/ any Government Department or Government Autonomous Organization in the relevant field in which admission is being sought.
		Ph.D. (Tech) • Pharmaceutics • Pharmaceutical Chemistry • Pharmacology • Pharmacognosy	
5.	Birla Institute of Technology and Science (BITS, Pilani) Vidya Vihar Campus Pilani - 333031 Rajasthan Tel: 01596 245073/4 www.bits-pilani.ac.in	B. Pharm. Four Years, Eight Semesters	• BITSAT Online Joint Entrance Examination (Pilani, Goa and Hyderabad) • The candidates should have passed the 12th examination of 10+2 system from a recognized Central or State board or its equivalent with Physics, Chemistry, and Biology or Mathematics and adequate proficiency in English. • The candidates should have obtained a minimum of aggregate 75% marks in Physics, Chemistry and Mathematics subjects (if he/she has taken Mathematics in BITSAT) or a minimum of aggregate 75% marks in Physics, Chemistry and Biology subjects (if he/she has taken Biology in BITSAT) in 12th class examination, with at least 60% marks in each of the Physics, Chemistry, and Mathematics / Biology subjects. • Direct Admission to Board Toppers - Direct admission to first rank students of all the central and state boards to B. Pharm. from PCB stream, irrespective of their BITSAT-2017 score.
		M. Pharm. • Pharmaceutical Chemistry • Pharmaceutics	• M. Pharm of BITS or its equivalent with a minimum of 60% aggregate. • Candidate with an M Sc/B.E or an equivalent with a minimum of 60% will also be considered for provisional admission to the Ph D programme.
		Ph. D. • Pharmaceutical Chemistry • Medicinal Chemistry • Organic Chemistry • Pharmacology	• M. Pharm./M.S. (Pharmacology and Toxicology/ Regulatory Toxicology)- GATE/GPAT qualified
6.	National Institute of Pharmaceutical Education and Research, (NIPER) Balanagar	M.S. (Pharm.) • Medicinal Chemistry • Pharmaceutical Analysis	• NIPER Joint Entrance Examination (Ahmedabad; Guwahati; Hajipur; Hyderabad; Kolkata; Raebareli; S.A.S. Nagar) • All other details same as for NIPER SAS Nagar above.

	Hyderabad - 500 037 Tel: 040 23074750 (Extn. Nos: 2001 to 2024) www.niperhyd.ac.in	• Pharmacology and Toxicology • Pharmaceutics • Regulatory Toxicology M.Tech. (Pharm.) • Pharmaceutical Technology (Process Chemistry) M.B.A (Pharm.) • Pharmaceutical Management	
		Ph.D. • Medicinal Chemistry • Pharmaceutical Analysis • Pharmacology and Toxicology • Pharmaceutics • Pharmaceutical Technology (Process Chemistry)	
7.	Manipal College of Pharmaceutical Sciences Manipal Academy of Higher Education, Madhav Nagar Manipal – 576 104 Tel: 09243777733 https://manipal.edu/mcops-manipal.html	B. Pharm. Four Years, Eight Semesters B. Pharm., Three Years Lateral Entry to 2nd Year	• Indian nationals. • Only those who have completed 17 years of age by 31st December are eligible. • Pass in 10+2 examination with Physics, Chemistry and English with Mathematics or Biotechnology or Computer Science or Biology as optional subjects. • Admissions are done on the basis of rank in the All India Manipal Academy of Higher Education Online Entrance Test (MAHE-OET) 2018. • Indian nationals. • Diploma holders in Pharmacy from an institution recognised by the Pharmacy Council of India. • Admissions are done on the basis of marks obtained in the qualifying examination and there is no Entrance Test for this course.
		Pharm. D. 5 years plus 1 year internship	• Indian nationals. • Only those who have completed 17 years of age by 31st December are eligible. • Pass in 10+2 examination with Physics, Chemistry and English with Mathematics or Biology as optional subjects.

			• Admissions are done on the basis of rank in the All India Manipal Academy of Higher Education Online Entrance Test (MAHE-OET) 2018.
		D. Pharm. Two years Course	• Indian nationals. • Only those who have completed 17 years of age by 31st December are eligible. • Pass in 10+2 examination with Physics, Chemistry and English with Mathematics or Biology as optional subjects. • Admissions are done on the basis of marks obtained in the qualifying examination and there is no entrance test.
		M. Pharm. • Pharmaceutical Chemistry • Drug Regulatory Affairs • Pharmacology • Pharmaceutics • Industrial Pharmacy • Pharmacognosy • Pharmacy Practice • Pharmaceutical Marketing • Pharmaceutical Administration • Pharmaceutical Quality Assurance • Pharmaceutical Biotechnology	• Indian nationals can apply under the General Category. Foreign nationals or Non Resident Indians or Indian nationals supported by NRI relatives can apply under the Foreign/NRI Category. • B. Pharm. from an institution recognized by the Pharmacy Council of India with minimum of 50% marks in aggregate. • Admissions are done on the basis of rank in the All India Manipal Academy of Higher Education Online Entrance Test (MAHE-OET) 2018. • Foreign/NRI Category: Admissions are done on the basis of marks obtained in the qualifying examination.
8.	JSS College of Pharmacy Ooty "Rocklands" Post Box No.20 Udhagamandalam – 643 001, Tamil Nadu Phone: +91-423-2443393 / 2443647 / 2443847 www.jssuni.edu.in	B. Pharm. Four Years, Eight Semesters	• Candidate shall have passed 10+2 examination conducted by the respective state/central government authorities recognized as equivalent to 10+2 examination by the Association of Indian Universities (AIU) with English as one of the subjects and Physics, Chemistry, Mathematics (P.C.M) and or Biology (P.C.B /P.C.M.B.) as optional subjects individually. Any other qualification approved by the Pharmacy Council of India as equivalent to any of the above examinations. • The students possessing 10+2 qualification from non-formal and non-classrooms based schooling such as National Institute of Open Schooling, open school systems of States etc. shall not be eligible for admission to B. Pharm program. • Student should complete the age of 17 years on or before 31st December of the year of admission to the programme. A pass in D. Pharm. course from an institution approved by the Pharmacy Council of India

		B. Pharm lateral entry to third semester of B. Pharm	under section 12 of the Pharmacy Act.
		D. Pharm 2 years	• A pass in any of the following examinations with Physics, Chemistry and Biology or Mathematics. ▪ Intermediate examination in Science; ▪ The first year of the three year degree course in Science ▪ 10+2 examination (academic stream) in Science; ▪ Pre–degree examination; • Any other qualification approved by the Pharmacy Council of India as equivalent to any of the above examination
		M. Pharm • Industrial Pharmacy • Pharma Quality Assurance • Pharma Regulatory Affairs • Pharmaceutical Analysis • Pharmaceutical Biotechnology • Pharmaceutical Chemistry • Pharmaceutics • Pharmacognosy • Pharmacology • Pharmacy Practice	• B. Pharm degree examination of an Indian university established by law in India from an institution approved by Pharmacy Council of India and has scored not less than 55 % of the maximum marks (aggregate of 4 years of B. Pharm.) • Provided that, every student, selected for admission to M. Pharm. program in JSS University, Ooty should have obtained registration with the State Pharmacy Council or should obtain the same within one month from the date of his/her admission, failing which the admission of the candidate shall be cancelled.
		Pharm. D. 5 years study plus one year internship	10+2 examination with Physics and Chemistry as compulsory subjects along with one of the two subjects: Mathematics or Biology. • A pass in D. Pharm course from an institution approved by the Pharmacy Council of India under section 12 of the Pharmacy Act. • Any other qualification approved by the Pharmacy Council of India as equivalent to any of the above examinations. • Provided that a student should complete the age of 17 years on or before 31st • December of the year of admission to the course. • Provided that there shall be reservation of seats for the students belonging to the Scheduled Castes, Scheduled Tribes and other Backward Classes in accordance with the instructions issued by the Central Government/State Government/Union Territory

		Pharm. D. (Post Baccalaureate) 3 year course (two years of study and one year internship)	• A pass in B. Pharm from an institution approved by the Pharmacy Council of India under section 12 of the Pharmacy Act: • Provided that there shall be reservation of seats for the students belonging to the Scheduled Castes, Scheduled Tribes and other Backward Classes in accordance with the instructions issued by the Central Government/State Government/Union Territory Administration as the case may be from time to time.
		PG Diploma in Pharmacy	• A candidate who has passed B. Pharm degree examination of any recognized University and has secured not less than 50% of the maximum marks (aggregate of four years) prescribed for the qualification examination shall be eligible for the admission to the following PG Diploma courses. 1. Pharmaceutical Quality Assurance (PG Dip.PQA) 2. Pharmaceutical Regulatory Affairs (PG Dip.PRA) 3. Nanotechnology (PG Dip. Nanotech.) 4. Bioinformatics (PG Dip. Bioinfo.) • A candidate who has passed B. Pharm, MBBS, BDS, BAMS degree examination of any recognized University and has secured not less than 50% of the maximum marks prescribed for the qualification examination shall be eligible for the admission to the following PG Diploma courses. 1. Pharmacovigilance 2. Clinical research 3. Herbal Products and their standardization
		Ph. D. • Industrial Pharmacy/ Pharmaceutics • Pharmacy Practice • Pharmacology • Pharmaceutical Chemistry	• Admission will be made through an Entrance Test/Interview conducted at National Level by the University. Candidates who qualify UGC / SLET / GATE / NET / UGC / CSIR (JRF) / teaching fellowship / M. Phil programme are exempted from Entrance Test/Interview. The interview will assess the candidates and their research interests. • Candidates who have obtained postgraduate degree in the concerned subject under various faculties of the University or its equivalent with a minimum of 55% of marks (50% in case of SC/ST/Cat-I) in the qualifying examination, are eligible for admission to PhD course. The qualifying degree has to be registered with the respective Councils, if applicable. • Candidates with qualification as per 3(a) above and who shall be involved in full time research activities in the concerned department are eligible to be admitted as "Full Time" candidate. • Candidates with qualification as per 3(a) above and who are working as regular faculty member in the concerned department are eligible to be admitted as "Part Time Internal" candidate. • Candidates with qualification as per 3(a) above and regular faculty members with not

			less than ten years of teaching experience of which five years shall be at the postgraduate level and having a minimum of three research publications either as a principal author or as a co author in any indexed journal are eligible to admit for the PhD degree without a guide as "Part Time Independent Research" Candidate. • However, such candidates shall seek the guidance/assistance of not less than three experts in the concerned field, who shall be members of faculties not below the rank of Associate Professors and possess the qualifications prescribed by the University for being a guide. They need not go through the scrutiny committee. • Candidates with qualification as per 3(a) above and working in a recognized institution/ organization with research agreement/MoU with the University are eligible for admission as "Part Time External" candidate.
9.	NIPER Gandhinagar Opposite Air force Station Palaj, Gandhinagar-382355, Gujarat, India. Phone : +91 79 66745555, www.niperahm.ac.in	MS Pharmacy • Medicinal Chemistry • Pharmaceutical Analysis • Pharmacology & Toxicology • Pharmaceutics • Natural Products • Biotechnology • Medical devices	• NIPER Joint Entrance Examination (Ahmedabad; Guwahati; Hajipur; Hyderabad; Kolkata; Raebareli; S.A.S. Nagar) • Online test shall be conducted at the following centres: Ahmedabad, Bengaluru, Bhopal, Chennai, Chandigarh, Dehradun, Guwahati, Hyderabad, Jaipur, Kolkata, Lucknow, Mumbai, Nagpur, New Delhi, Thiruvananthapuram, Pune • B. Pharm, M.Sc. (as relevant: Biological Sciences, Organic Chemistry) • The candidate should have passed the qualifying degree with a minimum of 60% marks in aggregate or CGPA of 6.75 on a 10 point scale wherever grades are awarded or equivalent (Percentage of marks or CGPA so calculated will be based on the norms fixed by the concerned University/Institution or aggregate marks or CGPA scored by the candidate for all years of the qualifying degree, in case University/Institution has not prescribed any norm for calculating such percentage or CGPA). • It is mandatory to bring GPAT/GATE/NET score card at the time of counseling/Group Discussion and Interview
		PhD in pharmaceutical sciences • Biotechnology • Medicinal Chemistry • Medical Devices • Natural Products • Pharmaceutics • Pharmaceutical Analysis • Pharmacology & Toxicology	• NIPER Joint Entrance Examination (Ahmedabad; Guwahati; Hajipur; Hyderabad; Kolkata; Raebareli; S.A.S. Nagar) • Online test shall be conducted at the following centres: Ahmedabad, Bengaluru, Bhopal, Chennai, Chandigarh, Dehradun, Guwahati, Hyderabad, Jaipur, Kolkata, Lucknow, Mumbai, Nagpur, New Delhi, Thiruvananthapuram, Pune • Based on the performance in the online test, selected candidates will be called for interview • Admission to the Ph.D. Programme will be based on the combined merit obtained by a candidate in the entrance examination and interview. • Limited number of seats will also be available for candidates having their own fellowships from CSIR/ UGC/ ICMR/ DBT/ DST INSPIRE, RGNF etc. in the Department of Medicinal Chemistry; Pharmacology & Toxicology; Pharmaceutics; Biotechnology and

			Pharmaceutical Technology (Process Chemistry), (Natural Products) etc. Candidates who have appeared for NET-JRF Examination of the CSIR/ UGC/ ICMR/ DBT/DST etc. in the above disciplines but are yet to get the result are also eligible to apply. However, such candidates will be required to produce the proof of having qualified the NET-JRF examination at the time of interview. • Seats are available for Self-Financing Foreign Nationals and Foreign Nationals under various scholarship schemes of the Ministry of Human Resource Development/ Ministry of External Affairs, Government of India. These seats are over and above the available seats mentioned above. Such candidates have to arrange for the clearance from the Ministry of External Affairs, Govt. of India, before they can be admitted, if selected. • Seats are available for candidates sponsored by Government Departments, Research and Development organizations, Public Sector Undertakings/Reputed Pharmaceutical Enterprises. • Candidate should have passed the qualifying degree with a minimum of 60% marks in aggregate or CGPA of 6.75 on a 10 point scale wherever grades are awarded or equivalent as determined by Board of Studies and Research of NIPER (Percentage of marks or CGPA so calculated will be based on the norms fixed by the concerned University / Institution or aggregate marks or CGPA scored by the candidate for all years of the qualifying degree, in case University /Institution has not prescribed any norm for calculating such percentage or CGPA). Passing of GPAT/GATE/NET is an essential qualification except for the following categories of candidates. ▪ Candidates holding M.D; M.V.Sc. ▪ Foreign nationals. ▪ Sponsored candidate from Government Departments, Research and Development organizations, Public Sector Undertakings/Reputed Pharmaceutical Enterprises
10	JSS College of Pharmacy JSS Medical Institutions Campus Sri Shivarathreeshwara Nagara Mysuru – 570 015 Tel: 0821-2548416 / 400 https://jssuni.edu.in	D. Pharm 2 years	• A pass in any of the following examinations with Physics, Chemistry and Biology or Mathematics. • Intermediate examination in Science; • The first year of the three year degree course in Science, • 10+2 examination (academic stream) in Science; • Pre–degree examination; • Any other qualification approved by the Pharmacy Council of India as equivalent to any of the above examination.
		B. Pharm. Four Years, Eight Semesters	• Candidate shall have passed 10+2 examination conducted by the respective state/central government authorities recognized as equivalent to 10+2 examination by

<table>
<tr><td></td><td></td><td>B. Pharm
Lateral Entry to Third Semester of B. Pharm.</td><td>the Association of Indian Universities (AIU) with English as one of the subjects and Physics, Chemistry, Mathematics (P.C.M) and or Biology (P.C.B /P.C.M.B.) as optional subjects individually. Any other qualification approved by the Pharmacy Council of India as equivalent to any of the above examinations.
• The students possessing 10+2 qualification from non-formal and non-classrooms based schooling such as National Institute of Open Schooling, open school systems of States etc. shall not be eligible for admission to B.Pharm program.
• Student should complete the age of 17 years on or before 31st December of the year of admission to the program
• A pass in D. Pharm. course from an institution approved by the Pharmacy Council of India under section 12 of the Pharmacy Act.</td></tr>
<tr><td></td><td></td><td>M. Pharm
• Cosmeceutics
• Industrial Pharmacy
• Pharma Quality Assurance
• Pharma Regulatory Affairs
• Pharmaceutical Analysis
• Pharmaceutical Chemistry
• Pharmaceutics
• Pharmacognosy
• Pharmacology
• Pharmacy Practice</td><td>A Pass in the following examination
• B. Pharm degree examination of an Indian university established by law in India from an institution approved by Pharmacy Council of India and has scored not less than 55 % of the maximum marks (aggregate of 4 years of B. Pharm.)
• Provided that, every student, selected for admission to M. Pharm. program in JSS University, Mysuru should have obtained registration with the State Pharmacy Council or should obtain the same within one month from the date of his/her admission, failing which the admission of the candidate shall be cancelled.</td></tr>
<tr><td></td><td></td><td>Ph. D.
• Industrial Pharmacy/ Pharmaceutics
• Pharmacy Practice
• Pharmacology
• Pharmaceutical Chemistry</td><td>• Admission will be made through an Entrance Test/Interview conducted at National Level by the University. Candidates who qualify UGC / SLET / GATE / NET / UGC / CSIR (JRF) / teaching fellowship / M.Phil programme are exempted from Entrance Test/Interview. The interview will assess the candidates and their research interests.
• Candidates who have obtained postgraduate degree in the concerned subject under various faculties of the University or its equivalent with a minimum of 55% of marks (50% in case of SC/ST/Cat-I) in the qualifying examination, are eligible for admission to PhD course. The qualifying degree has to be registered with the respective Councils, if applicable.
• Candidates with qualification as per 3(a) above and who shall be involved in full time</td></tr>
</table>

			research activities in the concerned department are eligible to be admitted as "Full Time" candidate. • Candidates with qualification as per 3(a) above and who are working as regular faculty member in the concerned department are eligible to be admitted as "Part Time Internal" candidate. • Candidates with qualification as per 3(a) above and regular faculty members with not less than ten years of teaching experience of which five years shall be at the postgraduate level and having a minimum of three research publications either as a principal author or as a co author in any indexed journal are eligible to admit for the PhD degree without a guide as "Part Time Independent Research" Candidate. • However, such candidates shall seek the guidance/assistance of not less than three experts in the concerned field, who shall be members of faculties not below the rank of Associate Professors and possess the qualifications prescribed by the University for being a guide. They need not go through the scrutiny committee. • Candidates with qualification as per 3(a) above and working in a recognized institution/ organization with research agreement/MoU with the University are eligible for admission as "Part Time External" candidate.
		Pharm. D. 5 years plus 1 year internship	A pass in any of the following examinations: • 10+2 examination with Physics and Chemistry as compulsory subjects along with one of the two subjects: Mathematics or Biology. • A pass in D. Pharm course from an institution approved by the Pharmacy Council of India under section 12 of the Pharmacy Act. • Any other qualification approved by the Pharmacy Council of India as equivalent to any of the above examinations. • Provided that a student should complete the age of 17 years on or before 31st December of the year of admission to the course.
11.	Birla Institute of Technology Mesra, Ranchi - 835215 Phone: 0651-2275444 / 896 / 2276496 www.bitmesra.ac.in	B. Pharm, 4 years (8 semesters)	• Candidates must have appeared in JEE (Main) 2018 or National Eligibility cum Entrance Test 2018 (NEET-UG) • Candidates must have passed Class 12 / I.Sc. or equivalent qualifying examination. • Candidates must have passed in English, Physics, Chemistry and Mathematics /Biology in Class 12 / I.Sc. or Equivalent Qualifying Examination with minimum 50% marks (45% for SC/ST/PwD) Marks in Class 12 to be computed as average of following 4 subjects - English, Physics, Chemistry, and Mathematics / Biology.
		M. Pharm, 2 years • Pharmaceutics	• Candidates must hold a B.Pharm degree from a PCI and AICTE approved Institute. Candidates must have minimum 55% marks in average (50% for SC/ST) in graduation.

		• Pharmaceutical Chemistry • Quality Assurance • Pharmacology • Pharmacognosy	• Candidates should preferably be GPAT qualified. Non-GPAT candidates may also apply. However, their applications will be considered only after applicants who have qualified in GPAT have been considered, admitted (for details, please see the selection procedure.
		PhD in Pharmaceutical sciences	The Institute offers Ph.D. programme twice in a year January / July in disciplines at Mesra and its Off Campuses
12.	Annamalai University Department of Pharmacy Faculty of Engineering & Technology Annamalai University Annamalainagar-608 002 Tel Number: 04144-239738 http://annamalaiuniversity.ac.in	D. Pharm	• A pass in Higher Secondary Examination or an equivalent examination with Physics and Chemistry, along with Biology (or) Botany & Zoology (or) Mathematics. • A pass in B.Sc. Degree with Physics, Chemistry, and Biology/Mathematics subjects either at the Higher Secondary level or at the graduate level. • The selection will be based on the marks obtained in the qualifying examination only. Rank list will be prepared based on the percentage of total marks obtained by the candidate in Higher Secondary course conducted by the Tamil Nadu State Board / any other equivalent Board.
		B. Pharm	• Candidate should be a Citizen of India. • Selection of candidates will be made on the basis of the performance of the candidates in the qualifying examination only
		B. Pharm (Lateral Entry)	Candidates who have obtained Diploma in Pharmacy with an aggregate of not less than 50% marks in the first and second year D.Pharm examinations from this University or any other University or Board recognized as equivalent thereto by this University.
		M. Pharm • Industrial Pharmacy • Pharmacy Practice • Quality Assurance • Pharmacology • Pharmaceutical Chemistry • Industrial Pharmacognosy	• Candidates who have passed the GATE examination will be eligible to get a stipend from AICTE • Candidates who have passed Bachelor of Pharmacy Degree Programme with not less than 50% of marks, of this University or any other University recognised as equivalent thereto by this University, are eligible for admission to the Master of Pharmacy Programmes. For SC/SCA/ST candidates, the eligibility is a pass in the B. Pharm. Degree Programme. • An entrance examination followed by an interview will be conducted for all the eligible candidates at Annamalai Nagar only.
		Pharm D (6 Years)	• A pass in10+2 examinations with Physics and Chemistry as compulsory subjects along with one of the following subjects: Mathematics or Biology or Botany and Zoology • A pass in Diploma in Pharmacy Course from an institution approved by the Pharmacy Council of India, under section 12 of the Pharmacy Act

			• Any other qualification approved by the Pharmacy Council of India as equivalent to any of the above examinations. • Other State Candidates can also apply. However, their selection will be subjected to following conditions: Irrespective of the category, they will be considered only under open competition and they will be considered after exhausting all the candidates from Tamil Nadu. • The selection will be based on the marks obtained in the qualifying examination only. Rank list will be prepared based on the percentage of total marks obtained by the candidate in higher secondary course conducted by the Tamil Nadu State Board / any other equivalent board.
		Pharm D (Post Baccalaureate)	• The selection will be based on the marks obtained in the qualifying examination only. Rank list will be prepared based on the percentage of total marks obtained by the candidate in all Semesters/Years.
13.	SVKM Narsee Monjee Institute of Management Studies V.L. Mehta Road Vile Parle (W), Mumbai – 400 056 www.nmims.edu/pharmacy	B. Pharm 4 Years	
		D. Pharm 2 years	
		M. Pharm • Pharmaceutics • Pharmaceutical Quality Assurance • Industrial Pharmacy • Pharmaceutical Technology	Two year programme
		B. Pharm + MBA (Pharmtech)	Five year programme
		M. Pharm + MBA (Pharmtech and Health Care Management) PhD (Full time and industrial sponsored) Pharmaceutical Sciences	Three year programe
14.	SRM Institute of science and	B. Pharm	• H.S.C / (+2) or equivalent qualification with Physics, Chemistry, Biology or Mathematics

	technology, Chennai SRM Nagar, Kattankulathur - 603 203 Kancheepuram District, Tamil Nadu. 044- 27417000, 27417499 www.srmuniv.ac.in		with a minimum aggregate of 50 % marks. • Qualified in SRMJEEH (UG)
		M. Pharm • Pharmaceutical Analysis • Pharmaceutical Chemistry • Pharmaceutical Quality Assurance • Pharmaceutical Regulatory Affairs • Pharmaceutics • Pharmacognosy • Pharmacology • Pharmacy Practice	• Bachelor of Pharmacy with 55% aggregate marks • SRMJEEH (PG)
		Pharm D 5 Years + 1 Year internship	Candidate must have passed any of the following examinations: • HSC / 10+2 or equivalent qualification with Physics and Chemistry as compulsory subjects along with one of the following subjects: Mathematics or Biology with 80% aggregate marks • Pass in D. Pharm course Existing Content an institution approved by the Pharmacy Council of India as equivalent to any of the above examinations, provided that a student should be 17 Years of age on or before 31st December of the Year of admission to the course with 80% aggregate marks
		Pharm D (Post Baccalaureate) 3 Years programme	Bachelor of Pharmacy with 55% aggregate marks
		Post Graduate Diploma in Clinical Research 1 Year	Graduates obtained a minimum of 50% in the respective qualifying examinations are eligible for admission: • B. Pharm/M. Pharm • Bachelor Degree/Post Graduate degrees in Biotechnology/Bioinformatics/Biochemistry/Microbiology

			• MBBS/BDS/BVSc • Graduate/Post Graduate degrees in alternate systems of medicine • B.Sc Nursing/M.Sc Nursing
		PhD	
15.	Amrita College of Pharmacy Amrita Vishwa Vidyapeetham University AIMS Health Sciences Campus, AIMS P. O. Ponekkara, Kochi 682041 https://www.amrita.edu/	B. Pharm 8 Semesters (4 years)	For B. Pharm 1st Year Candidate shall have passed 10+2 examination conducted by the respective state/central government authorities recognized as equivalent to 10+2 examination by the Association of Indian Universities (AIU) with English as one of the subjects and Physics, Chemistry, Mathematics (P.C.M) and or Biology (P.C.B / P.C.M.B.) as optional subjects individually. Any other qualification approved by the Pharmacy Council of India as equivalent to any of the above examinations.
		B. Pharm lateral entry (to third semester)	A pass in D. Pharm. course from an institution approved by the Pharmacy Council of India under section 12 of the Pharmacy Act.
		Pharm D 5 Years + 1 Year internship	10+2 examination with Physics and Chemistry as compulsory subjects along with one of the following subjects: Mathematics or Biology. or A pass in D. Pharm course from an institution approved by the Pharmacy Council of India under section 12 of the Pharmacy Act. or Any other qualification approved by the Pharmacy Council of India as equivalent to any of the above examinations. Provided that a student should complete the age of 17 years on or before 31st December of the year of admission to the course.
		Pharm D (Post Baccalaureate)	A pass in B. Pharm from an institution approved by the Pharmacy Council of India under section 12 of the Pharmacy Act.
		M. Pharm (2 years – 4 semesters) • Pharmacy Practice • Pharmaceutics • Pharmaceutical Chemistry • Pharmacology	
		Ph D	Pass in M. Pharm in any specialization or Doctor of Pharmacy (Pharm D)
16.	Poona College of Pharmacy Erandwane, Paud Road, Pune-411 038 Tel: 02025461046 http://pcp.bharatividyapeet	B. Pharm. Four Years, Eight Semesters	• Passed 10+2 with English, Physics, Chemistry and either Mathematics/ Biology/ Biotechnology/other vocational courses or • Must have passed Diploma in Pharmacy or its equivalent examination by Board of Technical Education or equivalent examination with not less than 50% of marks in the

	h.edu		aggregate of all subjects taken together at the Final Year Examination.
		B. Pharm, Three Years Lateral Entry to 2nd Year	• Candidate who has passed the final examination leading to the Diploma in Pharmacy conducted by the Board of Technical Education, Maharashtra State or equivalent examination from the institute approved by the Pharmacy Council of India and with a minimum First Class (60% i.e.600 out of 1000 at part-II examination for the Diploma in Pharmacy Course)
		Pharm. D. 5 years plus 1 year internship	• 10+2 examination with Physics and Chemistry as compulsory subjects along with one of the following subjects, Mathematics or Biology. • Pass in D. Pharm course from an institution approved by the Pharmacy Council of India under section 12 of the Pharmacy Act. • Any other qualification approved by the Pharmacy Council of India as equivalent to any of the above examinations. • Provided that a student should complete the age of 17 years on or before 31st December of the year of admission to the course.
		M. Pharm. • Pharmaceutical Chemistry • Pharmaceutics • Pharmacology • Pharmacognosy • Quality Assurance Techniques • Drug Regulatory Affairs • Pharmaceutical Biotechnology	• Passed B. Pharm. degree examination of any statutory/recognized University with atleast 60% of aggregate marks or equivalent grade (55 % for S.C./S.T., teacher and sponsored candidates. • As per the AICTE guideline, few seats are reserved for the candidates having qualified GPAT score and atleast 60% marks at the B. Pharm. examination. • The candidate must have appeared at All India Entrance Test conducted by Bharati Vidyapeeth University.
		Ph. D. • Pharmaceutical Chemistry • Pharmaceutics • Pharmacology • Pharmacognosy • Quality Assurance Techniques • Drug Regulatory Affairs • Pharmaceutical Biotechnology	

17.	Faculty of Pharmacy Kalabhavan The Maharaja Sayajirao University of Baroda Vadodara-390001 www.msubaroda.ac.in	B. Pharm Four Years, Eight Semesters	Admission process is done by ACPC, L. D. College of Engg. Ahmadabad. Visit www.jacpc.ldce.ac.in. Once the list of admitted candidates is declared by ACPC, those who are allotted seat at Faculty of Pharmacy, The Maharaja Sayajirao University of Baroda, must apply online for temporary registration on http://msub.digitaluniversity.ac
		M. Pharm 2 years, four semesters • Pharmacognosy and Herbal Drugs • Pharmaceutical Analysis • Pharmaceutics • Pharmaceutical Chemistry • Pharmaceutical Technology • Pharmacology	Admission process is done by ACPC, L. D. College of Engg. Ahmadabad. visit www.jacpc.ldce.ac.in. Once the list of admitted candidates is declared by ACPC, those who are allotted seat at Faculty of Pharmacy, The Maharaja Sayajirao University of Baroda, must apply online for temporary registration on http://msub.digitaluniversity.ac
		Ph. D in Pharmacy	• M. Pharm. degree with minimum 50% marks • GATE/GPAT qualification or PET (M.S. University of Baroda) qualified candidates • Ph.D. admission would be as per the University ordinance (O.Ph.) and subject to availability of seats with concerned teachers.
18.	Punjabi University Pharmacy Department, Gol Market Road, Opp. University Food Court, Urban Estate Phase II, Falauli, Patiala 147002 www.punjabiuniversity.ac.in	B. Pharm. Four Years, 8 Semesters	• 50% Marks in 10+2 with English, Physics, Chemistry and one of the following subjects: Biology/Biotechnology/ Mathematics
		M. Pharm. • Pharmaceutical Analysis • Pharmaceutical Chemistry • Pharmaceutical Quality Assurance • Pharmaceutics • Pharmacognosy • Pharmacology	• B. Pharm. from AICTE/PCI approved Institutions/ Universities with valid GPAT score • Entrance test conducted by Punjabi university.

		Ph.D. in Pharmacy	• GPAT-qualified students are registered from time to time for Ph.D., depending upon the availability of seats under different projects/schemes/fellowships sponsored by different agencies, including industry.
19.	Banasthali Vidyapith Deptt. of Pharmacy Banasthali University P.O. Banasthali Vidyapith Distt. Tonk, Rajasthan-304022 Tel: 01438-228341 www.banasthali.org	B. Pharm	• 60 % aggregate in 10 + 2 (Senior Secondary) with Physics, Chemistry and Biology • The admission to B. Pharm. course is provided on the basis of the merit which is drawn on the criteria of 50% marks of All Indian Entrance Test (conducted by the Banasthali University) and 50% marks of normalized aggregate percentage in 10+2 (Senior Secondary) school examination.
		M. Pharm • Pharmaceutical Chemistry • Pharmaceutics • Pharmacology	• The admission to M. Pharm. course is provided on the basis of the merit which is drawn on the criteria of 50% marks of All Indian Entrance Test (conducted by the Banasthali University) and 50% marks of B.Pharm. • 60 % in B. Pharm.
		PhD in Pharmacy	
20.	Sri Ramachandra Institute of Higher Education and Research, Chennai - 600016 Tel: 044-24765512 www.sriramachandra.edu.in	B. Pharm	Pass in HSC (+2) or Equivalent qualification with Physics, Chemistry, Biology or Botany and Zoology or with English, Physics, Chemistry, Mathematics and any other subject with 50% marks in the aggregate.
		Pharm. D – 6 academic years (5 years curriculum + 1 year internship)	HSC/CBSE/ISC (with physics and chemistry as compulsory subjects along with one of the subjects – Maths/Biology)/D. Pharm
		M. Pharm • Pharmacy Practice • Pharmaceutics • Quality assurance • Pharmacognosy • Pharmacology • Pharmaceutical Analysis	Candidates should possess B. Pharm Degree awarded by any recognized University.
		Pharm. D. (Post Baccalaureate) 3 academic years (2 years curriculum + 1 year	B. Pharm

		internship)	
		PhD	Full-Time: Candidates with UGC/ CSIR/ ICMR/ DBT/ DST NET-JRF/ AICTE-GATE/ AYUSH/ INSPIRE Fellowship or having qualified other UGC recognized national eligibility test with a valid fellowship at the time of entrance exam or who work in funded projects as JRF/SRF fellows in research projects in the Deemed University are exempted from appearing for Entrance Examination and interview and they will be called directly for counseling and admission. They should submit application and meet eligibility criteria as outlined in the Prospectus uploaded in the Deemed University website.
21.	Nirma University Institute of Pharmacy Sarkhej-Gandhinagar Highway, Post: Chandlodia, Via Gota, Ahmedabad - 382 481 Tel: 2717 - 241900 to 04 www.nirmauni.ac.in/IPNU	B. Pharm (4 years course)	• 85 Seats (out of 100 approved intake) are being admitted by ACPC (Admission committee for professional courses), Gujarat state. Candidate needs to apply to ACPC for centralized admission process. Eligible candidates would be allotted admission as per merit prepared considering results of qualifying exam (12th HSC Board exam) and GUJCET of current year. • If the seats remained vacant after completion of admission process by ACPC (i.e. after final round of allotment), then admission on vacant seats would be processed directly by Institute as per norms and instructions by ACPC. • Supernumerary Seats on TFW Scheme as well as for J & K Migrant are also being filled by ACPC, Gujarat State for candidates fulfilling the required conditions of eligibility. • For more information, Visit - www.jacpcldce.ac.in • 15 Seats are admitted by Institute as NRI category (NRI self / NRI ward / NRI sponsored) as per norms of ACPC.
		M. Pharm Two year (4 Semesters) • Pharmaceutics • Pharmaceutical Chemistry • Regulatory Affairs • Pharmacology • Pharmaceutical Analysis	• The candidates must have passed the qualifying examination (B. Pharm.) from a recognized university with minimum aggregate marks or equivalent Cumulative Grade Point Index (CGPI) or any other qualifying degree examination considered as equivalent of B. Pharm. degree by Nirma University, Ahmedabad. (*as per AICTE & PCI norms) • Candidates who are appearing for the final semester of qualifying examination (B. Pharm.) can also apply. In such case, the candidate is required to submit the result as soon as the same is available either by email or by fax (scanned image). • If applicant has passed qualifying examination (B. Pharm.) from a University other than Nirma University, then he/she will be required to obtain an eligibility certificate from Nirma University. The arrangement for obtaining the same will be made on the spot at the time of admission on payment of Rs. 1,000/- (Rupees One Thousand Only). • One seat is reserved in each branch for students who have passed their B. Pharm from Institute of Pharmacy, Nirma University, Ahmedabad. • Stipend would be given to All Admitted Students GPAT Qualified Student : Rs. 12,400/- per Month and Non-GPAT Student : Rs. 5,000/- per Month

		PhD Programme	• Candidates for admission to PhD programme shall have a Master's degree or a professional degree declared equivalent to the Master's degree by the corresponding statutory regulatory body, with at least 55% marks in aggregate or its equivalent grade 'B' in the UGC 7-point scale • An Entrance Test shall be qualifying with qualifying marks as 50%. The syllabus of the Entrance Test shall consist of 50% of research methodology and 50% shall be subject specific. • The list of candidates clearing the entrance test shall be declared on the notice board/ website of the University. • An interview/viva-voce to be organized by the University when the candidates are required to discuss their research interest/area through a presentation before Department Research Committee. • The candidates who qualify the UGC-NET (Including JRF) UGC-CSIR NET (Including JRF) SLET/ GATE/GPAT with a valid score in terms of cut-off marks and duration, teacher fellowship holder or who have passed M. Pharm programme shall be exempted from appearing in the entrance test and deemed to be qualified for personal interview
22.	KLE College of Pharmacy JNMC Campus Belgaum - 590010 Tel: 0831-471399, 0831-2472777 www.klepharm.edu	B. Pharm The course of study for B. Pharm shall extend over a period of 8 semester and six semesters for those admitted to second B. Pharm through lateral entry.	• Candidates who have passed two year P.U.C. examination of Karnataka Board or an equivalent examination of any other approved Board or university with not less than 45% with Physics and Chemistry as compulsory subjects along with any one of the subjects viz. Mathematics/Biology/Computer Sciences/ Biotechnology/ Technical vocational subject. • 5 % relaxation in minimum eligibility criteria for candidate belonging to reserved category • Candidates who have scored less than 45% marks in (10+2) but who have completed B.Sc. Degree with Chemistry as one of the compulsory subjects in combination with any two of the following subjects, namely, Physics or Mathematics, or Microbiology, or Botany, or Zoology, or Biotechnology, or Computer Sciences or Electronics securing not less than 40% marks in aggregate are eligible for admission to first year B. Pharm course. • Candidates who have passed D. Pharm course with minimum 50% marks and approved by Pharmacy Council of India shall also be eligible to this course and shall be admitted directly to 3rd Semester course, 10% over and above the sanctioned intake. Student shall have to study, Computer science of First semester of B. Pharm in addition to the third semester of B. Pharm subjects.
		M. Pharm • Pharmaceutical Chemistry	• A candidate who has passed B. Pharm degree examination of KLE University or B. Pharm examination of any other recognized Indian University established by law in India or any other degree courses in pharmacy recognized as equivalent by KLE

		• Pharmaceutics • Pharmacology and toxicology • Pharmaceutical Quality Assurance • Biotechnology • Pharmacy Practice • Pharmacognosy and phytochemistry	University or Pharmacy council of India (PCI) and/or All India Council of Technical Education (A I.C.T.E,) for this purpose and who has secured not less than 50% of the maximum marks (aggregate of four years) prescribed for the qualifying examination shall be eligible for admission to the M. Pharm course. • 5% relaxation in minimum eligibility criteria of candidate belonging to reserved category.
		MSc Clinical research	• A graduate in Health sciences [Medicine, Dental, Pharmacy, Nursing, Ayurveda, Homeopathy, Unani] or Life science graduates [biotechnology, botany/zoology]
		Pharm D	a) Pharm. D. Part-I Course – A pass in any of the following examinations - • 10+2 examination with Physics and Chemistry as compulsory subjects along with one of the following subjects: Mathematics or Biology. • A pass in D. Pharm course from an institution approved by the Pharmacy Council of India under section 12 of the Pharmacy Act. • Any other qualification approved by the Pharmacy Council of India as equivalent to any of the above examinations. Provided that a student should complete the age of 17 years on or before 31st December of the year of admission to the course. • Provided that there shall be reservation of seats for the students belonging to the Scheduled Castes, Scheduled Tribes and other Backward Classes in accordance with the instructions issued by the Central Government/State Government/Union Territory Administration as the case may be from time to time. b) Pharm D (Post Baccalaureate) Course - • A pass in B. Pharm from an institution approved by the Pharmacy Council of India under section 12 of the Pharmacy Act: Provided that there shall be reservation of seats for the students belonging to the Scheduled Castes, Scheduled Tribes and other Backward Classes in accordance with the instructions issued by the Central Government/State Government/Union Territory Administration as the case may be from time to time.
		PhD	
23.	ISF College of Pharmacy, Ferozepur GT Road, N.H. 95, Ghal Kalan, Moga 142001 Punjab Phone: 98786 96688, 87250 55460	D. Pharm 2 years full time course Affiliated with Punjab State Board of Technical Education	• 10+2 with PCB or PCM securing at least 50% marks in the aggregate and also in the aggregate of PCB or PCM.

	www.isfcp.org		
		B. Pharm 4 years full time course (8 semesters)	• 10+2 with Medical or non-medical securing at least 50% marks in the aggregate. • Completed the age of 17 years on or before 31 December of the year of taking admission as per PCI norms
		B. Pharm [Lateral Entry] Direct Admission to 2nd Year (3rd Semester)	For B. Pharm (Lateral), the candidate must pass D. Pharm degree from a recognized university.
		Pharm. D Doctor of Pharmacy 6 years full time course	Candidate should have passed the 10+2 or equivalent exam from a recognized board with minimum 50% marks in aggregate with Physics, Chemistry, Mathematics/Biology to be eligible to apply for Pharm.D, courses.
		Pharm. D (Post-Baccalaureate) Doctor of Pharmacy 3 years full time course after B. Pharm	B. Pharm degree with minimum 55% marks from a recognized university.
		M. Pharm 2 years (4 Semesters) full time course in following disciplines • Pharmaceutics • Pharmacology • Pharmaceutical Chemistry • Pharmaceutical Analysis • Pharmacognosy • Quality Assurance	• B. Pharm degree with minimum 55% marks from a recognized university. • Candidates who have appeared and qualified GPAT will be given preference for M. Pharm admission.
		Ph.D. in Pharmaceutical Sciences As per University Guidelines Affiliated with Maharaja Ranjit Singh State Technical University, Bathinda	• The minimum eligibility for admission in the Ph.D. program is M. Pharm degree with minimum 60% marks from a recognized university. • Admission to Ph.D. is done on the basis of entrance examination and personal interview conducted by the university.
24.	Bombay College of Pharmacy Kalina, Santacruz (E), Mumbai 400 098 www.bcp.edu.in	B. Pharm 4 years	Admissions are based on PCB Score of class XII HSC and qualified Maharashtra state CET Or Must have passed Diploma in Pharmacy or its equivalent examination by Board of Technical Education or equivalent examination with not less than 50% of marks in the aggregate of all subjects taken together at the Final Year Examination.

		B. Pharm., Three Years Lateral Entry to 2nd Year	• The candidate who has passed the final examination leading to the Diploma in Pharmacy conducted by the Board of Technical Education, Maharashtra State or equivalent examination from the institute approved by the Pharmacy Council of India and with a minimum First Class (60% i.e.600 out of 1000 at part-II examination for the Diploma in Pharmacy Course)
		M. Pharm • Pharmaceutical Chemistry • Pharmaceutics • Pharmacology and toxicology • Pharmacognosy and phytochemisry. • Pharmaceutical Analysis	• Passed B. Pharm. degree examination of any statutory/recognized University with atleast 60% of aggregate marks or equivalent grade (55 % for S.C./S.T., teacher and sponsored candidates. • As per the AICTE guideline, few seats are reserved for the candidates having qualified GPAT score and atleast 60% marks at the B. Pharm. examination.
25.	Amity University Sector-125 Noida – 201313 Tel: 0120-4392000 www.amity.edu	B. Pharm	• Candidate should be 10+2 pass with 60% marks in PCB/PCM • B. Pharm Lateral Entry: Diploma in Pharmacy, Govt. approved Institute/University, directly into 2nd year of the programme
		M. Pharm • Drug regulatory affairs • Pharmacology • Pharmaceutics	• B. Pharm (min 60%) from PCI recognized Institute
		PhD in Pharmaceutical Sciences	• Master's Degree in Pharmacy from any accredited Indian or Foreign University with a minimum of 55% marks or grade point average.
26.	Delhi Institute of Pharmaceutical Sciences and Research Mehrauli-Badarpur Road, Pushp Vihar Sector 3, New Delhi 110017 Tel: 29553771, 29553594 www.dipsar.ac.in	D. Pharm. Two years Course	• 10+2 with English as one of the subjects and Physics, Chemistry, Mathematics (P.C.M) and/or Biology (P.C.B / P.C.M.B.) as optional subjects with 55% or above marks in aggregate and individually in theory of the three Science subjects (Physics, Chemistry and Biology or Mathematics) • Completed the age of 17 years on or before 31 December of the year of taking admission as per PCI norms.
		B. Pharm. Regular and SFS Four Years, Eight Semesters	• 10+2 with English as one of the subjects and Physics, Chemistry, Mathematics (P.C.M) and/or Biology (P.C.B / P.C.M.B.) as optional subjects with 55% or above marks in aggregate and individually in theory of the three Science subjects (Physics, Chemistry and Biology or Mathematics)

			• Completed the age of 17 years on or before 31 December of the year of taking admission as per PCI norms.
		B. Pharm. II Year (Regular and SFS through lateral entry)	• Must have passed D. Pharm. course from an institution approved by the Pharmacy Council of India under section 12 of the Pharmacy Act as per regulation 4.B. of the Bachelor of Pharmacy course Regulations, 2014.
		M. Pharm. • Pharmaceutical Chemistry • Pharmaceutics • Pharmacology • Pharmaceutical Quality Assurance • Clinical Research • Hospital Pharmacy	• B. Pharm. Degree examination of an Indian university established by law in India from an institution approved by Pharmacy Council of India and has scored not less than 55% of the maximum marks (aggregate of theory II, III and IV yrs/or III to VIII semesters of B. Pharm.) • Every student, selected for admission to post graduate pharmacy program in any PCI approved institution should have obtained registration with the State Pharmacy Council or should apply for the registration of the same within one month from the date of his/her admission, failing which the admission of the candidate shall be cancelled. • It is mandatory to submit a migration certificate obtained from the respective university where the candidate had passed his/her qualifying degree. • Candidate seeking admission to the M. Pharm and MBA course must have passed the Bachelor of Pharmacy examination with at least 55% in the aggregate of theory of II, III and IV year from national capital of Delhi. • GPAT QUALIFIED CANDIDATES SHALL BE CONSIDERED FOR ADMISSION FIRST. • In case GPAT candidates are not available, Non GPAT candidates can be considered for admission, on the basis of merit. • First 15% of the total seats will be filled by Non-Delhi candidates with valid GPAT score and completed B. Pharm. examination with 55% from recognized University. • Remaining 85% of the total seats will be filled by graduates passed out from Delhi colleges/universities with valid GPAT score in order of preference of disciplines. The merit list of candidates for admission to 85% seats from Delhi will be in accordance with the following criteria: ▪ 50% weightage for marks in theory II, III and IV yrs (or III to VIII semesters) ▪ 50% weightage for GPAT score In case of more than one candidate with the same score, preference will be given to the candidate who is older in age. In case no GPAT students available in 15% Non-Delhi category, then student from Delhi category with GPAT will be considered.
27.	Lovely Professional University Delhi G.T. Road Phagwara - 144411, Punjab	B. Pharm 4 years course	Pass with 60% aggregate marks in 10+2 (with English, Physics, Chemistry and Biology or Maths) or equivalent, subject to qualifying LPUNEST Merit in qualifying examination, subject to eligibility criteria.

	Tel: 1824-404404 Tollfree: 1800 102 4431 https://schools.lpu.in/pharmaceutical-sciences/		
		B. Pharm Lateral Entry	• Pass with 60% aggregate marks in Diploma (Pharmacy) (2 years after 10+2) (Diploma should be recognized by PCI) or equivalent, subject to qualifying LPUNEST • In case marks scored in Diploma are 80% or above, then LPUNEST will be exempted and candidate may apply for admission
		M. Pharm • Pharmaceutics • Pharmacology • Quality Assurance • Analysis	• Pass with 60% aggregate marks in B. Pharm or equivalent, subject to qualifying LPUNEST or GPAT • In case marks scored in graduation are 70% or above, then LPUNEST and GPAT will be exempted and candidate may apply for admission.
		PhD • Pharmaceutical Chemistry • Pharmacognosy	• Master's degree with 55% aggregate marks in a relevant discipline or equivalent, subject to clearing LPUNEST and Interview • Other conditions as prescribed in the Guidelines for Degree of Doctor of Philosophy (Ph.D.) programmers. (5% relaxation to SC/ ST/ OBC (non-creamy layer)/ differently-abled candidates)
		PhD Ayurvedic Pharmacy	• Master's degree with 55% aggregate marks in a relevant discipline or equivalent, subject to clearing LPUNEST and Interview • Other conditions as prescribed in the Guidelines for Degree of Doctor of Philosophy (Ph.D.) programmes. (5% relaxation to SC/ ST/ OBC (non-creamy layer)/ differently-abled candidates)
28.	Department of Pharmaceutical sciences Dibrugarh University Dibrugarh-786004, Assam, India Tel No.: 0373-2370097 www.dibru.ac.in	B. Pharm	For admission to the First Semester of the B. Pharm. Course, one must have passed either- • 10+2 Examination (Science stream) of the Assam Higher Secondary Council, or any other examination recognised by the Dibrugarh University as equivalent to this examination, securing not less than 50% (45% for candidates belonging to Schedule Castes and Scheduled Tribes) marks in the aggregate of Physics, Chemistry and Biology OR • Two-Year Diploma in Pharmacy Examination of Assam or of any other Institution is recognised by the Pharmacy Council of India and AICTE securing not less than 50% marks in the aggregate • Mode of Selection is by Counseling of sort listed candidate based on merit- (i) Percentage of H. S. Marks in the aggregate of Physics, Chemistry and Biology. (ii) Percentage of marks in two years Diploma in Pharmacy Examination.

		M. Pharm • Pharmaceutics • Pharmaceutical Chemistry • Pharmacognosy	• For admission to the First Semester of the M. Pharm. Course, one must have passed Four year Bachelor Degree Course in Pharmacy securing not less than 55% marks from Dibrugarh University or from any other University recognized by the Dibrugarh University, PCI and AICTE • Candidates applying under Sponsored category should have a minimum of two years of teaching experience after obtaining B. Pharm. Degree (Candidates from academic institutions) or two years of industrial experience with Approval as a Chemist from the respective Drugs Control Authority (Candidates from industrial organizations) • Counseling of sort listed candidate based on merit- (a) GPAT score (b) Percentage of marks in B. Pharm. Examination • Candidates having valid score of GPAT or equivalent examination get preference.
		PhD	• Candidate seeking admission to the Doctor of Philosophy (Ph.D.) programme shall have to obtain at least 55% marks in Master's Degree OR equivalent grade point. • All applicants seeking admission to the Doctoral programme of the University [except foreign students applying for admission] must clear the Dibrugarh University Research Admission Test (DURAT) • DURAT is conducted annually by the University. The mode of conducting the DURAT is decided by the Research Council time to time • Foreign candidates intending to pursue the Ph.D. Programme of Dibrugarh University are exempted from DURAT. All other matters related to the foreign candidates are governed by the Dibrugarh University Rules for Foreign Students • All eligible candidates of Ph. D programme have to undertake a Six-Month Pre-Registration Course Work in the Dept. of Pharmaceutical Sciences and pass the course work examination before submitting application for Registration in the Ph. D programme.
29.	The Rashtrasant Tukadoji Maharaj Nagpur University Chhatrapati Shivaji Maharaj Administrative Premises Ravindranath Tagore Marg Nagpur 440001 https://www.nagpuruniversity.org/rtmnu/home/	B. Pharm	As per direction No. 57 / 2016 of PCI
		M. Pharm • Pharmaceutics • Pharmaceutical	As per direction No. 58 / 2016 of PCI

		Chemistry • Pharmacology • Pharmacognosy • Biotechnology • Quality Assurance • Industrial Pharmacy • Pharmacoinformatics • Clinical Pharmacy • Natural Products • Pharmaceutical Management	
30.	Dr. Bhanuben Nanavati College of Pharmacy Gate No.1, Mithibai College Campus, V.M. Road , Vile Parle (West), Mumbai 400 056 Phone : 022-42332052 / 58, 022 – 26134557 / 58 http://bncp.ac.in	B. Pharm	• 10+2 with 60% marks conducted by the Central Board of Secondary Education (CBSE) or any equivalent exam conducted by any State Board or Equivalent.
		M. Pharm • Pharmaceutics • Pharmacology • Quality Assurance	• 60% in B. Pharmacy with valid GPAT score • Candidates can apply through MHT CET or apply through GPAT OR PGECET Entrance test.
		PhD • Pharmaceutical Chemistry • Pharmaceutics	
31.	L. M. College of Pharmacy Lallubhai Motilal College of Pharmacy Post Box no. 4011 Navrangpura Ahmedabad - 380 009 Tel: 079-26302746 LMCP.IN	D. Pharm	• For D. Pharm, candidates must have passed 10+2 in Science stream with Physics and Chemistry as their main subject of study in addition to either Mathematics/Biology as one of the subjects • Admission to D. Pharm is done on the basis of merit scored in the qualifying examination and valid score obtained in GUJCET 2018.

		B. Pharm	• Applicants who have passed 10+2 with minimum 50% marks in Science stream with Biology as the core subject for B. Pharm program. • Admission to B. Pharm is done on the basis of valid score obtained in NEET UG 2018 entrance examination
		M. Pharm	• Candidates who have passed B. Pharm with 60% marks from a recognized board are eligible to apply for M. Pharm. • Admission to M. Pharm is done on the basis of valid score obtained in NEET PG/ GATE/ GPAT 2018.
		Pharm D	• For Pharm D, candidate must pass in 10+2 with Physics and Chemistry as compulsory subjects and Mathematics or Biology as optional subjects. • Admission to Pharm D is done on the basis of merit in the qualifying examination.
		PhD	• For Ph.D., candidates must have passed Master's degree or M. Phil with 55% marks in the relevant discipline is considered eligible. • Admission to Ph.D. is done through the marks scored in the UGC NET 2018. • The college offers 5% relaxation in the eligibility criteria for candidates belonging to SC/ST categories.
32.	Maharshi Dayanand University Department of Pharmaceutical Sciences Rohtak, 124001 Phone: +91 1262 393222 http://mdu.ac.in	B. Pharm	10+2 examination of the Board of School Education, Bhiwani or any other Board/University, recognized by this University, with Physics and Chemistry as compulsory subjects alongwith any one of the subjects, viz. Mathematics/Biology/ Biotechnology/Computer Science securing 50% marks in the above subjects taken together. The candidate must have attained the age of 17 years on or before 31st December of the year of admission to the Course.
		M. Pharm • Pharmacology • Industrial Pharmacy • Pharmacognosy • Pharmaceutical Chemistry • Regulatory Affairs	B. Pharm. with at least 50% marks in aggregate or any other examination recognized by M.D. University, Rohtak as equivalent thereto, and must possess a valid GPAT score. In case GPAT qualified students are not available, the seats will be open to the other candidates on merit basis, on the basis of aggregate score of B. Pharm.
		Ph D	
33.	NGSM Institute of Pharmaceutical Sciences, Deralakatte, Mangaluru – 575 018 Karnataka	D. Pharm	• Pass in 10+2 with Physics, Chemistry & Biology/Mathematics/ Computer Science/Electronics/Biotechnology and English as one of the languages of study.

	Tel: 0824 – 2203991/ 2203992 www.ngsmips.nitte.edu.in		
		B. Pharm	• Pass in 10+2 with 45% in Physics, Chemistry & Biology/Mathematics/Computer Science/Electronics/Biotechnology and English as one of the languages of study. Candidates with more than 70% marks in all the subjects are preferred. • Lateral Entry (B. Pharm) • D. Pharm Marks cards -Original + 3 attested copies • D. Pharm Completion Certificate - Original + 3 attested copies • Industrial Training Certificate -Original + 3 attested Copies • PCI Registration Certificate Original + 3 attested Copies
		Pharm D	Pass in 10+2 examination with Physics, Chemistry and Biology / Mathematics and English as one of the languages of study. Pass in D. Pharm course from an approved institution. Candidates with more than 70% marks in all the subjects are preferred.
		Pharm D (Post Baccalaureate) 3 Years	Pass in B. Pharm from a college recognized by PCI
		M. Pharm • Pharmacology • Pharmaceutics • Pharmaceutical chemistry • Pharmacy Practice • Pharmaceutical quality assurance • Drug Regulatory affairs	
		PhD	
34.	AU College of Pharmaceutical sciences, Andhra University, Visakhapatnam - 530 003 Andhra Pradesh Tel: 0891 - 284 4922, 2844923 andhrauniversity.edu.in	B. Pharm	• 10+2 or High School Senior Secondary exam by the Central Board of Secondary Education (CBSE) or any equivalent exam conducted by any State Board or Equivalent.
		Pharm D	
		Pharm D (PB)	

		M. Pharmacy • Pharmaceutical Technology • Pharmaceutical Biotechnology • Pharmaceutical Chemistry • Pharmaceutical and Food Analysis • Pharmacology • Pharmacognosy and Phytochemistry • Pharmacy Practice • Pharmaceutical Management • Drug Regulatory Affairs.	
		PhD	
35.	Guru Jambheshwar University of Science and Technology Department of Pharmaceutical Sciences Delhi Road, Hisar – 125001 (Haryana) Tel: 01662-263580 www.gjust.ac.in	B. Pharm	• Candidate shall have passed 10+2 examination conducted by the respective state/ central government authorities recognized as equivalent to 10+2 examination by the Association of Indian Universities (AIU) with English as one of the subjects and physics, Chemistry, Mathematics (P.C.M.) and or Biology (P.C.B./ P.C.M.B.) as optional subjects individually. Any other qualification approved by the Pharmacy Council of India as equivalent to any of the above examinations. • For admission to Bachelor of Pharmacy through (LEET) (to third semester) semester candidate must be pass in D. Pharm course from an institution approved by the Pharmacy Council of India under section 12 of the Pharmacy Act
		M. Pharm • Pharmacognosy • Pharmacology • Pharmaceutics • Pharmaceutical chemistry	• Bachelor of Pharmacy with atleast 55% marks (52.25% for SC candidates) • Admission to all M. Pharm programs will be made on the basis of merit of valid GPAT score. When sufficient GPAT qualified candidates are not available, admission may be given to non-GPAT candidates on the basis of merit of entrance test score • Fellowship is available to the candidates with valid GPAT Score subject to the receipt of fellowship from AICTE.
		PhD in Pharmaceutical Sciences	
36.	Y B Chavan College of Pharmacy Post Box No 33, Rauza Bagh, Harsool, Dr. Rafiq	B. Pharm	• Candidate should be an Indian National and should have passed the HSC (Std. XI) examination of Maharashtra State Board of Secondary and Higher Secondary Education or its equivalent examination with subjects English, Physics, Chemistry, and Mathematics/ Biology/ Biotechnology/ Technical Vocational subject.

	Zakaria Marg, Aurangabad-431001, Maharashtra Phone: 0240-238-1129 www.ybccpa.ac.in		• Secured minimum 45 % marks (minimum 40 % marks in case of candidates of Backward class categories and Persons with Disability belonging only to Maharashtra State) in the subjects Physics, Chemistry, and Mathematics/ Biology/ Biotechnology/ Technical Vocational subject added together (Maximum of marks obtained in Mathematics/ Biology/ Biotechnology/ Technical Vocational subject shall be considered for the purpose of addition). • Obtained a non-zero score in subjects Physics, Chemistry, and Mathematics/ Biology added together at MT-CET 2017 • Rounding of the percentage of marks for deciding eligibility for admission. • In case percentage, marks (converted out of 10) in the subjects Physics, Chemistry, and Biology/ Mathematics/ Biotechnology/ Technical Vocational Subjects added together at HSC (Std.XI), comes in fraction then percentage of marks shall be rounded off as explained in the example for the purpose of deciding the eligibility of the candidate. • If seats remain vacant, Diploma holders who have passed the Diploma course in Pharmacy with minimum of 45% marks and medium of instruction as English from AICTE approved Polytechnics can be considered for admission to First Year B. Pharm., as per the government Rules.
		B. Pharm Lateral Entry	The Candidate must be an Indian National and should have passed Post-SSC or Post-HSC Diploma Course in Pharmacy with at least 50.00 % marks (45.00 % marks in case of candidates of Backward class categories belonging only to Maharashtra State) from an AICTE approved Institution with English as the medium of instruction at Diploma level
		M. Pharm • Quality Assurance Techniques • Pharmaceutics • Pharmacology • Pharmaceutical Chemistry	• The candidate should be an Indian National and who possess bachelor's degree of equivalent in Pharmacy from any AICTE approved institution, with at least 55% marks (at least 50% marks in case of SC/ST category AND Persons with Disability candidates belonging to Maharashtra State only). • Should have non-zero Score in MAH-MPH-CET 2017, if the candidate has neither appeared for GPAT 2016 nor having valid and qualified GPAT 2016 All India Rank / Total Score. • In case percentage, marks in the B. Pharmacy Examination comes in fraction then the percentage of marks shall be rounded off as explained in the example for the purpose of deciding the eligibility of the candidate. • Qualifying the Graduate Pharmacy Aptitude Test (GPAT) is compulsory for awarding any fellowship. However, it is not mandatory for seeking admission to the M. Pharm. Course.
		PhD • Pharmaceutics • Pharmacology	

		• Pharmaceutical Chemistry • Pharmacognosy	
37.	PSG College of Pharmacy Peelamedu, Coimbatore – 641 004 Tel: 0422 -2570170 www.psgpharma.ac.in	B. Pharm	• Should have completed the age of 17 years on or before 31st December of admitting year. • **Candidates** belonging to all categories except Scheduled Castes/Scheduled Tribes for admission to the Pharmacy course must have obtained individual pass marks in Physics, Chemistry, Biology or Botany & Zoology or Mathematics both in theory and practical with a minimum of 35% marks. Not less than 40% aggregate marks in the above subjects is mandatory at the qualifying examination (Academic Stream) after a period of 12 years of study i.e.10+2 pattern of education. • Candidates belonging to Scheduled Caste / Scheduled Tribes not less than 35% aggregate marks. • Candidates qualified in the Diploma in Pharmacy examination **conducted** by the Board of Examinations of the Government of Tamil Nadu or any other Board of any other state recognized as equivalent thereto by the authority of Medical University
		M. Pharm • Pharmaceutics • Pharmacology • Pharma Analysis • Pharmacy Practice	Candidates for admission to first year of the Master of Pharmacy shall be required to have passed the B. Pharm degree of The Tamil Nadu Dr. M.G.R Medical University or any other University recognized as equivalent thereto by the authority of the Medical University
		Pharm D	A pass in any of the following examinations: • 10+2 examination with Physics and Chemistry as compulsory subjects along with one of the following subjects : Mathematics or Biology • Pass in D. Pharm course from an institution approved by the Pharmacy Council of India under section 12 of the Pharmacy Act • Any other qualification approved by the Pharmacy Council of India as equivalent to any of the above examinations
		Pharm D (PB)	Pass in B. Pharm from an institution approved by the Pharmacy Council of India under section 12 of the Pharmacy Act
		PhD	
38.	Department of Pharmacy, Guru Ghasidas University Koni, Bilaspur 495 009 (Chattisgarh) Phone: 07752-260027 www.ggu.ac.in	D. Pharm	50% in 10+2 with PCB/PCM from any recognized board or equivalent
		B. Pharm	50% in 10+2 with PCB/PCM from any recognized board or equivalent

		M. Pharm	• B. Pharm degree with 55% marks and valid GPAT Score card • Through VET (Vishwavidyalaya Entrance Test) for non GPAT candidates
		PhD	Through VRET
39.	Shoolini University Village Bajhol, P.O. Sultanpur, Solan 173229, Himachal Pradesh Tel: 9625233301, 9625233302, 9625233303 http://shooliniuniversity.co m/b-pharmacy-le	B. Pharm	• 10+2 (PCB/PCM) with at least 55% marks; Lateral Entry to 3rd Semester for Diploma in Pharmacy qualified candidates with minimum of 50% marks. • Admission criteria Through JEE (15% marks)/NEET/HPCET(20% marks) or 60% marks in +2 or any equivalent entrance test recognised by HP Government.
		B. Pharm (Practice)	• Diploma in Pharmacy with 50% marks from an institution approved by the Pharmacy Council of India and registered as pharmacist with Pharmacy Council and with minimum of four years of pharmacy practice in a community or hospital. • Admission is done by merit of qualifying examination
		M. Pharm • Pharmaceutics • Pharmacology • Pharmaceutical chemistry	• B. Pharmacy with at least 55% marks. • Admission criteria is by Merit of HPTU/GPAT Entrance Test or 60% marks in B. Pharmacy or any other equivalent test followed by Personal Interview.
		PhD Pharmacy	• Master's Degree in Pharmacy or any other related discipline with at least 55% marks. • Admission criteria is through Shoolini University entrance test followed by personal interview before the admission committee of the university. • JRF/NET/SET/M.Phil qualified candidates are exempted from entrance test.
40.	Integral University Dasauli, Bas-ha Kursi Road, Lucknow – 226026 Tel: 0522- 2890730, 2890812 www.iul.ac.in	B. Pharm	• A candidate must have passed 10+2 with Physics, Chemistry and (Maths/ Biology) with minimum 45% marks in aggregate from a recognized Board/ University. • Admission on the basis of merit in IUET(Integral university entrance test)-2018 • For Lateral Entry a candidate must have passed D. Pharm with 45% marks in aggregate from a recognized Board/ University.
		Pharm .D	• 10+2 with Physics, Chemistry and Maths/Biology with minimum 50% marks in aggregate from a recognized university/board. • Admissions on the basis of merit in IUET-2018
		M. Pharm	• A candidate must have passed B. Pharm with minimum 55% marks in aggregate. Weightage will be given to GPAT qualified candidates • Admission on the basis of merit in IUET-2018
41.	Maharishi Markandeshwar	B. Pharm	The Candidate should have passed 10+2 examination with Physics, Chemistry, English,

	Ambala - Yamunanagar Highway Mullana - Ambala, 133207 1800-2740-240 www.mmumullana.org		Mathematics and/ or Biology as optional subjects individually. Obtained at least 45% marks (40% in case of candidates belonging to reserved category) in the above subjects taken together. OR Passed Diploma examination with at least 45% marks (40% in case of candidates belonging to reserved category), subject to vacancies in the First Year, in case the vacancies at lateral entry are exhausted.
		B. Pharm Lateral Entry	The candidate should have passed in D. Pharm course with minimum 45% marks from an institution approved by the Pharmacy Council of India under section 12 of the Pharmacy Act
		M. Pharm • Pharmacology • Quality Assurance • Pharmaceutics	The candidate should have passed Bachelor in Pharmacy with minimum least 55% marks (50% in case of candidates belonging to reserved category) in the qualifying Examination.
		Pharm D 5 + 1 Years	10+2 examination with Physics and Chemistry as compulsory subjects along with one of the following subjects: Mathematics or Biology. OR A pass in D.Pharm course from an institution approved by the Pharmacy Council of India Under Section 12 of the Pharmacy Act. OR Any other qualification approved by the Pharmacy Council of India as equivalent to any of the above examinations. Provided that a student should complete the age of 17 years on or before 31st December of the year of admission to the course.
		Pharm D (Post Baccalaureate) 2 + 1 Years	The candidate should have passed in B.Pharm from an institution approved by the Pharmacy Council of India undersection 12 of the Pharmacy Act.
42.	R. C. Patel Institute of Pharmaceutical Education and Research Karwand Naka, Shirpur - 425 405 Tel: 02563-255189, 251809 rcpatelpharmacy.co.in	B. Pharm	• Candidate should be Indian National and should have passed HSC (XII) Examination of Maharashtra State Board of Secondary and higher Secondary Education or its equivalent examination with subject English, Physics, Chemistry & Biology/Mathematics and secured minimum 45% marks. ie: Not less than 135 marks out of 300 Marks (minimum 40% Marks i.e. Not less than 120 marks out of 300 marks in case of Candidate of Backward Class category belonging only to Maharashtra State) in the subjects of Physics, Chemistry and Biology / mathematics added together (maximum of marks obtained in biology/mathematic shall be considered for the purpose of addition. • Candidate should be Indian National and should have passed Post SSC or HSC Diploma

			Course in Pharmacy with at least 50 % marks (45 % marks in case of candidates of backward class categories belonging only to Maharashtra State) from an AICTE/PCI approved institutes with English as the medium of instruction at diploma level.
		M. Pharm • Pharmaceutics • Quality assurance • Pharmaceutical Chemistry • Pharmacology • Clinical Pharmacy • Pharmacognosy	• Students who have passed B. Pharm from approved college only are eligible for admission to M. Pharm. They Must have obtained at least 50 % marks in B. Pharm (for reservation and sponsored candidates 45%)
43.	Goa College of Pharmacy 18th June Road, Panaji, Goa, 403001 Tel: 0832 222 6882 http://gcp.goa.gov.in	B. Pharm	• A candidate must have passed 10+2 with Physics, Chemistry and (Maths/ Biology) with minimum 45% marks in aggregate from a recognized Board/ University. • Admission on the basis of merit in GCET(Goa common entrance test)-2018
		M. Pharm • Pharmacognosy • Pharmacology • Pharmaceutics • Quality Assurance	• B. Pharm degree with 55% marks and valid GPAT Score card • Admission on basis of merit in GCET.
		PhD in Pharmaceutical sciences	
44.	Chitkara University, Rajpura Chandigarh-Patiala National Highway (NH- 64), Village Jansla, Rajpura 140401 Punjab Tel: 09501105714 chitkara.edu.in/pharmacy	B. Pharm	• XII with a minimum aggregate of 50% marks (Physics, Chemistry, Biology/Maths as compulsory subjects)
		B. Pharm (Practice)	• A pass in Diploma course in Pharmacy from an institution approved by the Pharmacy Council of India | A registered pharmacist | Minimum of 4 years of pharmacy practice experience along with experience proof and 'No Objection Certificate' from the employer •

		M. Pharm	• B. Pharmacy from a recognized University with a minimum aggregate of 50%. A candidate has to appear for the Entrance exam followed by a personal interview.
		Pharm. D	• XII with a minimum aggregate of 50% marks (Physics, Chemistry, Biology/Maths as compulsory subjects)
		Pharm D (PB)	• B. Pharm with a minimum aggregate of 50%. The candidate will join the program in the 4th year of Pharm D and will subsequently complete the course
45.	Dr. D. Y. Patil Institute of Pharmaceutical Sciences & Research Sant Tukaram Nagar Pimpri, Pune 411018 Tel: 020-27420261/ 020-27421549 pharmacy.dypvp.edu.in	B. Pharm	• Candidate should be an Indian National • Passed HSC or its equivalent examination with Physics and Chemistry as compulsory subjects along with one of the Mathematics or Biotechnology or Biology and obtained at least 50 % of marks (at least 45% marks in case of candidate of backward class categories and persons with disability belonging only to Maharashtra state) in the above subjects taken together • Obtained Score in MHT-CET 2018.
		M. Pharmacy • Pharmaceutics • Quality Assurance • Pharmacology	• Candidate should be an Indian National • Passed Bachelor's degree in Pharmacy from any AICTE or PCI or Central or State government approved institutions with at least 55 % of marks (at least 50% marks in case of candidate of backward class categories and persons with disability belonging only to Maharashtra state) in the above subjects taken together • Obtained score in GPAT conducted by AICTE • For sponsored candidates minimum of 2 years of full time work experience in the relevant field in which admission is being sought
		Pharm D	• Candidate should be an Indian National • Passed HSC or its equivalent examination with Physics and Chemistry as compulsory subjects along with one of the Mathematics or Biotechnology or Biology and obtained at least 50 % of marks (at least 45% marks in case of candidate of backward class categories and persons with disability belonging only to Maharashtra state) in the above subjects taken together Or • Passed Diploma Course in Pharmacy from institutes affiliated to State Board and having approval of competent central authority and State Government and obtained at least 50 % of marks (at least 45% marks in case of candidate of backward class categories and persons with disability belonging only to Maharashtra state • Candidate should have appeared in all the subjects and obtained non zero score in the CET conducted by the Competent Authority

		PhD • Pharmaceutics • Pharmacology • Pharmaceutical Chemistry • Pharmacognosy	
46.	Sri Padmavati Mahila Visvavidyalayam Near West Railway Station, SVU Staff Colony Padmavathi Nagar Tirupati, 517502 Phone: 0877 228 4592 https://www.spmvv.ac.in/	B. Pharm	A Pass certificate in the Intermediate Examination/Higher Secondary Certificate (Multipurpose). Pre-University science course with Bi.P.C. M.P.C. and qualification in EAMCET Examination. Selection and allotment of seats will be made by the competent authority on the basis of EAMCET ranking in the ratio of 20:20 for M.P.C., Bi.P.C. Four students with D. Pharm qualification and based on ECET rank will be directly admitted to 2nd year B. Pharm.
		M. Pharm • Pharmaceutical Chemistry • Pharmacology • Pharmaceutics	B. Pharm Degree with a minimum of 50% marks on the Aggregate. The Admission is based on a valid GPAT Score/PGECET.
47.	College of Pharmacy, Madras Medical College Near Park Town Station, Park Town, Chennai – 600003 Tel: 044 2530 5000 www.mmc.ac.in	B. Pharm	• Candidates belonging to all categories except scheduled Castes / scheduled Tribes for admission to B. Pharm course must have obtained individual pass marks in Physics, Chemistry, Biology or Botany and Zoology or Mathematics both in theory and practical with a minimum of 35% marks. Not less than 50% aggregate marks in the above subjects is mandatory at the qualifying examination (academic stream) after a period of 12 years of study i.e.10 + 2 pattern of education. • Candidates belonging to scheduled castes / scheduled tribes must have obtained Individual pass marks in Physics, Chemistry, Biology or Botany and Zoology (or) Mathematics both in Theory and Practical with a minimum of 35% marks and with not less than 40% aggregate marks in the above subjects. • Pass in English with a minimum of 35% marks is mandatory for all categories for admission to the course. (OR) • Candidates qualified in the Diploma in Pharmacy examination conducted by the Board of Examinations of the Government of Tamil Nadu or any other Board of any other State recognized as equivalent thereto by the authority of this University.
		M. Pharm	Pass in the B. Pharm Degree of The TN Dr.M.G.R. Medical University or any other University recognized as equivalent thereto by the authority of this University.
		PhD	
48.	University Institute of Pharmacy, Pt. Ravishankar	B. Pharm	• 50% in 10 + 2 with PCM /PCB • The C.G. state Pre –Pharmacy entrance test to be qualified for the admission

	Shukla University Raipur 492010 Chhattisgarh Tel: 0771-2262832 www.iopraipur.ac.in		• Admission to B. Pharm 2nd Year through Lateral Entry : • D. Pharm with first class marks from the institute approved by Pharmacy Council of India (PCI), New Delhi/AICTE, New Delhi.
		M. Pharm Pharmaceutics	• B. Pharm 60% (55% for SC/ST) with GATE/GPAT preferred.
		PhD	• M. Pharm & University Entrance Test (GATE/GPAT/NET qualified exempted from entrance test).
49.	Bharati Vidyapeeth's College of Pharmacy Sector - 8, C.B.D. Belapur, Navi Mumbai - 400 614. Tel: 022 27571122 http://bvcop.in	B. Pharm	• The candidate should be an Indian National • Passed HSC or its equivalent examination with Physics and Chemistry as compulsory subjects along with one of the Mathematics or Biotechnology or Biology and obtained at least 50% marks (at least 45% marks in case of candidates of Backward class categories and Persons with Disability belonging only to Maharashtra State) in the above subjects taken together • Obtained Score in CET • NRI / OCI / PIO, Children of Indian workers in the Gulf countries, Foreign National.- (i) The candidate should have passed the HSC or its equivalent examination with Physics and Chemistry as compulsory subjects along with one of the Mathematics or Biotechnology or Biology, and obtained at least 50 % marks in the above subjects taken together ; (ii) Any other criterion declared by appropriate authority from time to time. • Direct Second Year (Lateral Entry) Admission,-For Maharashtra State Candidature Candidate and All India Candidature Candidate,- (i) The Candidate should be an Indian National; (ii) Passed Diploma Course in Pharmacy with at least 45 % marks (at least 40 % marks in case of candidates of Backward class categories and Persons with disability belonging to Maharashtra State only) from an All India Council for Technical Education or Pharmacy Council of India or Central or State Government approved Institution or its equivalent. (iii) Any other criterion declared by appropriate authority from time to time
		M. Pharm • Pharmaceutics • Pharmaceutical Chemistry • Pharmacology • Pharmacognosy • QA Techniques • Biotech	• Candidate should be an Indian National • Passed Bachelor's Degree in Pharmacy from any All India Council for Technical Education or Pharmacy Council of India or Central or State; Government approved institution, with at least 55% marks (at least 50% marks in case of Backward Class category and Persons with Disability Candidates belonging to Maharashtra State only) • Obtained score in Graduates Pharmacy Aptitude Test (GPAT) conducted by All India Council for Technical Education; (iv) For sponsored candidates, minimum of two years of full time work experience in a registered firm/ company/ industry/ educational and/

			or research institute/ any Government Department or Government Autonomous Organization in the relevant field in which admission is being sought • NRI / OCI/ PIO, Children of Indian workers in the Gulf countries, Foreign National.- (i) Passed Bachelor's Degree in Pharmacy from any All India Council for Technical Education or Pharmacy Council of India or Central or State; Government approved institution, with at least 55% marks; (ii) Any other criterion declared by appropriate authority from time to time.
		Pharm D	• Candidate should be an Indian National • Passed HSC or its equivalent examination with subjects Physics and Chemistry as compulsory subjects along with one of the Mathematics or Biotechnology or Biology and obtained at least 50 % marks (at least 45 % marks in case of candidates of Backward class categories and Persons with Disability belonging only to Maharashtra State) in the above subjects taken together Or • Passed Diploma Course in Pharmacy from institutes affiliated to State Board and having approval of competent central authority and State Government and obtained at least 50 % marks (at least 45 % marks in case of candidates of Backward class categories and Persons with Disability belonging only to Maharashtra State) • The candidate should have obtained at least 50% marks in the CET
50.	Acharya Nagarjuna University College of Pharmaceutical Sciences Nagarjunanagar Guntur 522510 Phone: 0863 234 6459 http://www.nagarjunauniversity.ac.in/pharmdepartment.php	B. Pharm	10+2 passed with at least 60% marks from a recognized school with subjects English, Physics, Math, and Chemistry /Biotechnology /Biology/ Technical Vocational subject.
		M. Pharm Pharmaceutics Industrial Pharmacy Pharmacology Pharmaceutical Chemistry Pharmaceutical Analysis	A bachelor's degree or an equivalent degree from a recognized university with 60% or equivalent CGPA and valid GPAT/GATE are eligible for admission.

www.ingramcontent.com/pod-product-compliance
Lightning Source LLC
Chambersburg PA
CBHW080930240926
51849CB00003BA/423
9789390211890